D1739236

NAVAJO STORIES

Editor
BRODERICK H. JOHNSON

Illustrators
RAYMOND JOHNSON and TEDDY DRAPER, JR.

Composition
PUBLICATION SERVICES, INC., *Tempe, Arizona*

Cover Photo by
ED McCOMBS© *Director, Navajo Community College Press*

Printing & Binding
GILLILAND PRINTING, INC., *Arkansas City, Kansas*

of the Long Walk Period

COLLECTION OF MATERIAL CONTAINED IN THIS BOOK WAS MADE POSSIBLE BY A GRANT FROM THE WEATHERHEAD FOUNDATION OF NEW YORK CITY

Published by
NAVAJO COMMUNITY COLLEGE PRESS
Tsaile, Navajo Nation, Arizona 86556

Original material in this book was gathered

in the Navajo language

under the supervision of Ruth Roessel

NAVAJO COMMUNITY COLLEGE PRESS
TSAILE
NAVAJO NATION, ARIZONA 86556

International Standard Book Number 0-912586-16-8
Library of Congress Catalog Card Number 73-78328

FIRST PRINTING, MAY, 1973
SECOND PRINTING, APRIL, 1975
THIRD PRINTING, MARCH, 1994
Printed in the United States of America

Contents

Contents (Continued)

This Book is Dedicated

to the Members of the Board of Regents
of Navajo Community College and to the
Late Dr. Ned A. Hatathli, Former President
of the College – All of Whom

had the vision and courage
to require publication
by Navajos, for Navajos, about Navajos

NAVAJO COMMUNITY COLLEGE
BOARD OF REGENTS

Phillip Bluehouse, President

Larry Emerson, Vice President

Dr. Alyse Neundorf, Secretary

Marilyn Lujan-Atcitty, Treasurer

Dr. Guy Gorman, Sr.

Anita Pfeiffer

Daniel Tso

Leonard Tsosie

Andre Cordero, Student Representative

THE PRESIDENT OF THE COLLEGE
Tommy H. Lewis, Jr., Ed.D.

THE VICE PRESIDENT OF THE COLLEGE
James K. McNeley, Ph.D.

JOHNSON

Foreword

THIS BOOK REPRESENTS a very significant study made by the Navajo people. For the first time one of the great tragedies of our country's history – one in which the Navajos were the victims – is being presented from the Navajo point of view and by the Navajos themselves. This places emphasis upon the fact that it is exceedingly important that the Navajos have a version of their history as prepared and interpreted by their own people. In accomplishing this formidable task many problems and obstacles have occurred.

In the first place, it is obvious from the material collected for the book that, while the events themselves are vivid and clear in the minds of Navajos even today, time and sequence have become blurred and perhaps confused. A telescoping of time relative to some storytellers seems to be evident in that events that might have been separated by as many as 50 or more years are described as having occurred simultaneously with events that are known to have taken place many years later. An example of this is the story of the Navajo Massacre in a cave in Canyon del Muerto. This story, told, or referred to, in several accounts, is presented as occurring at the same time that the soldiers went into Canyon de Chelly to force the surrender of the Navajos during the Navajo Wars of the 1860s, when, in fact, it took place about 1805, with Spanish soldiers as the aggressors. It may be true that there was, indeed, a second "Massacre Cave" experience for the Navajos, or – more likely – it may be that the telescoping of time explains the close identification of these two events.

Tradition such as that involved in these Navajo stories is not deeply concerned with exact times. This, of course, is to be expected inasmuch as the Navajos did not have written records, and the stories that are collected herein have been handed down by word of mouth for many years. It is interesting, however, to note that the stories are far more specific in terms of place than they are in terms of time. The specific locations where events occurred and the nature of those events are well remembered, while the specific dates usually are not.

In the second place, these stories reflect an interesting dilemma which in the end goes unresolved. The dilemma concerns who was at fault. Who was basically responsible for the "Long Walk"? These stories, almost without exception, discuss the question, but, if there is any consistency in them, it is the inconsistency regarding places, groups or people to blame. Some stories place the blame for the "Long Walk" at the doorstep of all Navajos. Others put the culpability on only a few Navajos who did do the things that resulted in gross retaliation and punishment. Some attempt to describe the tragedy in terms of the government trying to save the Navajos from persecution and possible annihilation by their enemies. Still other narrators place all blame squarely on the shoulders of the U. S. Government, the white people, the Mexicans and hostile Indian tribes.

In spite of the obvious lack of agreement in terms of whom to blame for the "Long Walk," it is extremely interesting and significant to note that many of the Navajos who told these stories were willing to place the fault at the doorstep of the Navajo people themselves. This is a type of honesty that usually is not found in historical accounts of other major catastrophies such as the Revolutionary War, the Civil War, World War I, World War II and so forth. Most nations interpret history in a manner which makes them faultless, and the blame thus accrues to others who are outsiders – either individuals or nations. The honesty of the Navajos in this regard is very refreshing.

In the third place, this book provides important insights into the Navajos' interpretation of specific Navajo historical events. Because people in general see their history through their own glasses, their view of an event usually is different from the view of an outside observer, and certainly it is unlike that of a different participant. As one reads these stories, a most revealing factor is the close identification, on the part of the Navajo storytellers, of the events with their religion. Time and again the Holy People come to the aid of the Navajos and are responsible for assisting them in returning home and being restored to their land. One reads the stories which relate to the Coyote ceremony held at Fort Sumner which, in the eyes of the tellers, was responsible for the change of heart in the Army that previously had refused to allow the Navajos to return home, but which, after the ceremony had been held, allowed the *Diné* to go back to their country.

Other penetrating perceptions into the Navajos' interpretation of their own history include the extreme awareness felt by the Navajos in connection with being alone in the world – beset, besieged and surrounded by enemies.

The stories in this book are full of the attacks and raids by other Indian tribes and Mexicans, as well as by the Army, against the Navajos. There is almost a feeling of persecution on the part of the Navajos in terms of the raids directed against them by others.

An interesting insight is the Navajos' knowledge that they were not only beset and surrounded by enemies but that their enemies possessed far superior weapons. Time and again the stories discuss the use of bows and arrows against guns. Certainly the bravery of the Navajos in facing that kind of weapon is clearly demonstrated.

Yet another point relates to the Navajos' knowledge that many of their people never went to Fort Sumner (Bosque Redondo). While other historical accounts make it clear that there were Navajos who did not go to Fort Sumner, it is very interesting to read these stories and to learn of the large numbers of Navajos – as told by descendants of those Navajos – who actually never went to what in reality was a prison camp. It would be revealing to be able to determine the approximate percentage of the Tribe that did not make the "Long Walk."

A further perception relates to the fact that the Navajos were well aware of the possibility of being removed from Fort Sumner to some place other than their homeland. Many of the stories tell of their desire not to go to Oklahoma or what was then Indian Territory, and one of the stories mentions the objection to the possibility of being moved down to the Phoenix, Arizona, area. In any event, the stories indicate that the Navajos were gravely concerned and aware of the possibility that they would not be allowed to return to their beloved land.

An additional exciting point, one which is particularly appropriate today, is the question raised by several of the narrators about the matter of justice. They question how a nation that has been governed by laws and respect for justice could allow that kind of a tragedy to occur. The fact that Navajos today are relating the "Long Walk" to the entire subject of justice and human rights is most significant.

It also is of interest to learn that some Navajos went to live with certain Apache tribes to escape Fort Sumner. Historical accounts mention this, but here for the first time we have a story which tells of a person who actually went there; and several stories tell what the Navajos learned from the Apaches during the period of living with them. The acquisition by the Navajos of the Chiricahua Wind Chant ceremony, which is held frequently today, is an ever-present reminder of that association.

This book is not meant to be a collection of specific historical events that can be placed chronologically in an exact time sequence. Rather, it is a collection of stories which have been handed down by the Navajo people themselves and which reflect the Navajos' view of the events described. The intention of this laborious work is primarily to enable the Navajos themselves to learn through their own eyes and ears about events which took place in the past in which their ancestors were involved.

No American ever would allow all of his history books to be written by residents of Germany, the Soviet Union or any other foreign country. And yet, for more than a hundred years, this is exactly what transpired with regard to the Navajos. They had a history – and they had no history. They had a history in the sense that they had traditions and stories and events that took place in the past; in another sense, they had no history because it never was interpreted, presented nor published by the Navajos – only by white historians and anthropologists.

Now, for the first time, Navajo history is looked at, interpreted and presented by Navajos for Navajos.

Ruth Roessel, Director
Navajo and Indian Studies Program
Navajo Community College
Tsaile, Arizona

April, 1973

JOHNSON

Acknowledgments

THIS BOOK IS ANOTHER IN A SERIES of publications by the Navajo Community College Press in keeping with the mandate by the College's Board of Regents that books be published about, for and by the Navajo Indians.

Collection, translation and organization of the book's contents were made possible through a grant by the Weatherhead Foundation of New York City. Without the assistance of the Foundation, the publication would not have been possible, and the wishes of the Navajo people to have books about, for and by themselves could not have been fulfilled.

The President of the Board of Regents, Guy Gorman, Sr., specifically requested that the following statement be included in the acknowledgments: "We are very grateful for, and most appreciative of, the support of the Weatherhead Foundation. As a result of that support we have been able for the first time to collect material and prepare it for publication so that Navajo students and others can learn about Navajo history as experienced by the Navajos themselves."

Navajo Studies at Navajo Community College will continue to publish books dealing with important events and periods in the Tribe's history as described by the Navajos. It is not an easy task, but it is in keeping with the explicit mandate given to the Navajo Studies Program by the Board of Regents.

All of the material contained in the book was collected by Navajos from Navajos and translated by Navajos.

A great deal of credit must go to everyone involved. First, of course, we extend our thanks to some 40 Navajos, most of them elderly, who did their parts magnificently by taping (in the Navajo language) their versions of the Long Walk and other events which occurred more than a hundred years ago and which had come down to them by word of mouth. The name of each man or woman, together with a brief identifying sketch, accompanies his or her story.

Navajos at the College whose work contributed in an especially significant manner to the preparation of the material in the book were Harrison Bia, Raymond Johnson, Kee Jackson, Ruth Begaye and Teddy Draper, Sr.

Mr. Bia, of Many Farms, Arizona, field coordinator and chief interviewer, worked long and hard in traveling over a large area of the Reservation, frequently on narrow sandy, muddy or rocky roads, to locate and talk, in Navajo, with many of the storytellers who then made the tapes. He also assisted in translating the tapes and in organizing the work in connection with the College's Navajo Studies Program. Mr. Johnson, of Shiprock, New Mexico, one of three artists, made the illustrating of this book his primary interest throughout the greater period of its preparation. Mr. Jackson, of Shonto, Arizona, worked patiently and painstakingly in his task as a key translator. He also went to remote areas of the Reservation and did interviewing. Miss Begaye, of Many Farms, typed much of the manuscript in its original version from the hand-written translations, even though she was, at the same time, secretary to the entire Navajo Studies Department. Mr. Draper, of Chinle, Arizona, in addition to contributing a long story, was the overall translating consultant and labored many extra hours in checking tapes and working with the Director of the Navajo Community College Press in clarifying the usage of, as well as the spelling and highly complex accenting of, the difficult Navajo words and expressions prevalent throughout the book. He did this while teaching full-time as a Navajo language instructor at the College.

Other Navajos who contributed heavily to the tedious but rewarding preparation of the material were Teddy Draper, Jr., of Chinle – artist-illustrator; Miss Rita Paddock, of Smoke Signal, Arizona – artist-illustrator; Miss Arlene Tso, of Page, Arizona – translator and secretary to the group working on the book; Max Denny, of Piñon, Arizona – translator; Eugene Teller, of Del Muerto, Arizona – translator; Milton Denny, of Piñon – who assisted in translating for a time, and Leonard Begaye, of Many Farms – who helped in typing the translations.

Mrs. Caroline Verhelst, of Mesa, Arizona, retyped the edited original stories.

A special word of appreciation is in order for Broderick H. Johnson, Director of the Navajo Community College Press. Mr. Johnson took the translated and typed materials, edited them carefully and made every effort to retain the original and distinctive Navajo wording, flavor and concepts. Then, he was responsible for all of the many tasks leading to actual publication of the volume. His unusual abilities in guiding a book through the stages of publication, coupled with his knowledge and understanding of the Navajos, are evident in this volume – as they are in many others; and we are most grateful for his patient assistance.

R.R.
1973

JOHNSON

Navajo Kinship

IT SHOULD BE NOTED THAT NAVAJO KINSHIP is an extremely complex subject – that the Navajos think of such relationships in a much broader and different sense than does the general American population. Consequently, references to relatives in the stories in this book may be confusing to many readers.

Following is a brief discussion of the kinship concept:

The first and most easily defined level is the **biological family**, consisting of husband, wife and unmarried children. With the Navajos the main line of descent is through the mother.

Second is the **extended family** which is made up of a husband and wife, their unmarried children and their married daughters with the latters' husbands and unmarried children. However, this is only a general description. Some biological families live away from the group as separate units; and frequently other relatives are present. In any case, the extended family lives as a group, occupying from two to perhaps five or six hogans or other types of homes and within shouting distance of each other.

The third level is the **outfit**, which signifies two or more extended families, or one or more extended families with one or more biological families, cooperating in farm work, herding and other tasks, as well as in sponsoring ceremonials. The various units of this wide circle of relatives may live miles apart.

Fourth is the **clan** in which the members are not necessarily – in fact, most of them are not – blood relatives. Relatives are not thought of as being restricted to biological connections, and members of a clan use "sister" and other blood-relative terms in referring to other members and even to members of "linked" clans. A Navajo belongs to the clan of his or her mother, but he or she is said to be "born for" the clan of the father; and all members of the father's clan are relatives. As a result, a Navajo might say, "I am *Kinyąą'áanii* (Towering House People), born for *Tsínaajinii* (Extended Dark Trees People). The writer once saw a list of approximately 75-80 clans, but a number of them had disappeared. In a recent study at Navajo Community College, Teddy Draper, Sr., Navajo language instructor, developed a list of 43 existing clans. Many of the clan names seem to indicate origins based upon geographical areas.

Thus, clans provide a large number of "relatives"; and they offer ties for Navajos who have no blood relationship, may live in widely separated localities – indeed, may never see each other. The ties, however, are there, and Navajos will make great efforts to do favors for, or to assist, clan relatives.

The final level consists of **linked clans**, with every clan being connected with one or several others. This probably is a result of divisions among original single-clan units caused by geographical separation, quarreling, lack of cooperation or forming of new clans through association with other tribes.

[Readers who are interested in a more complete discussion of Navajo kinship concepts are referred to Gladys Reichard, *Social Life of the Navaho Indians*, Columbia University Contributions to Anthropology, 1928, and to Kluckhohn and Leighton, *The Navaho*, Natural History Library Revised Edition, 1962.]

An example of clan relationships is that involving Teddy Draper, Sr., one of the book's storytellers and consultant in Navajo language aspects of the manuscript preparation. It is described thus in his own words:

"I belong to four different clans. My main clan is *Ashįįhí* (Salt People). I am related to *Tsénjíkiní* (Honey-Combed Rock People), *Dibé Łizhiní* (Black Sheep People) and *Mą'ii' Deeshgiizhnii* (Coyote Pass People). However, I have more clans that are related to me through my father. My father belongs to the *Tó'aheedlíinii* (Water Flowing Together People).

"All male *Tó'aheedlíinii* clan members are related to me as my little fathers, uncles and cousins. The females become my little mothers, aunts and cousins. The males' female children become my little mothers and cousins. The males' and females' children's children become my grandchildren, and all who become inlaws by marrying into the clan are my inlaws.

"The other clan related to my father is in the same manner in the relationship system. It is the *Naakaii Dine'é* (Mexican People). The *Naakaii Dine'é* are related to me in the same way as the *Tó'aheedlíinii's* clan system. Also, the members of the *Kinyąą'áanii* clan (Towering House People) are my *shinálí* (grandfathers) and *shinálí* (grandmothers) because it is my father's father's (paternal) clan. It is the same way with my mother's father's (maternal) clan which is *Tódich'íinii* (Bitter Water People). They are my *shicheii* and *shimásání* (grandfathers and grandmothers). My father's uncles, *shinálí*, are my grandfathers, too. On my mother's side, all of her brothers are my uncles, and my mother's mother's brothers are my *shicheíí* (grandfathers).

"ALL *Ashįįhí* people (my main clan) are my mothers, sisters, brothers, uncles, grandfathers, grandmothers, nephews, nieces, grandnieces, grandnephews, great-grandmothers and so on. The other three clans (on my mother's side) are the same as the *Ashįįhí* clan system; so I have many relationships within six existing clans. I was born INTO my mother's *Ashįįhí* clan; so I became a member of the *Ashįįhí* clan. I am not nearly as close to my father's clans as I am to my mother's clans. But I am born FOR my father's main clan. I have MANY relatives throughout the Navajo Reservation."

–THE EDITOR

Howard W. Gorman

Mr. Gorman, who lives in Ganado, Navajo Nation, Ariz., has been a member of the Navajo Tribal Council for the past 36 years – since 1937 – and was its Vice Chairman from 1938 to 1942. He was 73 years of age at the time of publication of this book. He has been a member of the Board of Regents of Navajo Community College since its founding in 1968. He was born into the *Tódich'íinii* (Bitter Water) clan, and his account of the Long Walk and the Fort Sumner experiences was passed down to him by various ancestors.

THIS STORY IS ABOUT THE LONG WALK to Fort Sumner. There are two points of view regarding it – the White Man's and the Navajo's. Many books have been written and many references made to the Long Walk, but always from the White viewpoint; and they usually are distorted and not true. This book gives a Navajo viewpoint – as I learned it from my ancestors.

The Long Walk to Fort Sumner – what was the cause of it? It began because of the behavior of a few *Diné*. A handful, here and there, riding horseback, killed white people and others that were traveling overland, and took their belongings. So the soldiers, commanded by Kit Carson, were ordered out. Carson was nicknamed *Bi'éé' Łichíí'ii* (Red Clothes).

A man named *Ałtsą́ąbinii'í* (Double Face), a very stubborn man, known as a thief and a killer, killed white people, and he and his group took their property. Today, they could be referred to as gangsters. He and his men troubled the camps of the white people who were traveling overland westward seeking gold. They killed the Whites, taking their mules, horses and other belongings. Then, to the white people, they would say, "We are not harming anyone and don't expect a conflict."

Unexpectedly, *Bi'éé' Łichíí'í* (Red Clothes' Soldiers) arrived, destroying water wells – contaminating them, breaking the rocks edging the waterholes or filling up the holes with dirt so that they became useless. They also burned cornfields and the orchards of

Kit Carson's soldiers destroyed or contaminated water sources so that they were useless.

peaches. That is what they did to us unexpectedly and unreasonably, because most of us were not harming anybody. In the open fields we planted squash and corn. And we lived peacefully, not expecting a conflict. We naturally were a peaceful people. We were not warlike; but, still, we had those soldier visitors.

During that time women were very skilled in weaving, and the *Diné* always were dressed well. Many men were skilled in silver-smithing, and there was a lot of silver for them. They even made bridles; they depended upon no one. They had everything they needed. Then the word was heard about Red Clothes and his soldiers, over near *Nazlini*, at a place called *T'iisnidiitsooí* (Yellow Cotton Slope), up the ridge near the white rocks where my ancestors lived. They were living there when they heard of the soldiers. Around *Lók'aahnteel* (Ganado) they invaded, killing anything, even some of the *Diné's* sheep and horses, and destroying the waterholes. Those who wondered and asked why and what was going on – and refused to take orders – were shot or were killed with other weapons. Then, upon the ridge near *T'iisnidiitsooí*, one evening, with a fire built outdoors, we were warned by the lights of other fires which showed across on the red ridge near a place called *Be'ek'idhatsoh* (Big Lake). The troops were on the move over there. *Diné* living down in the valley also were warned of the lights from a lookout on top of Red Mesa, also called Kit Carson Mesa. It was from this mesa that the soldiers were seen.

Word was sent out warning the *Diné* that troops were on the move, destroying property, having no pity on anyone. Those living in the area at the time were my closely related clan, such as my uncles; some were of the *Mą'ii' Deeshgiizhnii* (Coyote Pass) clan and some of the *Tódich'íinii* (Bitter Water) clan. When the *Diné* were warned of the invaders, they gathered their bedding and other property and started to move out over the snow-covered ground. I don't know which month it was; it could have been January. The Navajos headed north toward *Chííhłigai* (Red Clay). Canyon de Chelly was their only hope of survival. You could follow their trail easily because of their plowing through the deep snow. They moved all night, throughout the morning and into the late afternoon, when they reached a place called *Tsé Náá'deezbáál* (Blanket Wall Cave) in the canyon, where, below the cliff dwelling, they built a fire to warm themselves. On the steep walls were steps carved into the rock. These steps probably are still there. Down them during the day the ice had melted, and, in the evening, it had frozen again – right after sundown. When the Navajos arrived, the steps were covered with ice, which made it impossible to go up; so they built a fire below the cliff dwelling and settled for the night. Unfortunately, however, the soldiers caught up with them. They must have seen fires at the homes the *Diné* had left, and they had followed the trail through the snow to the place called *Tsé Náá'deezbáál*. The Navajos heard horses' hoofs, and a figure was recognized in the approaching group which was a man named *Naakaii Chílii* (Small Mexican). He was an enemy to the Navajos and helped the military. At a very young age he had been captured and had been raised among the *Diné*. He had escaped and had been picked up by the enemies. Later, he led the military to the hide-out of the *Diné* because he knew where it was.

Navajos who asked what was going on or refused to take orders were killed by the soldiers.

Fires over on a ridge warned the Navajos that the troops were on the move.

One man escaped by jumping off a high cliff onto some bushes below that were covered with deep snow.

Many *Diné* were killed, but one man, *Baa' Haaidiiłééh* (Preparing a Warrior) was a hunch-backed man, and he survived by jumping from the cliff on the canyon wall onto some bushes below which were covered with deep snow. He ran from there, receiving no injury from the jump. That is how it was told. Most of the rest were killed. One received a wound across the forehead, and blood trickled down. He raised his hand and yelled, "What is happening, and why are you doing this? Wait! Wait!" When he waved and shouted, *Naakaii Chílii* ordered his men to stop what they were doing. Also, someone supposedly tried to escape with a child, but left it behind. The little girl lay there in her cradle, with her face down. The headboard, arching over the child's head, must have protected it from injury. A soldier walked over to the child and picked her up; and the wounded man was treated with a bandage on the wound across his forehead. The place was a tragic sight. Many of those who had been attacked were my clan relatives.

The wounded man was taken as a captive, and the soldiers moved away on the trail. They already were camped at *Ch'ínílí* (Chinle). A few days later the captive was ordered into *Tséyi'* (Canyon de Chelly); and, to make sure he would return, he was told, "If you don't return, you will be killed just like the rest. Now go into *Tséyi'* and order all those that live in the canyon to move out. From here we'll go to *Tséhootsooí* (Fort Defiance). We'll be leaving soon."

Sixteen Navajos came out from the canyon, even though they didn't want to, but they knew that the *Nóóda'í* (Ute Indians) were on the loose, riding horseback, and that they were dangerously aggressive. When the sixteen were evacuated, the journey began, but a few remained in the canyon. Those that stayed feared the enemies too much to move. It was impossible to go across to *Dził Łijiin* (Black Mountain). Earlier, many had moved toward *Naatsis'aan* (Navajo Mountain) before the enemies started raiding; and many had settled there. It is a really desolate area. It's a torn-up area. To this day people get lost, even Boy Scouts.

Navajos had moved into the Navajo Mountain area for permanent settlement, driving their horses and sheep. This took place before the soldiers arrived.

After the events described, the Utes scouted *Tséyi'* (Canyon de Chelly) where there were the few survivors. The leader of the Utes, named *Tsii'bálígaii* (Grayhair), led the group. The Navajos killed him through the use of witchcraft, as the story goes. After his death the Utes moved out of the canyon with the body, which seemed to settle the raids for the time being. A singing chant had been performed to kill him. The Utes departed from the area after losing their leader. They were known for their dangerous aggressiveness. One story goes like this: Near the edge of *Tséyi'*, climbing on horseback almost to the top of the canyon, one of the Utes, speaking in the *Diné* language, called, "*Diné*, let me shoot at you. If I miss you, I'll leave this rifle, some ammunition and smoking tobacco for you."

So a Navajo agreed to let the Ute shoot at him. The man fired and missed. He left the rifle, other things and the tobacco, and he got on his horse and rode off. This one time a *Nóóda'í* (Ute) was beaten. But the Navajos took chances in picking up the weapon and other articles because they feared and had a suspicious feeling that the Ute had polluted the gun and tobacco with poison.

They stayed there for no longer than a month; then about seventeen *Diné* left *Ch'ínílí* (Chinle). They moved on top of the *Tséyi'* (edge of the canyon rim) to *Ni'iíjiihásání* (Old Sawmill) and to *Tséhootsooí* (Fort Defiance). Somewhere close to Old Sawmill there was a boundary line. If you made an escape over the boundary line in fleeing from an enemy *Nóóda'í*, the Ute would just let you go. He would throw tobacco at you or yell good-bye or wave at you. The Utes' main job was keeping the *Diné* from crossing the line.

The *Nóóda'í* were furnished with these things: Two horses, saddles, rifles, ammunition, blankets, food, tobacco – all by the government in *Wááshindoon* (Washington). The *Nóóda'í* were hired by the government, and paid by it, to help scout with the soldiers to take Navajos as captives. The Utes also moved into the *Naatsis'aan* (Navajo Mountain) area before their leader, *Tsii'bálígaii* (Grayhair), went into *Tséyi'* (Canyon de Chelly). Kit Carson and his soldiers didn't go as far as *Naatsis'aan.* They went as far as *Denihootso* (Dennehotso) in the Kayenta area. East of *'Ooljéétó* (Moon Water) there's a place called *Naakaii To'hayiiłkáadí* (Mexican Canyon). The Navajos noticed the Utes moving toward the canyon. Along the only path that leads into the canyon on the east side there are curved canyon walls, with the tops and bottoms being extremely wooded areas.

Into this beautiful curved canyon the Utes moved. Only four Navajos saw the enemies moving toward them. So these four planned to fight the Utes. Because the Utes were powerful enemies, the Navajos planned real carefully. Soon the Navajos were ready for them, knowing that the leader, *Tsii'bálígaii* (Grayhair) and his band were dangerous. Up on top of the curved canyon the Navajos gathered firewood and piled it with cedar bark to build bonfires. They built several piles some distance apart, and one of the *Diné* told the other men, "Three of you be sure and be ready with your *honooyééł* (cedar bark torches). Light your torches when I give you the signal." Then this man went to meet the approaching *Nóóda'í.* He warned them to turn back because it was impossible for them to go on. He said, "There are many *Diné* up there ready with their bows and arrows, also rifles." But the Utes didn't believe what he told them. So the Navajo made a sign to his three men who started lighting the wood piles which they had made. Soon huge clouds of smoke went up.

"See up there!" The Navajo said to the Utes. "Those are the Navajos. Many of them are up there." And the Ute leader replied, "All right." They saddled their horses and moved out. That is how the story is told. Then, not long before the Long Walk to Fort Sumner, while the *Diné* were still being taken captive, the Utes and American soldiers scouted around for them. The Utes and soldiers moved up toward *T'áábiich'įįdii* (Aneth, Utah), and back down around *Denihootso* in the Kayenta region; also, up on top of *Dził Łijiin* (Black Mountain), and from there toward the east, through

Ho'yéé' (Steamboat Canyon) and to *Lók'aahnteel* (Ganado, Arizona). From there they went to *Kinteel* (Wide Ruins) and to *Tséhootsooí* (Fort Defiance). They concentrated on these areas mostly, including the *Ch'ínílí* (Chinle) area. When it seemed that there was not a sign of any more *Diné*, they quit scouting around and reported back to their headquarters. They decided that more searching was useless.

From Fort Defiance the Navajos started on their journey. That was in 1864. They headed for *Shash Bitoo'* (Fort Wingate) first, and from there they started on their Long Walk. Women and children traveled on foot. That's why we call it the Long Walk. It was inhuman because the Navajos, if they got tired and couldn't continue to walk farther, were just shot down. Some wagons went along, but they were carrying army supplies, like clothes and food. *Jaanéèz* (mules) pulled the wagons. So the Navajos were not cared for. They had to keep walking all the time, day after day. They kept that up for about 18 or 19 days from Fort Wingate to Fort Sumner, or *Hwéèldi*.

On the journey the Navajos went through all kinds of hardships, like tiredness and having injuries. And, when those things happened, the people would hear gun shots in the rear. But they couldn't do anything about it. They just felt sorry for the ones being shot. Sometimes they would plead with the soldiers to let them go back and do something, but they were refused. This is how the story was told by my ancestors. It was said that those ancestors were on the Long Walk with their daughter, who was pregnant and about to give birth. Somewhere beyond *K'aalógii Dził* (Butterfly Mountain) on this side of *Bilín* (Belen), as it is called, south of Albuquerque, the

When Navajos were tired or ill and could not walk farther they were shot down.

The pregnant daughter of the narrator's ancestors was shot when she no longer could keep up with the others.

daughter got tired and weak and couldn't keep up with the others or go any farther because of her conditon. So my ancestors asked the Army to hold up for a while and to let the woman give birth. But the soldiers wouldn't do it. They forced my people to move on, saying that they were getting behind the others. The soldiers told the parents that they had to leave their daughter behind. "Your daughter is not going to survive, anyway; sooner or later she is going to die," they said in their own language.

"Go ahead," the daughter said to her parents, "things might come out all right with me." But the poor thing was mistaken, my grandparents used to say. Not long after they had moved on, they heard a gunshot from where they had been a short time ago.

"Maybe we should go back and do something, or at least cover the body with dirt," one of them said.

By that time one of the soldiers came riding up from the direction of the sound. He must have shot her to death. That's the way the story goes.

These Navajos had done nothing wrong. For no reason they had been taken captive and driven to *Hwéeldi* (Fort Sumner). While that was going on, they were told nothing — not even what it was all about and for what reasons. The Army just rounded them up and herded them to the prison camp. Large numbers of Navajos made the journey. Some of them tried to escape. Those who did, and were caught, were shot and killed.

As I said, a large number of our people went on the Long Walk, and, when they started back several years later, more than 7,500 made the return trip. Since many of them had died, this means that there must have been a great number who walked to Fort Sumner. I don't know exactly in what formation they walked. Maybe they marched in two lines or went in single file. That is one thing I never have heard. "We were just being driven," they said afterward. And when they reached *Hwééldi*, which was located across a river, they saw that, on the other side of the river, some adobe or mud shelters were being started. The *Diné* helped build those shelters.

The Army selected some of the Navajos to be in charge of their people. The captives were divided into groups. The selected men were put in charge – one for each group. If these leaders wanted to go somewhere for a short while, they had to get permission, or a pass, from the Army officers. They were not allowed to leave confinement without permission, and they had to have good causes and special reasons. The Navajos had hardly anything at that time; and they ate the rations but couldn't get used to them. Most of them got sick and had stomach trouble. The children also had stomach ache, and some of them died of it. Others died of starvation. The prisoners begged the Army for some corn, and the leaders also pleaded for it for their people. Finally, they were given some – one ear of corn for each member of the *Diné*. Some boys would wander off to where the mules and horses were corraled. There they would poke around in the manure to take undigested corn out of it. Then they would roast the corn in hot ashes to be eaten. They had nothing to grind corn with at that time, like the stone corn grinders that the Navajos have now.

Also, the water was bad and salty, which gave them dysentery. They were given medical treatment, but extreme hardships stayed with them for about a year after they arrived at Fort Sumner, and they had a bad time throughout the imprisonment. Large numbers of the *Diné* lost their lives. A few would ask permission to hunt small game like *gah* (rabbits), and permission sometimes was granted. The *Diné* also hunted *na'azísi* (gophers) along the river bank and used them for food.

That's the way it went with our people for at least a year. Then, after about two years, in the autumn, some of them were allowed to leave confinement and were granted permission to go farther to hunt bigger game. There were mountains toward the east, southeast and south; so the *Diné* decided to hunt deer in those mountains. Only those who were trusted and "settled" were permitted to hunt, and they were told not to get into trouble. It was said to them, "You Navajos have been in all kinds of trouble back in your homeland – stealing, raiding and killing the White Men. Many White Men have been killed, and all of these things are charged against you. You are held responsible for them. They charged you people with these things from the east or *Wááshindoon* (Washington). So now you have to settle down, and some day you might return to your homes and lands. Think about yourselves; think straight!"

Although they were told all those things, the Navajos still didn't like what they were being taught. They said among themselves, "What did we do wrong? We people here didn't do any harm. We were gathered up for no reason. The ones that were doing all the killing and raiding of the White Men probably are still doing the same thing back home – raiding and stealing from the White Men, and killing. We harmless people are held here, and we want to go back to our lands right away."

The Navajos would say those things quietly among themselves. Of the few *Diné* who were permitted to hunt in the mountains, some brought back deer meat. Others returned without it. Those were the unlucky ones. There was one thing that took place that I want to tell about, however. All of the captive Navajos were blamed for it and were almost killed. While hunting in the mountains, three Navajos came upon a ranch. The cowboy, or white rancher, had about 25 head of cattle. Sometimes he would put the cattle inside the corral, and, at other times, leave them out in the pasture. This rancher was big and husky. He had some horses, too, which were noticed by the three *Diné*, who planned to make a move. A woman was seen coming out of the hut, or shelter, but there were no signs of children. A big dog, grayish colored, was noticed by the Navajos. So they made plans; and, at dusk, they watched from a distance as the rancher put the horses in the corral. Then he placed logs across the entrance, which were a lot easier for the Navajos to remove silently than to open a gate. A candle was burning inside the hut. When the cowboy put his stock in the corral he tied his dog by the side of the corral entrance. Soon after he walked inside the hut the candle went out. He and his wife must have gone to sleep, and that was when the Navajos made their move.

They crawled one behind each other, the strongest one in front and the others in the back line. The front Navajo was carrying a knife. They approached the corral quietly from behind. Then the one with the knife jumped on the dog and stabbed and killed it. The dead dog was dragged aside, and the logs across the corral entrance were taken out slowly and carefully; and the Navajos drove the horses out quietly. They drove them until morning, and continued driving them for I don't know how long. In time, they held up, killed and butchered one of the horses. They roasted and ate some of the meat, some was put in a tree for safekeeping, and they took the rest with them. Then they started driving the horses again, saying, "We'll come back for the rest of the meat some time!"

One Navajo stabbed the dog; then they removed the logs and began to drive out the horses.

But before they reached Fort Sumner a band of *Naałání* (Comanches) caught up with them. These Comanches were friends of the rancher. East of *Hwéeldi* there was a hill behind which the *Diné* had a battle with the Comanches. Several Navajos were killed. Then a Navajo named *Tsóósí* (Tsosie) came from the camp and hollered to the fighting men, "That's enough! Stop!" Somehow they must have heard him. They obeyed his orders, and the fighting broke up. The Comanches got on their horses and rode off, with some Navajos from the camp shooting at them. The Navajos then were gathered up by the Army and driven back to confinement. They were asked the cause of the fight, and they told the reason – why the fighting had started between them and the Comanches.

So, the Navajos ruined their privilege of hunting game; and, because of this, some of them slipped away to *Yootó* (Santa Fe) to see the Indian Commissioner, who they thought was a friend of the *Diné.* The Navajos explained to him the problems they were having at *Hwéeldi* where they were being held captive for no reason, and that the Army was guarding them with guns. One of the Commissioner's inspectors was sent to Fort Sumner to see what was going on. Nothing was said during the checking around; but, later, one of the officers told them, "You Navajos are foolish and senseless. You are here to learn discipline. If you keep on getting into mischief you are going to be driven on to *Halgai Hatéél* (Oklahoma)." They also were told that the Indian Commissioner in Santa Fe had ordered them to give up their bad habits.

In the second and third years the *Diné* tried to plant corn, but it was no use. It didn't grow. They were told to plant it in the way of the *Bilagáana* (White Men). But still it didn't grow. So they were given corn from somewhere else which they survived on.

Within about another year, when it was planned to transfer the *Diné* someplace else, the *Bi'éé Łichíí'í* (Red Clothes, referring to the soldiers) somehow sent out a message. We don't know how it was delivered. Anyway, the soldiers got a message to a man by the name of *Yichi'dahyiłwóh* (Barboncito), far beyond *Tónaneesdizí* (Tuba City), where the little Colorado River and the San Juan River meet. That was where Barboncito camped. A certain Navajo by the name of *'Ahidigishii* (Finger Signal) was not a good man. He had shot a woman as she sat on a horse. While Barboncito was there to settle that matter the message reached him to move to Fort Sumner at once. He was told, "You are to move to *Shash Bitoo'* (Fort Wingate) first; then on. The *Diné* at *Hwéeldi* are getting senseless and making all kinds of trouble. They were thought to be more sensible, but they are getting worse. Pretty soon they will just jump into the river and drown themselves. They are being taught something, but they don't understand. It seems like they are not even interested in work, like planting corn."

Everything they did was explained to Barboncito; so he made ready to move. It was believed that he had two wives. *Yichi'-dahyiłwóh* or *Hastiin (Hastį́į́) Dahghaa'í* (Barboncito) was of the *Mą'ii' Deeshgiizhnii* (Coyote Pass) clan. He was my grandfather on my father's side. A man by the name of *Bilátł'ah* (Palm of Hand) was his close relative, and that man, *Bilátł'ah*, was my real grandfather on my mother's side. So Barboncito started off with all his belongings — his cattle, sheep and horses being driven along. They journeyed south of the *Kiis'áanii* (Hopi) territory and through *T'áálá'í Hooghan* (One

Home) on beyond *Jadító* (Jeddito) to *Lók'aahnteel* (Ganado). From there they went to *Tséhootsooí* (Fort Defiance) and on to *Shash Bitoo'* (Fort Wingate).

Barboncito chanted or gave a ceremony while he traveled with his family – a wife, son, daughter and son-in-law. He took everything that belonged to him. *'Adool'íseek'ego* (Toe-by-Toe) is the name of the ceremony. I don't know what kind that was. I have asked, but nobody seems to remember it. Anyway, that is how he conducted his chant or ceremony all the way to *Shash Bitoo'*. From there on I don't know what kind he used. *Hastįį (or Hastiin) Dahghaa'í* wasn't driven to Fort Sumner with the others; he was sent on a special assignment. His duty was to talk to his fellow Navajos and to rehabilitate their minds and make them think about coming back to their own land and not to be sent to *Halgai Hatééł* (Oklahoma). At that time some of the *Chíshí Dine'é* (Chiricahua Apaches) had been taken to *Halgai Hatééł*. Some *Naałání* (Comanche) chiefs also had been sent there. These people were known to be aggressive and dangerous.

Some of the Chiricahua Apaches still live in Anadarko, Oklahoma. Not all of them live on the Mescalero Reservation. For the same reason that had been used against the *Diné*, they had been taken there; and the Navajos were supposed to be sent there, too. But there was a much larger number of Navajos – more than 7,000 of them, and it wasn't easy to put that number in Oklahoma. That was one reason the government didn't think much of taking them there.

When Barboncito got to *Hwééldi* he began talking to the people, and he was asked many questions. Barboncito was a chanter, or medicine man, it was said. He told them, "You people, my fellow men, back on your land there are weeds where you used to plant, and your corn patches lie just as you left them. Why are you doing the things that you shouldn't do?"

But the Navajos didn't like what he said. They just asked, "Who are you, anyway? Where did you come from? We don't know you." They didn't like him a bit.

Later, it was during the fourth year at Fort Sumner, a man by the name of *Hatáłii Yázhí* (Little Singer) said one day, "It looks like this man knows what he is talking about. This *Hastiin Dahghaa'í* sounds like he is right about what he is trying to tell us, my fellow people, and I am satisfied with what he says. Maybe we should listen to him and then be allowed to return to our homeland. There are places back there whose names we have forgotten."

[I want to say here that some of the Navajos still lived at *Naatsis'aan* (Navajo Mountain), and some had managed to go back there after taking off from *Hwéeldi* by themselves. Others had jumped into the river, trying to escape. They were watched by the military. If they crossed all right they were not shot at; but, if the river was too deep, there was no chance for them to cross, and they were just carried away. A number of them were drowned. Others crossed and were not shot at.

As an example of things that happened at camp, there was a time when somebody stole bread from the bakery, and the *Diné* were mistreated for that. Two of them were put in jail.]

These are just a few of the incidents that took place at Fort Sumner. There are lots of stories. I remember them in connection with it being all right for *Hatáłii Yázhí* (Little Singer) to believe in what Barboncito said. He added, "This Barboncito is telling the truth. We should be good and try to be allowed to return to our homeland."

At about this time they saw one of the Army's lieutenants riding into Fort Sumner with an arrow in his back, right between his shoulders, and dead! The arrow didn't appear to be a *Diné* type. It might have been one made by the *Naashgalí Dine'é* (Mescalero Apaches), who had been in trouble with the Army before. Now, they might have been getting even with the soldiers. The *Naałání* (Comanches) also were enemies of the Army. But the Navajos didn't know which tribe the arrow belonged to. They were sure, though, that it was not a Navajo arrow. If it had been, the Navajos would have been driven to *Halgai Hatéél* (Oklahoma) for sure. It was a good thing that the arrow wasn't one of theirs, especially after they had called themselves harmless people.

Wood became harder and harder to find. There were no trees around, like cedar and piñon. Out at a great distance – many miles – there was some mesquite, the roots of which were dug out and brought home for firewood. Some little trees were around, but they were not good for firewood, giving a blue flame like butane, and they were tough. Anyway, wood was the hardest thing to get; and the Navajos suffered their worst hardships in winter when it got real cold.

Finally, the *Diné* began to make plans to return to their homeland, and the Army was in contact with *Wááshindoon* (Washington), explaining that the *Diné* wanted to make treaties and to go home.

One of them, *Hastiin Dahghaa'í*, said that from the Rio Grande west was their homeland, that what they were staying on was not. A man by the name of *Tótsohnii Hastįį́* (Big Water Clan Man) agreed. He said, "I'm not about to give up my life here – even to think of dying here. I would rather return to my homeland and die there." And that's exactly what happened to him. Years ago, he passed away in *Lók'aahnteel* (Ganado, Arizona). The Army officials reported these things to Washington, and the result was the old treaty of 1868. It was made at about the end of the fourth year at Fort Sumner, around May or June.

Finally, a United States Army general arrived from the east (or Washington), and the treaty began to take shape. On one side sat the general or *haskééjínaat'áá'* (war chief) and beside him a White Man who spoke Mexican and English. Beside the White Man sat a Navajo by the name of *Tsóósí* (Tsosie) who spoke Mexican and *Diné*. At the end of the line sat *Hastiin Dahghaa'í* (Mr. Mustache), the man also known as Barboncito. When the general spoke it would be to the man who spoke English and Mexican. He would translate in Mexican to *Tsóósí*, who understood that language; and *Tsóósí* would translate in the *Diné* language to *Hastiin Dahghaa'í*.

Then Mr. Mustache would answer in the Navajo language to *Tsóósí*, and *Tsóósí* would translate in Mexican to the White Man, who would translate to the general in English. There was no time for the *Diné* to talk to each other. That was how the treaty was made in 1868 – about one hundred and four years ago.

There was one thing that isn't mentioned in the White Man's histories. A wooden post was put in the ground, and a big billy goat was hit in the mid-section with a stick so that he struck the post repeatedly with his head and horns. I don't know how long this continued. But, after a while, the brains of the goat came out, and that's when they got through with him. Then the general turned to the Navajos and said, "Nowhere, at no time in the future, whatever you do, don't break this treaty. If you get in trouble with Washington or the U. S. Government again and do the things you should not do, that is what is going to happen to you people." He meant what had happened to the billy goat.

In that way the Navajos were warned to go by the treaty and respect it. All of the *Diné* witnessed what took place, and one of the head men explained to them, He said, "Be careful about whatever you do. Don't break the treaty or kill any more enemies or White Men."

The *Diné* also were told to enroll their children in school and to let them be educated. They were strictly told this, and many Navajos say that we are still keeping our promise made in the treaty.

But the government didn't exactly keep its promise. For instance, now there are not enough classrooms for our children. There were supposed to be about 30 students to each classroom. But we

It is said that 27 head men signed the peace treaty (of 1868) with their thumb prints.

don't have that kind; and the government promised it when we were informed to enroll our children from age 6 to 16. We are doing that, but, because of a need for classroom space, lots of our children are not getting the education that they should have. The reason why lots of our children are out of school is that the United States government has not fulfilled its obligation according to the treaty. But we have stood by the treaty. We have carried out its stipulations clear through. About 27 head men signed the peace treaty agreement with their thumb prints, and those prints still are that way. The names of these Navajos were written in Mexican. *Hastiin Adiits'a'ii Sání* (the late Chee Dodge) knew the names. For myself, I don't have the list.

Barboncito was made *Hózhǫǫji Naat'aah* (peace commissioner). He was one of those who had been put in charge, and his first job was completed. That was why he had come to Fort Sumner.

On June 2, in the year of 1868, the treaty was made legal for the Navajos; so they started their journey back right away. They went to *Shash Bitoo'* (Fort Wingate) and then to *Tséhootsooí* (Fort Defiance), where they were given rations and two sheep to each family. That is how it is said in Navajo history. (Some people don't tell the story right. They just mention that the people were given sheep.) And the Navajos began to take real good care of their sheep. Even if they were hungry and had chapped lips in cold weather, instead of butchering a sheep they would hunt small game, like rabbits, rats and gophers; and they survived on these while they tried hard to increase their livestock.

Then, in the 1930s, the *Diné* were told that they were over-grazing their land with their livestock, and the stock reduction program took place.

According to written history, a little more than 7,500 Navajos returned from Fort Sumner to the Navajo Reservation. The government said our Reservation was bigger than it really turned out to be. In four directions were the sacred mountains – to the east *Sisnaajiní* (Blanca Peak), to the south *Tsoodził* (Mount Taylor), to the west *Dook'o'oosłíid* (San Francisco Peak) and to the north *Dibé Nitsaa* (La Plata Mountains). Inside these four sacred mountains the Navajos had lived many years ago. After their return from Fort Sumner the Reservation set aside for them was real small, perhaps like a little way from *Tséhootsooí* (Fort Defiance) up to *Dził Łijiin* (Black Mountain) and toward the southeast from there. Then, on back north to *Tooh* (San Juan River), that was the size of the land that the Navajos returned to. Their homeland had been much larger, but the *Diné* were told that if they would go by the treaty their Reservation would be increased in size.

It has been increased I don't know how many times. *Hastįį Adiits'a'ii Sání* (Chee Dodge) said some time ago that it had been added to 11 times toward the east. In the direction of Crownpoint, there's a place called *Hoołk'id* (Rolling Hills) and a neighboring area called *Diné Bitah* (Navajo Country) and also Cuba, New Mexico (or *Na'azísítóh* or Gopher Water) and *Kinkikai'í* (Prewitt, N.M.) – all these areas had been *Diné* territory, and the *Diné* got them back in 1904 when Theodore Roosevelt was President by executive order. But four years later, in 1908, Howard Taft became president, and the executive order land was repossessed. That was the idea of the white people who wanted the land for their livestock. That is the land that once was ours, and it isn't ours any more. The white people are settled on it now. The Navajos were to receive compensation in terms of money, but they were cheated out of it, and the claim wasn't settled right for them. We are satisfied with the territories that have been added to our Reservation, but the repossession of what I described kind of hurt our feelings. Even today, attorneys still complain about that deal.

When we were taken to *Hwéeldi* (Fort Sumner), a harmless people, for four years, the White Men got all our land – north to *Dibé Nitsaa* (the La Plata Mountains), toward the northwest to *Dził Ashdlá'ii* (La Sal Mountains) to the *Tó Dootł'izhí* (Green River), and beyond to the mountain with no name (Mount Henry). The Navajos used to have, and live on, that whole area. Later, the white people took most of that territory back.

As for *T'áábiich'įįdii* (Aneth) in Utah, the Montezuma area, land north of the San Juan River and toward the Colorado River, a place now called Blanding, also Monticello, Utah, Navajos living in those areas weren't taken to *Hwéeldi* because they had their own leader. They called him Calgalia or *K'ááyéłii* (Torch). He was the leader in the area around Moab, Utah, where the Colorado River and the San Juan River join. That was where many Navajos lived and had lands, and they never made the journey to Fort Sumner.

Also, a large number of Navajos – I think maybe 1,000 or 2,000 or more – moved down below *Naatsis'aan* (Navajo Mountain). While they were living there, the rest of the Navajos – around 8,000 – were herded to Fort Sumner where many lost their lives.

After the return, when it seemed that everything was settled down, people began moving out of the *Naatsis'aan* (Navajo Mountain) area. It's very rugged, with canyons. You could get lost in that place in a short time.

After coming back from Fort Sumner to Fort Wingate some of our people became scouts for the military police or the Army. The *Chíshí Dine'é* (Chiricahua Apaches) got in trouble with the Army, and the Navajo scouts fought with the Army. The Navajos helped in that way. Many of our people have told about this helping the Army, and some passed away still saying it.

As I have said, our ancestors were taken captive and driven to *Hwéeldi* for no reason at all. They were harmless people, and, even to date, we are the same, holding no harm for anybody. But other tribes, like the Utes, as well as the White Men, always started trouble. It was the same with the *Naakaii* (Mexicans). We *Diné* never caused trouble, and we don't intend to start it. That's the way I think of us. Many Navajos who know our history and the story of *Hwéeldi* say the same thing.

Teddy Draper, Sr.

Kiiłbáhí (Grayboy)

Teddy Draper, Sr., is a Navajo language instructor at Navajo Community College and was the translating consultant with regard to the spelling, accenting and exact meanings of the Navajo words and expressions used throughout this book. The following narrative of how a band of Navajos escaped the Long Walk by occupying Fortress Rock was told to him by his maternal and paternal grandmothers. Mr. Draper, 49 years old, lives in Chinle, Ariz., not far from his birthplace in Canyon del Muerto. He was born into his mother's *Ashįįhí* (Salt People) clan and for his father's *Tó'aheedlíinii* (Water Flowing Together) clan.

I WAS BORN about 19 miles from *Ch'ínílí* (Chinle), Arizona, in *Tséyi'* (Canyon del Muerto) on April 2, 1923. I lived in Canyon del Muerto until I was about 13 years old, when I started to attend the Bureau of Indian Affairs Boarding School at Chinle. Before I went to school, I never spoke a word of the English language which now is my second language. I am a full-blooded Navajo Indian.

My maternal and paternal grandmothers' mothers told a story about the expedition of soldiers to *Tséyi'* (Canyon de Chelly) [same word for both canyons] which is located east of Chinle. My grandmother on my mother's side and my grandmother on my father's side told me my paternal great-grandmothers' stories. They were very interesting stories. Both of my real grandmothers told me many, many stories about religion, tradition and the way the fighting and the Long Walk came about.

I was about nine years old when I was taking care of our peach trees and I was doing some hoeing. One day I came in for supper. I had blue cornmeal and hot goat's milk. Now my vision is reflecting back to my two grandmothers telling me stories. My paternal grandmother said, "This is your canyon, my grandson. Did you know that you're not a slave to the United States soldiers?"

When she said that I was confused.

She continued, "My grandson, sit down here, you were working hard today. Do you know the story of Navajo Fortress Rock?"

I said, "No."

My grandmother then said that it was the huge high wall rock at *Tséjiiní* (Black Rock Canyon) junction (with Canyon del Muerto) and that my great-grandmother [on my father's side] had told her:

The Navajos heard that there were many soldiers moving in at *Shash Bitoo'* (Fort Wingate, New Mexico). This was just about one year before the long walk to Fort Sumner. The soldiers had come to *Tsélání* (Many Fortress Rocks – Salina – which is now Salina Trading Post). It was in *Bini'ant'ą́ą́tsoh* (September) before *Bi'éé' Łichíí'ii* (Kit Carson – Red Clothes) and his soldiers came to Canyon del Muerto. Another trip was made by the soldiers to *DziłŁijiin* (Black Mountain), and the *Bi'éé' Łichíí'í* (all of the Red Clothes – the soldiers) killed more *Diné* there; also, the soldiers were settling at *Tséhootsooí* (Fort Defiance).

Now we heard that the soldiers would do more exploring in Canyon de Chelly. I was 16 years old and I [my great-grandmother] had my own bow and arrows. They called me *Asdzaan Naakaii* (Mexican Lady). I had experienced fighting against *Naakaii siláo* (Mexican soldiers). That's how I got my name. When I had been about 13 years old I remember the *Diné* saying that there were some enemies who tried to come into Canyon de Chelly. It wasn't the Mexicans. We had had closer relations with all of the *Diné* when I was about 10 years old, but some of the *Diné* became bad, maybe 20 of them, and now we heard those *'Aná'í Diné* (Enemy Navajos) were turning against us because the other *Diné* had chased them away from the Navajo land. Our *Diné* said that the Enemy Navajos were with the *Bi'éé' Łichíí'í* and helped to bring the soldiers to the canyon. I wasn't too afraid because where we were located was more of a safe place to hide. We had forest protection, men to protect us, and there were enough dried peaches and dried meat to eat.

All the *Diné* were making bows and arrows, especially arrows, to use if the enemies came to our territory. It had been some years that we had spent in this area, and not an enemy had come to where we were. This place had been home to me since I was born. It was a young man who told me that he and other warriors had gone to *Nazlíní* (Nazlini) where they heard about some Navajos stealing mules and oxen at Fort Defiance. The leaders talked about it. *Dahghaa'í* (Mustache – of the *Mą'ii' Deeshgíízhnii*, Coyote Pass clan) said that maybe the time had come for us to go to where we wanted to go. He said, "Many of you know where to move. The soldiers might come here. Many of you traveled from east, south, west and north. We are glad you came. We cannot take our livestock with us to *Tsélą́ą́'* (Navajo Fortress Rock). The men have been working on the trails for many days; so you can go to the safe place until the soldiers are gone. Some others have sent *Diné* to Fort Defiance to steal mules and oxen so the soldiers will not have any transportation to come soon. The soldiers are now on foot and we have time to go to the safe place. I want you to kill most of the livestock and prepare the meat. It is getting cold now, so we have to start in four days. We must be on the top of *Tsélą̨ą̨'* before it starts to snow. The men are still taking wood to the top. The ladders have been put up. I don't know, my people, why we have to do this. We never harmed anyone, but the enemies are hurting us. My people, be strong and be prepared to defend yourselves and your people. We will leave some men here at our village to take care of the livestock; that way we will not face starvation soon."

Dahghaa'í was a great leader, even though he was a very small man. I remember, he was one of the wealthy men with about 500 sheep and 20 horses. It was *Ghą̨ą̨jį̨* (October) when we made the move to *Tsélą̨ą̨'*. I helped a little girl whose name was *Asdzą́ą́ Ashįįhí* (Salt Lady) [my great-grandmother, on my mother's side]. She was about seven years old. She had no immediate family. It was hard climbing to the top of *Tsélą̨ą̨'*. We were on *Tsélą̨ą̨'* for about 20 days without any trouble happening. The word then came that some soldiers were moving east of Canyon de Chelly and another group was moving toward the mouth of the canyon. I remember that the leaders were saying that we could give up or we could cooperate with the soldiers but that they were very dangerous when they had rifles.

The top of *Tsélą̨ą̨'* was well fortified from any kind of enemies, with no danger from attack. It was pretty cold, but we all had enough food and shelter. Then it was *Niłch'itsoh* (December). The snow was pretty heavy, and the water supply was good. The preparation was excellently done by our men before we went on to *Tsélą̨ą̨'*. There were 13 natural water holes of different sizes – that is, hollow places in the rock, like bowls, where water collected. We had men going back to our village every day to visit the tenants and to bring back real fresh mutton. In time, everyone got used to living on the top of *Tsélą̨ą̨'*. About halfway down the trail *Diné* warriors waited for any kind of attack. The total number of *Diné* (on the rock and in the village) must have been over 300. It got to be *Yasniłtééz* (January) when the lookout watchers saw a group of soldiers coming down through Canyon del Muerto from the east. About 60 soldiers were coming, and they would be there in about two days. All mothers, children, older people and younger people were instructed to stay quiet until the soldiers passed us. It was the next afternoon when the soldiers moved closer through the canyon. From where I was they looked very small, but they were armed and they had good horses. They camped below us at the junction. Our men didn't try to attack them. The next day they moved down the canyon and disappeared. *Dahghaa'í* said: "There are about 75 more soldiers at the mouth of the canyon, and they have war commanding officers. The chief one's name is *Bi'éé' Łichíí'ii* (Kit Carson). He is a very pure White Man, and he has two commandants under him, and they will come back to fight us. *Bi'éé' Łichíí'ii* will never come to our stronghold. He is afraid he might get killed by the *Diné*. That's why he stays back behind his soldiers and just gives orders. He never has been in the canyon – just his soldiers. He is the one who doesn't understand his law that people are not to be killed. Now he knows where the large body of Navajo Indians is located. Let him and his soldiers try to attack us. We didn't do anything wrong. His rifle shots will not come to the secret rock, but be on the alert. They will come here again."

I didn't know how long we would be on *Tsélą́ą́'*, but, four days later, the white enemies were on the canyon rim across from us, and they fired at our location, but it was too far and they left again. After six days I was making peach stew when someone yelled, "They are coming back again from down the canyon." My aunt on my father's side said, "Come! So the soldiers think they can starve the Navajos." In the afternoon one group went in the south canyon and one group up the north canyon. To me there seemed to be about 75 soldiers altogether. I thought this might be the last Navajo war. Every preparation had been made to meet the white soldiers.

We heard there were some Navajos who had surrendered to the White Men already. *Hastiin Jaa'tł'óół Ninéézii* (Mr. Long Earrings) had come with his band a few days before, and he said, "My people, you have a very good place to fight the enemies. There are some *'Ańá'í Diné* with the white soldiers. The *'Ańá'í Diné* broke my treaty with the White Men. We will move some of the ladders if the enemies start to come up, but I don't think they will ever come to where we are now. Let them fight us, and we shall remain up here."

Tsélą́ą́' is almost separate from the main point of *Tséjiin* (Black Rock Canyon). There is a main point, but there is a great cracked gap between it and the rock. One long pine log had been placed across the gap which was now an icy pole. It would be impossible for the enemies to get across the first long pole. The next ledge was a well fortified area with about 200 Navajo warriors. They had very few rifles but plenty of bows and arrows. The trail led to more long poles which were ladders which could be pulled to the top of the rock. They were very long poles. Then two poles were across a gap caused by cracks high in the rock. Finally, another pole went right to the top. Those poles could be removed to the top. All these poles had been brought, with much hard labor, by our men last summer and fall from 15 to 20 miles away from *Tsélą́ą́'*.

We heard two shots down below that afternoon, and that was it for the day. The next day the soldiers were still in the canyon. Some of our people were shouting at the soldiers, calling them names, swearing, cursing and threatening them in the Navajo tongue. There were a few more rifle shots down below us. It started to snow, and the white soldiers left. We were safe again, but I don't remember what the soldiers yelled to us about coming back. There must have been some arguments by loud oral voice. It was cold because it was *Yasniłtéez* (January).

Some of our people were sick from the cold. Some families lost beloved ones, but it was natural to us. Our men were going across to other

The Navajos left their village, went down into Black Rock Canyon and then began the slow and laborious climb to the top of Navajo Fortress Rock where they sought safety from Kit Carson's soldiers. (The illustration depicts the south side of the rock, with Black Rock Canyon going to the right – approximately southeast – and the beginning of Canyon del Muerto at the left from where it cuts to the northeast.)

Navajo men climbed down 900 feet of the straight north face of the rock and silently drew water from a pool close to sleeping soldiers. It was on the dark side, away from the moonlight, where Canyon ael Muerto begins.

canyons, even if it was cold, with ice and snow on the trail. Some died from slipping off the rocks, poles and icy ground.

Still no enemies went to our village where our livestock was being cared for because it was almost impossible to reach it from any side unless you knew just where to go. Early in *Atsa'biyáázh* (February) we heard that the soldiers were returning to kill all the Navajos who didn't give up and go to *Tséhootsooí* (Fort Defiance). We heard that there were soldiers who were poisoning water and food so that the Navajos would die from it. If anyone wanted to leave, it was up to the individual. Sometime in *Atsa'biyáázh* (February) the soldiers returned to stay in the bottom of the canyon. The *yas* (snow) was starting to melt during the day, and the snow was going down. At first the soldiers didn't try to come up the trail. They camped for about 11 days without bothering us. They just patrolled in the canyons for other Navajos. The word we received was that many Navajos elsewhere were starving and dying. Many of them had already gone to Fort Defiance from Chinle. The number in our band was decreasing because some of them were captured while they were on missions. After 16 days the soldiers below us started shooting at the southeast side of *Tsélą́ą́'*. All day there was crying, yelling and shooting, and some wounded Navajos were brought to the top of *Tsélą́ą́'*. The next day the Navajo warriors came up, and they pulled up the poles. The following few days everything was silent, except those wounded warriors were yelling or moaning. The soldiers below fried bacon so that the smell would rise to the rock, making the Navajos hungry and persuade them to give up and come down to the soldiers' camp or starve.

About 20 of our warriors had died. They were buried on the west end of the flat rock. The soldiers stayed for another five or six days after the poles had been pulled up from the trail. Then we had a water problem. The wounded were thirsty, and the snow, ice and water were gone. *Hastį́į́ Jaa'tł'óół Ninéézii* (Mr. Long Earrings) put everybody to work to help with all kinds of ropes and jugs. There were ropes, made of yucca plants, that they used to pull up the poles, and we had some Mexican ropes. There were enough ropes to get some water from the bottom of the canyon where the soldiers were waiting. There was moonlight, but it didn't shine on the north side of *Tsélą́ą́'*. I don't remember how many *Diné* got water that night. The Navajos were getting it from the bottom of the dark side of the canyon all night long while the moonlight was bright elsewhere. It is about 900 feet of straight wall from where the Navajos got water – right close to the white soldiers' feet.

The soldiers left the next day, heading toward Chinle. The *Diné* placed the poles back on the trail. The warriors went down first to pick up the dead *Diné* and bury them. We were instructed not to leave until the soldiers left Chinle. According to one *'Anáʼí Diné*, the soldiers were starving; so they had to leave. But the Navajos on *Tsélą́ą́'* didn't starve. *Tsélą́ą́'* is one of the best earth mothers we have.

My paternal grandmother then said, "Let your other grandmother finish the rest of the story."

Now I (Teddy Draper, Sr.) am living at Chinle, Arizona, and I am employed by Navajo Community College as Navajo language instructor. During World War II, I was in the South Pacific Ocean area. It was 28 years ago, and more, when I was using fine American rifles against the Japanese in the battle of Iwo Jima as a member of the U.S. Marine Corp, 28th Regiment, 5th Division. While I fought on Iwo Jima Island, I thought of my grandmothers. My maternal grandmother had died of old age in 1943 while I was overseas. She was called *Asdzą́ą́ Ashįįhíni' Biche'é* (Salt Lady's Daughter). I remember what she told about after leaving *Tsélą́ą'* in Canyon del Muerto.

She said:

This is what your great-grandmother told me. Everybody was leaving early in *Woozhch'įįd* (March) from *Tsélą́ą'*. Before we went to *Tsélą́ą'* I came from the twin trail which is north of *Tsélą́ą'*, and all my close relatives were left there. I went with some of my kinship. I was alone at the edge of *Tsélą́ą'* where the trail starts down, watching everyone move down. No one seemed to want to help me go down on the difficult trail. Then, in the afternoon, an elderly man came by and said, "*Shi tsooí tį́ tséjiiní deesáagóó.*" ("My grandchild, let's go to the point of Black Rock Canyon.") He helped me all the way down the trail. In some shaded areas, there were still icy spots. I followed the people through Black Rock Canyon and up the trail to where our old village was. Then I knew who *Asdzaan Naakaii* was [my paternal great-grandmother]. She was beautiful like a *Háyoołkááł Atééd* (Dawn Girl). *Asdzaan Naakaii* helped me much because I didn't have enough clothes. She made me nice yucca shoes and a skirt.

One time *Asdzaan Naakaii* told me that she was thinking about going to Fort Defiance to live. It was spring when some of our people left for Fort Defiance to turn themselves in to the U.S. soldiers. *Asdzaan Naakaii* left me, and I was lonesome; but I didn't want to go because my uncle *Dahghaa'í* protected me and fed me. *Dahghaa'í* told me to stay and take care of the livestock; so I did. Then it was about *Bini'ant'ą́ą́ts'osi* (August), almost a year after we started having trouble with the enemies. *Dahghaa'í* told me he and some people would turn themselves in at Fort Defiance and would go to *Hwééldi*, but he said, "I will come back to visit in the future." We still had a great number of livestock. We stayed in the same area for a year after the soldiers left us. There were no enemies in our territory, and I know we were protected by our great ones who made us.

About another year, after lambing time, some people came into our village early before dawn. It was *Dahghaa'í* and other Navajos. They had horses, and there was something on the horse *Dahghaa'í* was riding. I looked at it, and he told me it was a saddle. He told us he had escaped from *Hwééldi* – two rivers away in the east where many Navajos were kept. He said, "We were on the journey for 22 days to get back here. I will return to *Hwééldi* sometime in the future."

They stayed with us for about a year and most of them went back to *Hwééldi*, but *Dahghaa'í* didn't go. His second wife and his older children went with him to Navajo Mountain, and he took some sheep and his horses because he was afraid someone might tell on him. He was not only protecting himself, but he was protecting us, too. He didn't want us to be discovered by the soldiers. His plans were to go far away from *Hwééldi* because he wanted to kill a Navajo man who had told lies about the Navajo people.

The man named *Jaa'tł'óół Ninéézii* (Long Earrings) left our band that year, too. We had about 80 Navajos camping there, but sometimes we had more, and sometimes we had not so many because some of them were traveling through or had escaped from *Hwééldi*. The following winter we had a bad time because we didn't have enough food to go around to all Navajos. Some babies were born, and the men kept the women fed. I was about 10 years old by then. We lost some babies and some of our older people from natural sickness. Some Navajos who came died, too, because they were wounded while they were escaping from *Hwééldi*. All these years were exciting to me.

A man called *Dahghaa'łtsoí* (Yellow Mustache) became our leader. He was *Ashįįhí* (Salt People) clan. I called him my grandfather. He gave me what I needed and taught me how to make yucca shoes and ropes and how to weave baskets into water jugs. I kept myself busy helping around in the village, but we were always guided by the elders. The boys were trained to become fighters.

In the summer we still planted our corn and squash on the Black Rock Canyon upper floor. The enemies never touched this floor in the canyon. The peach trees at our camp and in Black Rock Canyon gave us good crops all the time because the soldiers didn't destroy the trees or even visit the place.

In the third year we were not too afraid of the soldiers. We heard that our people would return to their land soon. At that same time we were over-crowding our village. One of my aunts escaped from *Hwééldi* that year, and she said, "I left *Hwééldi* 26 days ago with four others, but only two of us returned. The other three were killed by our enemies."

The fourth winter started and the snow began to fall. I got hungry sometimes, and our animals decreased very fast to very few!

All these years I didn't hear about my cousin, *Asdzaan Naakaii*, who had gone to *Hwééldi*. She must have been about 20 years old, and maybe she had a baby.

In 1946, after my return from the South Pacific campaign and the occupation of Japan, my grandmother on my father's side still lived in the canyon about three miles from *Tsélą́ą'*. She was old and grayhaired, but her eyes still saw clearly and her body was still very strong. She had been born at *Hwééldi* and was about 81 years old. She lived at the same place where she told me the story of *Tsélą́ą'* about 15 years before. She didn't recognize me when I came to her because I was wearing a uniform. I told her I was *Kiiłbáhí* (Grayboy). Then she cried and said, "*Ahaalaane'éé shiyáázh, doolá dó'ayoó át'ééda lá.*" ("My poor boy, it was very hard going"). I told her about my experiences throughout the South Pacific. I told her I could speak Japanese, too.

She was very proud of me. Her name was *Naakaii Asdzaaní' Biche'é'* (Mexican Lady's Daughter). I lost her in 1949. It was an accident. She went out at night and stumbled over a log and fell on a stone, hitting the right side of her head.

I told some of my war stories to my grandmother. They were chiefly about the invasion of Iwo Jima, but, also, about my fighting and serving, for a total of 32 months on the island of Guam, on Kwajelein in the Marshall Islands and in the occupation of Japan. About Iwo Jima, I told her of the four American soldiers raising the flag after the capture of Mt. Suribachi, with fighting going on all around. I showed her a picture of the event, and I told her about Ira Hayes, a Pima Indian from Arizona, being one of the four – and that I was about 100 feet away from the scene when the picture was taken.

I told her that, often, during the terrible fighting, when I was sweating and almost in a state of shock, I thought of my grandmothers and of Canyon de Chelly and Canyon del Muerto. I explained that it was a different kind of war from the fighting in the canyons and the suffering at *Hwééldi.* For one thing, we were using the best weapons in the world – not just bows and arrows.

I never saw my grandfather on my father's side, but I did see my grandfather on my mother's side. My parents now are living at Del Muerto. My father is 83 years old, and my mother is 76. They are both in good health. The Navajo language was used at certain times in the South Pacific during World War II, in place of a code, so that the Japanese could not understand our communications. They never "broke" it – never understood it. I was one of the "code-talkers." The Navajo language helped to win the war against the Japanese in World War II.

Navajo Fortress Rock at the junction of Canyon del Muerto and Black Rock Canyon in what is now the Canyon de Chelly National Monument. The photo was taken from the floor of Del Muerto, facing approximately south. The position of the first log bridge across the chasm at the left is drawn in black and indicated by an arrow. Climbing logs (ladders), which were visible from this point, are drawn in black to the left of the upper center and indicated by arrows. The top ladder, as described in the story, still is in place after more than 100 years.

View from the upper edge of Canyon del Muerto (northern rim) to the eastern part of the top of Fortress Rock. It was from this rim that Kit Carson's soldiers shot at the Navajos, but the distance was too great for the firing to be effective. The rock virtually is an island rising out of the canyon, separated by a chasm from the land shown in the upper left corner of the photo. The view is toward the southeast.

Western end of Navajo Fortress Rock as seen from the northern rim of Canyon del Muerto. Black Rock Canyon extends to the left, southeastward from the far side of the Rock. Canyon del Muerto continues to the right and later joins Canyon de Chelly. The Navajos climbed up the eastern end of the rock (not shown in this photo).

Western "point" of Fortress Rock – photographer standing in the junction and facing east. Canyon del Muerto is to the left; Black Rock Canyon is to the right. The village mentioned in the story was on top of the land showing at the left. Beyond the outcropping at the left was the area where the Navajos drew water, as told (and illustrated) in the account by one of Mr. Draper's ancestors.

Chahadineli Benally

Ch'ahádiniini' Bináli

This elderly Navajo, approximately 85 years old, lives near Valley Store, Ariz., between Chinle and Many Farms. He is a well-known medicine man and has a wide reputation as a storyteller and Navajo historian. The source of this story was one of his grandmothers who told him the true-to-life account. His main clan is the *Kinyąą'áanii* (Towering House People).

MY GREAT-GRANDMOTHER'S SISTER had four daughters and one boy. The youngest of the four daughters was taken captive by the enemies. The story was related to me by her (my late grandmother), and I will tell as much as I can remember. After all, it did not happen yesterday nor a year ago.

The family was living close to Black Mesa, west of the mesa where *Hastiin* (Mister) *Tsébícha'í* (Rock It Has a Hat) lives now. The enemies, the Mexicans, must have camped overnight in a nearby valley because it was early in the morning when they came to attack. They were out killing and capturing our people at the time.

One of the girls said her sister left the family camp early that morning without looking for enemies who might be close by or approaching from any direction. She took a five-year-old boy, a close kin, with her. They walked quite a distance from the camp to the cornfields, where there also was a small patch of potatoes which were ripe and ready for gathering. While the little boy played nearby, she dug potatoes. Suddenly she saw a group of Mexicans riding out from behind a large rock about half a mile away. They must have spotted the little boy for they headed in his direction, and there was nothing to do but to try and hide. The girl guessed that they had been spotted, but, if by any chance they had not been seen, which was possible, she crawled underneath a large bush of greasewood, pulling the boy with her.

The riders stayed on the main horse trail, but, just as they were passing, four of them turned their horses and headed toward the potato patch, searching for the two Navajos. They pulled their horses right up to the bush, and they all dismounted. They had long rifles in scabbards tied to their saddles. One of them stepped forward, held out his hand for the little boy and pulled him forward. A second man did the same to the girl who was to become my grandmother. One of the men opened a bag of potatoes that my grandmother had picked, glanced in it and threw it away. He put the boy behind him on his horse, and the girl was helped upon a horse behind another man with whom she rode all through the journey.

This is how they were captured, and the journey started through *Tsé'abe'í* (Breast Rock). Along about noon they stopped near *Tséłichíí' Dah Azkání* (Red Rock) where they unsaddled the horses and prepared to eat lunch. The little boy came running to my grandmother, crying. They were given a little food, and, together, they ate. The Mexicans threw an armful of fresh long-ear corn to the horses, and this looked very tempting. The girl, who still was hungry, wished she could get hold of some.

After lunch, the journey continued toward *Lók'aahnteel* (Ganado). Once in a while one of the men would pull something from his pocket, glance at it and put it back. (Later the girl came to know that it was called a watch. At that time it was kept in a pocket instead of on the wrist.) The journey slowly advanced toward *Tsé Bínii Dziní* (Rock Standing Against the Wall), and some of the riders were sleeping in the saddle as they rode along. Had there been an ambush, they would not have had a chance. They all would have been killed. Right above *Be'ek'idhatsoh* (Big Lake), where there was plenty of grass, they unsaddled their horses at sunset and prepared to camp for the night. One of the men tried to get the little boy to sleep with him, but the boy kept crying and wouldn't settle down; so the man brought him over, and the girl tucked him beside her and they went to sleep. The men were up at daylight and prepared breakfast. The captives were fed, as they were for the rest of the journey.

Preparations for the day's ride – packing several mules with blankets, food, etc. – took time. At last, the men covered the fire with sand, being cautious not to start a fire in the tall grass that grew all around. At noon they stopped for lunch at *Na'ásho'íító'í* (Snake Water). After lunch they went on below *Lók'aahnteel* (Ganado), and from there to *Łééyí'tó* (Klagetoh). Overnight camp was made not far from there. The next day, they stopped for lunch in the region of *Ch'ilzhóó'* (Chambers). That was as far as she knew the places, the areas and the names of them. From there everything was unfamiliar and strange. They traveled across deserts, plains, mountains and rivers, traveling toward some large mountains, very dimly seen in the

The Navajo girl was helped upon a horse behind a Mexican with whom she rode throughout the long journey. The little boy, a close kin, rode with another Mexican.

distance; and the journey continued toward those mountains heading straight south. She thought that she knew *Tsoodził* (Mount Taylor) near which they spent the night.

After another day, they camped across *Tooh* (Rio Grande River). Then there were more mountains which they traveled through, getting nearer to their destination which was in the territory of New Mexico. It had been very far, and it seemed to the girl like traveling would never end, when they finally came to a wide river. After crossing it the party separated; some of the men rode on, taking the little boy with them. The others lived near the river, and an older Mexican in the party took her to his house where she met his wife.

As they came into the room, his wife rushed to him, crying. They embraced and hugged each other for a while. The wife was an elderly woman with hair almost all white. The Navajo girl shook hands with her, and the woman said something, but all the girl understood was "my friend."

By that time she knew that she was pregnant with a baby for her husband whom she had left behind along with the rest of the family. Back home, they had been missed by the family that same day, and, from the tracks and evidence left behind, they knew what had happened. Some relatives went looking for them and saw the riders from a distance, with the woman and the boy, but they had no hope of saving them.

That evening, in the Mexican home, she was given two blankets and a sleeping pad, also space inside the same house that the couple lived in. From that time on she got acquainted with the Mexican woman, and she helped with the cooking, house work and whatever chores that needed to be done. Soon, the two women got so used to each other that they were almost inseparable. The Mexican man didn't bother her; he went about attending to his daily chores.

It was in the fall. Winter was just around the corner, and she was growing bigger with the baby inside her.

She caught on to the language fast, and soon the two women were communicating fluently in the Mexican language. The Mexican woman didn't like the idea of the girl being captured and held captive in her pregnant condition, and she expressed her opinion by saying, "This will not be permitted. No! We won't permit anything bad to happen, no matter what he says (referring to her husband). I don't like it! There is no sense in your captivity! There is no use in having you suffer. You will go home!"

My grandmother liked the idea.

After being there five months, a caravan of Mexican men approached, riding side by side in twos. The woman told her the purpose of the visit was to buy her. Then she added, "But I won't let them have you; my answer will be 'no'! You are already given to me; so you belong to me. I shall never agree to let them take you."

The couple had no children of their own – just the two of them living there. And now the Navajo captive. There were other neighbors, friends who lived close by who would come for visits. Sometimes they would get into conversation about the Navajos, and one elderly woman said, "The people named '*Diné*' are very brave; no other tribe can match their braveness. If the Navajo people as a whole would fight against a single tribe, the other tribe would not have a chance. They all would be killed. As it is now, almost all other tribes have become allies to fight against the Navajo people. They have no friends among other tribes here. Their only friends are *Beehaí* (Jicarilla Apaches), but they live far off up north; and one other tribe in the east." Then she added, to the girl, "But I am your friend and I am on your side. Should a time ever come that I would get captured by your people, I'm willing to live among them."

At the time the Mexican men came, slave trading went on not too far from the house. There was a special meeting house for the purpose. The caravan that arrived had camped there, and the old Mexican man was over there talking with the people. In the meantime, the two ladies were busy, preparing meals for the visitors, setting out food on the long table. When this was ready the men were called to come in to eat. As they went into the room, they gave the girl hard looks.

The next day, just as the morning star appeared, the two women started cooking again, and, at sunrise, the visitors had their breakfast. The trading was postponed to another date. The visitors brought their horses and prepared to leave. In the slave trading, the girl was one who was to be sold, but the Mexican woman kept her word. She had a hot discussion with her husband. The husband wanted to sell the Navajo, but her Mexican friend flatly refused. Later, the woman found out that there was some correspondence going on between her husband and another man who was interested in buying the woman, but he had kept the letters hidden from his wife. Somehow, she got hold of them. In one letter it was written that the man was willing to pay a high price for her and that he would come any day now. His wife was furious, tore up the letter and threw it in the fire, saying to her husband, "I will never permit you to do this." They had a fight over this, and some friends had to break it up. The man was pretty angry.

On the day of the appointment, toward sunset, the same caravan of Mexicans returned. After their arrival at the meeting place, the discussion of slave trading got started. Some time toward dawn, the girl's Mexican friend came back from the meeting and she told her what had taken place and how she absolutely refused to let her be sold, regardless of the cost. She had told the men that she wanted to have the Navajo lady keep her company now that she was in her old age. She had said, "Let her stay with me; I can't let you take her." With that she had left the room.

Afterward there was a long discussion, for the old man kept hoping his wife would give in. But, the next day, they left again after they ate breakfast.

Seven months had passed, and my grandmother's baby was growing bigger. The old Mexican man was still angry and pouting. He had left home for several weeks.

During that time, the Mexican woman made a plan for her. She said, "I don't want my husband to sell you. He'll never guess or find out how I'm to let you go. I want to release you to go home."

My grandmother hugged the woman to her, calling her sister in the Mexican language which she could understand and speak very well. The elderly woman said, "I know the journey will be very hard and fearful, but you'll make it back all right. The faith and belief within you will guide you home safe. I will let you take one of these long swords; there are a lot of them in there. It will come in handy in case you are attacked, perhaps by vicious animals. I will hide a sword along with a knife for you near the river." Then she added, after thinking a while, "A month from now they will return, and by then there will be a definite decision. I'm sure they'll take you then, if you still are here."

From that time she made plans and preparations for my grandmother's escape. She thought that, after the men returned, and while they were deeply involved with the meeting, would be a good time for her to take off; she started to get ready the things that the young woman would need to take on her journey. All these were to be fixed ahead of time so that there wouldn't be any delay when the day came for her to leave. The Mexican woman and her husband were in a happy mood, talking about the butchering of a steer for their visitors. Four days before their arrival a big animal was butchered, and the meat prepared for a feast. At the same time, the woman prepared some meat into jerky for her friend.

In the meantime, my grandmother was busy, too. Among other things, she cooked some blue corn and made it into heavy mush. Her food was packed into a container, along with a jug of water. The old woman also gave my grandmother two blankets, one black and one red, which were brand new. All the things were fixed into a bundle,

The storyteller's grandmother hugged the elderly Mexican lady and called her sister in the Mexican language which she quickly had learned to understand and to speak very well.

The girl could see that the search by the Mexicans mostly was in the direction opposite to where she was hiding.

tied with a rope on each end and arranged so that it could be carried over the back.

Toward evening on a certain day, the visitors arrived, tables were set with food and they all came in to eat.

The Mexican woman had given my grandmother instructions, telling her how to get across the river and how she should go toward a certain mountain and hide there until the men gave up looking for her. It was the opposite direction from where she had been brought. So, she slipped away late that evening, after the Mexican woman returned from the meeting house and said that it was safe for her to leave. She arranged the pack on her back and started for the river, following her friend's instructions. By that time she was about eight months pregnant. After crossing the river without any difficulty, she came upon some horses that were grazing. Had she got hold of one of them, no doubt she could have traveled a great distance in a single night. However, she climbed the mountain, just as the woman had told her; and, almost at the top, she found a good hiding place where she settled down. From that point, she barely could see the lights where the houses were. She kept looking, trying to see what was happening. Later, she knew that the search was on. She could see torches carried around by searchers, looking for her tracks. They finally gave up toward dawn.

However, early the next morning, just before sunup, they started gathering their horses, and, soon, a group of riders really were searching, riding around appearing to look for her tracks. The search mostly went on in the direction opposite to where she was hiding. The riders split into several groups as they searched. And they all did their searching in the other direction. Soon one group went over the hill toward another mountain, while the rest stayed behind, still looking for her tracks. This went on all day, and, finally, at sundown, they all came riding in to the houses.

In the meantime, my grandmother stayed hidden. Now and then she would look out and watch the activities in the distance below. She took a nap, and it was late in the afternoon when she awoke. Late in the evening she was ready to leave. She started walking carefully down the slope of the mountain. After reaching the bottom, she kept close to the slope, taking care not to make her tracks obvious, walking mostly on rocks and grass. She would take only a mouthful of water now and then because she wanted to make it last for as long as possible. By daybreak she had reached another mountain in the opposite direction from the house from where she had been. She found a cave where she hid because she didn't want to take a chance on being seen. She slept in the cave all day; then, as it was getting dark, she climbed out and started walking again. After she was sure she was going in the right direction, she walked all night. At dawn she crawled under a large cedar tree whose branches hung thickly to the ground, and she went to sleep. She still didn't want to take a chance on traveling in the daytime; so she slept during daylight and traveled at night.

Again, she started out when darkness came, and she traveled all night. By that time she knew she had put a great distance behind her and that there would be little danger of being seen, even if she traveled during the day; so she traveled day and night. She would stop just long enough to rest a while and eat a little of the food, saving it as long as possible. After traveling without sleep for almost two days, she was exhausted; and she found a place to spend the night.

Next morning, she came to the edge of a mountain from where she could see miles and miles in every direction. In one direction, she could see a white tent several miles away. "Probably a sheepherder's camp," she thought, and she avoided it. After traveling several more days and nights, toward evening, as she was still walking, she thought of continuing all night, but she heard the howl of a wolf, and she knew danger was approaching. Nearby were some large trees, thin of foliage at the bottom and thick with branches and leaves at the top. She climbed one of the trees and settled near the top, making herself as comfortable as possible – not knowing how long she'd be up there.

Soon the wolf came running, growling and showing his long white teeth. It kept charging up the tree, but fell each time. Then the woman heard another sound, and two more wolves appeared. They all would run and try to climb the tree. They were there all night. Finally, my grandmother got impatient. "This has gone on long enough," she thought; so she climbed down to near the bottom of the tree, the sword ready in one hand, prepared to attack the animals. She placed her legs wide apart ana planted one foot against a big branch, while she held onto another branch tightly with one hand. In the other she held the long weapon. One animal was very vicious, clawing the tree and growling. When it tried to climb the tree again she thrust the long sword into its throat. The wolf made a strangling noise, fell backward and died almost instantly. The other two wolves went over, sniffed the blood that was flowing from the mouth of the dead wolf and left, running fast over the hill and howling after they had gone quite a distance. Much later, they howled far off in the mountains.

At dawn she crawled under a large cedar tree the branches of which hung thick to the ground – and went to sleep.

After the danger had passed, my grandmother climbed down (it was daylight by that time), and she walked all day. There were few signs of life anywhere, not even many tracks. Once in a while she would come upon coyote tracks as she walked across the valleys, mountains, plains and desert lands. Before she reached another mountain, the sun disappeared, and it began to get dark fast. She was exhausted, and she started looking for a place to rest for the night. She came upon a small stream where she decided to stay. She took out her holy corn pollen and prayed to Mother Earth, saying, "Hear me! Let no one see me or find me throughout my journey as I go in the unknown direction. Let someone direct and guide me. Mr. Owl, I know you live above in the high cliffs. In time of trouble, I am in need of your guidance. I trust you will guide me."

After her prayers, she sat down and took out some cornmeal, which she ate with water. Before long, an owl hooted a short distance away. Soon it came to rest on top of a nearby rock. Once more, she pleaded with the owl, saying, "I will follow you. Hoot at intervals so that I will know which way I'm going as you guide me toward my homeland."

It was very dark as she started walking, following the owl. After a short distance the owl hooted again, and she walked in the direction from which the sound came. This continued all night – the owl hooting at intervals, and the woman following at a distance – until early dawn. At that time the owl left her. She had reached another mountain; and, after climbing to the top, she stopped to rest and to eat more blue cornmeal. From there she could see for miles around in all directions. In the far-off distance she could see a large herd of sheep grazing in a valley. Nearby was a tent, and she figured it was another sheepherder's camp.

After resting for several hours, she continued her journey through a wide section of mountain forest. Just as she reached the ridge of the mountain, she heard the barking of a dog behind her. It sounded quite close, and, with a frightened feeling, she looked around. She thought that search dogs might be coming after her, and she looked for a place to hide. Directly ahead she saw the shell of an old tree stump, with the insides rotted out. It would be a safe place, she thought, as she climbed inside the stump and stood there. At this moment, a big yellow dog ran up, with another (white with black spots) following right behind. Both dogs barked and ran back and forth. Then one charged up, ready to attack. The moment it came near my grandmother stuck the sword into its heart, and the dog fell dead. As the second one attacked, she did the same thing. She left both dogs lying there and walked away quickly, for she feared there might be riders behind them. She hastily went over the ridge and almost ran down to the level ground below. From there she could see a region thick with trees, and she aimed for them. The sun had gone down again.

She did not know how many days and nights she had traveled. She had come from the east, from somewhere beyond and below *Tóta'* (Farmington). That she later figured out, but, at the time, she didn't know. Upon her capture she had been taken toward the southeast. She thought that, somewhere, coming back, she had lost her way after she had made her escape from the Mexicans.

Anyway, she walked all night, until, at dawn, when she was almost exhausted, she came to an area where there was a lot of green grass; and she decided to rest. She unpacked her blankets and some food and prepared a bed on the ground. After eating and drinking a little water, she went to sleep. Just before sundown, a coyote howled back where she had come from; and, looking carefully, she saw the

One wolf was especially vicious, clawing, trying to climb the tree and growling. The girl killed it with her sword.

coyote tracking her. The animal saw her, too. It stood looking at her for a while, and then slowly advanced. It seemed to be uncertain of itself, hesitating a moment before each step. When it had come quite near, she said, "What is it?". The coyote slunk along the ground. She had frightened it. She tried to decide what she should do to it – perhaps kill it with the sword. Then, on second thought, she decided against this and decided to just plead with it to help her find her way home. "Mr. Coyote, that howls with the early dawn of the mornings, great things have been said about you. Turquoise you carried. I want to get home. I'm in very poor condition and barely making it on my journey."

As she talked, she noticed that the coyote was watching her. It tried to stand up, but it didn't seem able to raise its back end; so it dragged itself to within a short distance of her with its two front arms until, suddenly, it got up and ran over the hill without looking back.

She then fixed her pack and left. She started through *Tsénaajin* (Black Rock Cliff) and finally came to *Tooh* (San Juan River). She noticed that the river was running low. At the shore, she took all her clothes off, put them into a bundle, along with the rest of her pack, and prepared to cross the river. With both hands holding the bundle above her head, she got into the water and started to cross. Before

She came upon a small stream where she decided to rest. She distributed some of her holy corn pollen and said a prayer to Mother Earth.

long, the water was above her knees. About halfway across, it came up to her chest and soon was to her chin. However, she got across and sat down to get dry before putting her clothes on.

A familiar mountain was in view in the distance, and from there she recognized the different directions. From one of the Navajo late leaders she remembered hearing of an old horse trail that led from about where she was toward the mountain, and suddenly she knew exactly where she was. She realized that somewhere along the way she had lost the direction toward her homeland, but now she knew it. She began to walk again.

Her baby was about due. She stopped to rest, ate some blue cornmeal, which was about gone. She had filled the small jug with water at the river. Feeling very tired, she took a short nap before continuing her journey on through *Tsénaajin.* She finally found the horse trail that she had heard about. It was in the afternoon by the time she reached the other side of *Lók'ai'jígai* (Lukachukai) at a place called *Há'jishzhíís* (Where He Came Out Dancing). After walking through there, she came upon the ridge overlooking *Tó Dilhil* (Whiskey Creek). There she stopped to rest when she felt some sharp pains and knew her time was drawing near. She knew, too, that she would have to get prepared before the sun went down. But, first, she had to find a good place.

Her pains began to come at closer intervals as she worked. She cleared a hollow in the sand under a thick cedar tree, gathered some firewood and built a fire. Then she gathered a supply of wood. She also brought some big flat rocks and put them into hot ashes. Then she lay down, waiting for the rocks to get hot. After they were hot, she placed the rocks and ashes under her, right against her lower back. She was glad that she knew what to do in a case like this. She had observed, and helped with, some babies being delivered at home. Once in a while, she gave a good massaging to her abdomen. While she massaged she sang the sacred song for the safe arrival of the baby.

When the morning star rose over the horizon, the baby came. She tore a wide strip off one of the blankets and used it to wrap tightly around her waist for support. There was hardly any blood. The baby was alive, although very thin. So she had borne the baby after she had come back to her land and while she was barely making it to her home. She decided that she had no choice but to abandon the child. That would be the best way, she thought. She talked to the baby, saying, "What other way is there, my baby? I have been journeying in the poorest way, after being captured and allowed to escape. Now I must leave you behind. I ask of you not to let any evil come my way because of what I must do to you."

At sunup she was ready to leave. She ate the last of the blue cornmeal, with water, and then she walked away. Just before she went over a ridge, she looked back to where the baby was, and she saw crows flying nearby.

She became very exhausted as she walked on and on. In the region of *Díwózhiibii'tó* (Upper Greasewood, Arizona) she couldn't go any farther; so she set fire to an old stump and spent the night by the fire. In another day and a half she crossed the valley between *Tséhilį́* (Tsaile) and *Bą́ąnijigház* (Slip Off Mesa). By noon of that last day, she came back to the place where she and the boy had been captured. It had been almost nine months from the time they had been captured to when she returned.

Having the baby had made her very weak, and she got exhausted easily. So, once more, she stopped to rest under some thick greasewood. She had been seen by her relatives from a good distance, where the families were living. The people were curious, asking one another who it could be. A man (it happened to be her husband) went out to see. He kept out of sight as he walked toward the person, keeping his bow and arrows ready. By that time it was in the afternoon, and she felt rested and ready to continue her journey. The man was quite near, and he could see that it was a woman dressed in Mexican style. He stayed hidden as he watched her, and, when she started walking again, he recognized her. He was about to catch up with her when she saw him, carrying his bow and arrows. Suddenly, she recognized him, and she stood there, startled. He came and embraced her, with tears in his eyes.

It was the custom that when a person had been captured and held in captivity a certain length of time, upon his or her return, a certain ceremonial had to be performed over the person before he or she could begin to associate again with family and relatives. The husband took her pack and ran home ahead of her, bearing the news. The family was living right below *Ténineezí* (Tall Rock), where there are some authentic old hogans today. While she was walking in, the family started preparations for the ceremonial. Upon her arrival she undressed some distance from the hogan where the ceremonial was to take place. The medicine man came out of the hogan, singing and carrying a prayer stick in one hand. He extended one end of the prayer stick to her, and together they walked into the hogan where yucca soap was ready. She was bathed and then dried with white cornmeal. The medicine man started his prayers, which continued until evening. When they were over, she was greeted by each member of the family. Tears of joy were shed, and they were happy. Together they shared the blessing of yellow corn pollen.

Just before the girl went over the ridge she looked back to where she had left her baby, and she saw crows flying near it.

This is the story of how my grandmother came home from captivity. She was of the *Kinyąą'áanii* (Tall House) clan. She died of old age. Also, my grandfather died of old age. Both were buried with white corn, which is the custom when a person dies of old age.

The boy who was captured with her never was found. My grandmother never went to *Hwééldi* during the Long Walk period. She was living at *Tóhaalíní* (Water Pond or Spring) when the people returned.

The girl recognized her husband who ran up and embraced her with tears in his eyes.

Rita Wheeler

Mrs. Wheeler is a housewife who lives at Round Rock, Ariz. This is the story of the terrible sufferings of Fort Sumner as told by one of her grandfathers. Now in her sixties, she is of the *Táchii'nii* (Red Streak Extending Into the Water) clan.

WHAT I WILL TALK ABOUT INVOLVES my late grandfather, my late mother's grandmother and her grandfather.

Our ancestors lived generation after generation around this area, the place called *Da'ák'ehóteeł* (Large Corn Field). These particular events took place here where a group of families would live together side by side and move from area to area, seeking and gathering different kinds of food from growing herbs in a wide region. At that time people didn't live close together like they do today. *Da'ák'ehóteeł* was the name for fields where corn was planted annually by the families.

Bones from horses were the only source for making tools – like shoulder blades, large flat bone parts, were made into shovels and used to dig irrigation ditches among the corn. Another tool was called "*gish*," a long, hard stick of greasewood. This stick was made with a sharp-pointed end something like a pick. It also was used for irrigation. Tools were made during the winter months and ready for use by spring. It took a lot of time, patience and effort. Rough stones were used to smooth the bones and sticks into fine smooth ends and edges. My great-grandfather usually was responsible for making the tools and in planting corn and irrigating the fields – this with the help of the rest of the family.

My great-grandfather made the journey to Fort Sumner, along with one of his older sisters. They were children at the time. My great-grandfather was about 11 years old and his sister about 13 when they left.

My grandmother had a brother named *T'áátáhago'áhadit'ání* (Only One Joint). He was a small man, but he was a great runner. He could out-run a horse. He used to travel off to a great distance, from here all the way to *Tsébít'í* (Shiprock) and across the *Tooh* (San Juan River) where he hunted such animals as deer, antelope and wild turkeys; and, sometimes, he would bring some beef fixed into dry jerky. He used to talk about his trips, how he crossed the river and places where it was impossible to cross except over beaver dams.

Here at *Lók'ai'jígai* (Lukachukai), in various areas, different kinds of herbs grew seasonally. People would pick them for food, but sometimes they didn't grow to full bloom on account of bad weather or sudden freezes. Some of the herbs were *dzizé* (berries), *chiiłchin* (sumac plant) and seeds from various other types of plants.

The family had a few sheep and goats. At intervals, one of them was butchered and used sparingly among the family and close relatives; so there was no chance of having a large flock of sheep. The number always stayed the same.

Corn was one of the most important items of diet and one thing that the family always had. There was enough harvested from the previous season to last and last. Corn was ground into a fine powder to make mush, and it was fixed in many other ways. One of the favorite ways was with goat's milk, like mush or gravy; and goat's milk was also one of the very important diet items in the family, especially for children. A group of families lived together, working and sharing what was necessary to survive in the *Lók'ai'jígai* (Lukachukai) area called *Tsékoohootsooí* (Green Box Canyon).

Two of the important in-laws, a man named *Dinée Yázhí* (Little Man), *Tótsohnii* (Big Water) clan, and *T'ááłáhago'áhadit'ání*, were the two men who were the leaders of the small band, consisting of several families.

When my grandfather was still alive, he used to tell me about conditions and historical events or incidents that had taken place. Sometimes he would talk about tragic events, and that would frighten me a great deal. Sometimes, when I was out herding, I would wonder about those things and be afraid. The area was almost uninhabited for miles and miles around; and the few people who lived there moved from place to place where abundance of different kinds of plants and herbs grew. People were constantly on the move in search of food, storing it away for the hard winter months. There was no such thing as having permanent homes in one area, like they do today.

So it was that this group of families moved from Lukachukai all the way across the *Tooh* (San Juan River). They spent many days traveling, camping at night and moving on the next day. In this particular group, no one was emaciated from starvation, although food was hard to get. It was heard sometimes that a child or an elderly man or woman had died of starvation in other family groups, but that was not common until after the conflict among the tribes started.

So my grandfather's families, and several other families related by clans, spent some years across *Tooh* on the mountain at a place called *Dził Giizh* (Between Mountain, Cove, Ariz.). On their arrival, they found that it was true that different kinds of plants and herbs grew abundantly and could be easily gathered and made ready for meals. While there, the family continued to grow corn annually. The families increased in size, and the menfolks went hunting in the surrounding mountains.

The families were living happy and content when it was learned that another tribe, named *Nóóda'í* (Utes) were complaining, saying that the Navajos were hunting in their territory and that they should move elsewhere. They kept nagging the Navajos about it, and soon they were talking very dangerously, with the intention of waging war. For that reason the group practically fled from the area. It was in the winter, and snow was about a foot deep on the ground when the families started moving back in the same manner and in the direction they had come from. Crossing *Tooh* presented no problem. The families and animals crossed near a beaver dam where the current was not swift. Some men and animals that were good swimmers would cross that way, but women and children made their way over the beaver dam. The journey back took many days.

The group had to leave an old woman who was in very poor health and couldn't walk. Her son and a granddaughter stayed with her. The granddaughter, six or seven years old, she had raised from when she was a baby because of the death of the child's mother. The two young people didn't want to leave the grandmother, in spite of persuasion by her and the relatives. There was no way of moving the lady around because she was very old and ill. She was completely an invalid. The son and granddaughter wanted to stay with her regardless of consequences. The boy was older than the girl, and he would go out constantly to bring in wood and keep the fire going for his mother.

For several days after the rest of the family left them, the lady talked with the children. She told them they must leave and follow the relatives. She said, "It's no use. There is not much chance for me to live. Leave me here; I'll take whatever comes. Just leave me some wood and some food and go immediately. Eventually, the fire and the food will be gone and then I'll endure whatever comes to meet my death. My son, take very good care of your niece so that she may grow up into a fine woman, and someday she'll have a family of her own."

She pleaded and pleaded with them to leave. Finally, they gave in, but the girl clung to her grandmother, crying. The boy had to break her away. The grandmother was very brave. She did not shed a tear in front of them. Her son started carrying his niece, and finally he came to where they had to cross the river. It took about seven days to catch up with the families, which were moving slowly. Sometimes they would spend a couple of days at one place; then continue. Some families moved ahead of others; at times they were miles apart. Finally, after many days and months, they reached what is now *Tódínéeshzhee'* (Kayenta) and went on toward *Tó'naneesdizí* (Tuba City).

They had no particular destination. They just were fleeing from the *Nóóda'í* tribe. They wanted to go as far away from the *Nóóda'í* as they possibly could, and they finally arrived in *Dził Łibaii* (Gray Mountain), where they spent some years. There they found that plants, herbs and wild animals were scarce, and hunting trips took the menfolks great distances away, like over toward *Dook'o'oosłííd* (San Francisco Peaks). The Navajos gathered plants there, too. Soon trips were made into the *Kiis'áanii* (Hopi) territory where they started trading with the *Kiis'áanii*. The villages of the Hopis were in existence then, one of which was the *Íýákin* (Hotevilla) village. After several years, it was learned that the *Nóóda'í* were raiding the Navajos around this part of the land, and some families had to flee for safety.

After that, the conflict between tribes settled into what seemed like a long period of time. It was then that the families and relatives decided to go back to the east, back to Lukachukai, where the move many years before had begun. So the families started, advancing slowly eastward, through what is now Tuba City, over to the Hopi villages and finally through and over *Dził Łijiin* (Black Mesa or Mountain) and over and down the ridge of *Háájíbáhí* (Where Warrior Comes Up). The families had increased to a large number, and they settled within a big area. Some families moved farther away from the others, and they were practically scattered. Some even became close neighbors of the Hopis for a while. My own grandmother and other ancestors decided to move to *Da'ák'ehóteeł* (Large Corn Field) where there was plenty of water and a cornfield. After they went to *Da'ák'ehóteeł* is when different tribes started intruding upon their lives — tribes such as the *Nóóda'í*, *Naałání* (Comanches) and *Kiis'áanii*. The reason why they came to raid was because of a few Navajo men who had gone out to raid other tribes. Some even went into the territory of the Mexicans and brought back horses. This created tension and soon brought those people into the Navajo areas, raiding and waging war upon families. That was when they really became our enemies.

It was during this time that our own family and close relatives encountered the enemies. It was right after harvest, for the families had gathered corn and had dumped a mass of it into a pit. They has left it there to cook overnight. At early dawn the enemies attacked. My great-grandfather, named *Hastiin Lichíí* (Red Man), my great grandmother and her sister were among some relatives who fled; and, of course, my grandfather, who was a little boy then.

The families managed to flee across the valley to Black Mesa, but, just before they reached the top of the mountain, the enemies caught up with them and attacked on the slope of the mountain. The enemies traveled in groups, seeking Navajos, and this particular band of enemies had chased my ancestors across the valley. They raced their horses at high speed, while most of this particular Navajo family had to travel on foot. My grandfather said he was leading the goats. At that time, a herder didn't drive the sheep or goats; he just hollered and gave certain signals, and they started following in a single line.

Seven people were killed along the mountain slope, and a lot were injured; some managed to survive.

Bows and arrows were not the most effective weapons. *Tsiidítáán* (spear) was the best weapon used. It was a long spear with a very sharp point. A man could stick it right through the heart of an enemy or an animal. They were as good as guns. With them a lot of enemies were killed.

My grandfather said that at that time dogs didn't bark, even when an enemy was close by. They kept silent, and even sheep and goats didn't make noise unnecessarily. It seemed like they sensed danger and knew when to be quiet. Children and babies also usually were quiet, even when they were hungry; and this always was the case when an enemy was close by. I guess the Holy People had something to do with that.

It was at sunset when the attack took place, and it started raining very hard. It poured, with thunder and lightning going in all directions. Everyone got soaked. Fighting ceased, and the enemies turned back. The rest of the families kept moving in spite of the rain, until they knew for sure that they were far enough away from the enemies. Survivors then gathered together and discovered that the second wife of one of the men, named *Gábidáán* [a Spanish word], was missing, along with her two-year-old baby. The last time she had been seen she was riding with the baby tucked under one arm. Her mother, among the survivors, heard about her missing daughter, and she walked back without anyone noticing her. She hoped to find her daughter and granddaughter alive. It was dark and the rain was pouring. When she got to where the attack took place, she saw the dead bodies, all naked to the skin. The enemies had taken their clothes, although some womenfolks were wearing *biil'éé'* (squaw dresses) and *kénitsaaí* (high-topped moccasins). Of course, they had taken the jewelry that the women and men had been wearing. They left them completely nude.

From where she was, she could see the enemies gathered around a bonfire a couple of miles away. They had several other fires going, too. She searched for her daughter as she walked around in pitch dark. She looked and listened intensely as she wandered around. She had about given up hope when she heard something nearby. She stopped and listened. She heard it a second time, and it sounded like someone sobbing softly. She moved closer to where the sound came from, and she called out loud the names of the children in the family. When she called her granddaughter's name, the baby instantly responded. There the grandmother stood, water dripping to her feet.

She swung the baby to her back and started walking. It still was raining, with much thunder and lightning.

After she had walked some distance, she came upon some horses grazing, and they were the enemies' horses. She tried to get hold of one. She would slowly walk up to one, but it would turn and move away from her. Finally, a pinto stood still for her. She used one end of her belt to catch the horse's chin and the other end for reins. She tucked the baby under her arm, climbed on and started slowly. She traveled all night and, at dawn, she caught up with the rest of the family somewhere toward the far side of Black Mountain where the group had gathered.

That is how the story goes, according to my ancestors. I saw the woman myself – the one who, as a baby, had been found by her grandmother. She died of old age not many years ago near *Da'ák'ehóteeł* (Large Corn Field) at her own old homestead. A daughter whom she bore is now an old woman – very much alive. She's the older sister of my own mother.

After these tragic events, there was a long pause, something like three years, in which the people lived peacefully. Once in a great while they would hear of enemies raiding. It was during this period that our ancestors who had survived moved from Black Mountain back to *Lók'ai'jígai*, and, this time, they went up on the mountains where they knew for sure they were safe from enemies; and deer hunting was very favorable.

My own grandfather, *T'ááłáhago'áhadit'ání* (Only One Joint), still headed the family. He was a very brave man, the one who would travel great distances and could out-run horses. He kept the family well fed, and he held it together. One time, upon his return home, he told the group that he had seen on his trip where people were gathering at *Tséhootsooí* (Fort Defiance) from all directions. "Many leaders are there, and food is being distributed," he said. "I think we should go and get our share."

It was decided that they all would go as soon as possible.

The reason for the gathering and food distribution, according to my grandfather, was that the White Man said that all tribes had become our enemies, and that the White Man would help us survive.

The journey to *Hwééldi* (Fort Sumner) never was mentioned until it was time to leave Fort Defiance. My ancestors didn't realize that they would be confined even at Fort Defiance and that plans for the march to *Hwééldi* had been made which they were not aware of at the time.

The family owned a few goats, and my grandfather would not let go of them because the milk was the most important part of the diet for the whole family, especially the children. So, regardless of what, he kept the goats.

When the rest of the family had first started on the journey from the mountains to *Tséhootsooí*, my grandfather had stayed behind with a few sheep and goats, saying, "You go ahead. I will follow in a few days. It won't take me long to get there with the sheep and goats. And so it was. He spent only one night before he caught up with them, and they arrived in *Tséhootsooí* together. As they reached the top of a ridge overlooking *Tséhootsooí*, they could see a large settlement there already. Smoke was rising from many camps on the slope of the mountain. They found later that regular meetings were being held with Navajo leaders by White Men who told them that, in order for the people to survive, they had to move on to *Hwééldi*. I don't remember how long they were at *Tséhootsooí*, but, by that time, they were aware of their confinement.

Before the journey to *Hwééldi* (Fort Sumner) began, when the people started eating the strange food, they had diarrhea which caused a lot of deaths among babies, children, old people and even others. Many of these died on the way to *Hwééldi*. During the terrible trip, many deaths also resulted from starvation and exposure. My grandfather had warned his family about eating the strange food that was not good for them, especially for babies and children. Goat

Henry Chee Dodge learned English at Fort Sumner and, even when a little boy, became an interpreter.

milk was the main source of diet in his family; therefore, there were no deaths from diarrhea. Among other families, there was no choice; and they took their chances with the food. Furthermore, they didn't know how to fix it the proper way, which made the situation worse.

The move to *Hwéeldi* got under way with some large wagons hauling food and personal possessions; otherwise, the people traveled on foot, babies and some children being carried by their parents and relatives. It was a slow process, and soldiers escorted the people all the way. My grandfather made the journey on foot, leading what little herd the family owned. My other grandfather was in his teen-age years, along with his sister, who was older.

Adiits'a'ii Sání (Chee Dodge) was a little boy at *Hwéeldi* (Fort Sumner). People didn't know he was to become one of our well-known leaders at the time.

After arriving at *Hwéeldi*, the sister had to take care of the herd, while my grandfather was asked by one of the white leaders to come to his house to do some work for him daily, like chopping wood, bringing in wood, cleaning house, etc.

The people were given small shovels with which they built their shelters, which were just holes dug in the ground with some tree branches for shade over the top part.

Besides doing daily house chores for the white leader, my grandfather also took care of some horses that belonged to the soldiers. He would take the horses out to graze in the field. In the evenings, before he returned to his camp, he was given a small amount of flour or corn, just enough to be fixed for one meal. Sometimes, he would watch cooks prepare meals for the soldiers, and he would learn how different ingredients were used. Then he would teach his sister ways to prepare different meals.

Many people died at *Hwéeldi* — of various diseases, starvation, exposure and attacks by enemies. It was decided by some white leaders that two little boys, Chee Dodge and *Chaalátsoh* (Big Charley), should learn to read, write and speak the English language. The two boys began their lessons with an elderly white man for a teacher, and this continued for two years. At the end of that time, the two boys could understand the language well enough to help in interpreting between the Navajos and the White Men.

While confined at *Hwéeldi*, different tribes of enemies would sneak upon the camp to attack the Navajos. Wolves also were one of the worst enemies. People couldn't go outside their huts after dark. A few goats that were kept nearby gradually were killed off by the wolves during the nights until finally only four or five were left. My grandfather said, "Something has to be done if we're to keep any goats, and their milk is very important."

He went to the white leaders with his problem, saying he would like a day from his regular duties to fix up a good shelter for his goats. He was granted a day; so he got busy right away, digging another trench next to his own for the few goats that he had left. Things were all right after that, the goats being corraled right next to him at night. Soon, the goats multiplied, and before long he had to widen the trench into a bigger space.

After four years the people started pleading with the leaders to release them from *Hwééldi* to go back to their land. They begged and begged, and several *Déést'įį'* (Vision-Way) ceremonies were performed by the medicine men to find out whether they would be released. According to the medicine men who performed the Vision-Ways, they could see their release in the near future; so there was much hope among the people. In time, they were released, with the provision that several agreements which had been made were met.

One of the major reasons for the release was that the Navajos had agreed to let their children get the White Man's education. That's why all of the children were placed in the hands of the government to be educated, and the rule still holds today.

After arriving back at *Tséhootsooí*, some of the people spent several more months there. Then they scattered, going in all directions back to their old homesteads.

My grandfather and families went straight back to *Jádíní Bideetiin* (Deer Trail) where we now are situated. My grandfather, when he was alive, said that we originated here long before the journey to *Hwééldi.*

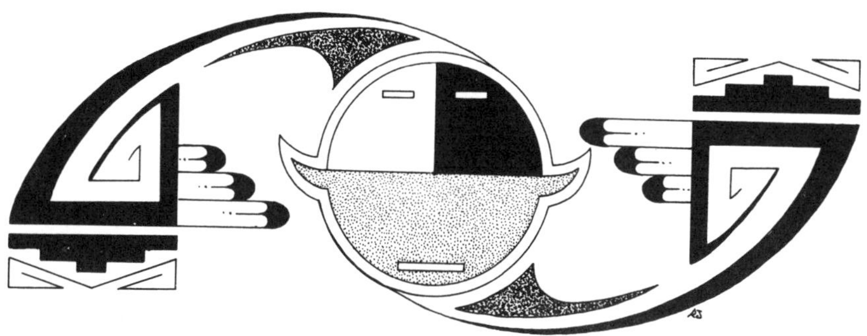

Frank Johnson

Frank Johnson, of Valley Store, Ariz., is a medicine man who here tells of the remarkable experiences of one of his grandmothers. About 70 years of age, Mr. Johnson is a member of the *Tótsohnii* (Big Water) clan.

THERE IS THE MOUNTAIN called *Tsézhin Náshjíní* (Black Round Cliffs). It curves in a kind of circle where, in time of fear of enemies, some *Diné* lived. Long ago, the Navajos were engaged in warfare with the *Nóóda'í* (Utes), *Naakaii* (Mexicans) and *Dziłghą'í* (Apaches).

Near *Tsézhin Náshjíní* (Black Round Cliffs), in time of conflict among these tribes, some Navajos hid and lived among some tall oak trees that grew thickly in that area.

Once, during this fearful period, three men ran up to the ridge of *Tséyi'* (Canyon de Chelly) seeking food. Toward the *Tséyi'* edge they discovered a large patch of *naaskáádii* (wheat grass), the seeds of which were used for food. Around the same area, some large flat cacti grew and also some pine trees. The inner layer of the pine bark also was used for food. One man ran back to the camp to tell the others about the food, and immediately a group of men and women went up to help gather it.

My grandmother told me that, during this time, she and her son, *Ashkíí* (the Boy) had followed the crowd seeking food. While everyone was busy collecting herbs, there was a loud noise nearby, and, all of a sudden, a large group of Mexican riders appeared and approached rapidly. The Navajos quickly disappeared through some large thick bushes; and my grandmother and her son ran fast through those bushes. They had gone a distance when the riders caught up with them. Being captured, they were put together on one horse, with their feet tied under the abdomen of the horse, and they were led away to a large camp of Mexicans. After that, the whole caravan started moving toward *Nitsxaazni'áhí* (Big Hill) and on to *Tséhilį́* (Tsaile).

There, a group of riders left the caravan behind. They carried small axes. Somewhere beyond *Sǫ'silá* (Chee Dodge's Mountain – Sonsela) they chopped down cedar trees and made a corral. After the arrival of the caravan, the captives were herded into the cedar corral where they were left under the watchful eyes of some Mexican women.

That night my grandmother made plans for her son to escape and to return to *Tsézhin Náshjíní* (Black Round Cliffs). The idea was for the boy to crawl out under the cedar corral and run as fast as he could. He did escape after the guards had gone to sleep, and he ran all the way to *Hootsoh* (Green Meadow) where he stopped just long enough to hide from the Mexican riders who were after him. The boy had been discovered missing; so a group of riders started searching for him. They finally gave up their search, however, and went back to their camp. After the Mexicans left, the boy started his journey again and got back to *Tsézhin Náshjíní* that same night.

The next day the Mexican caravan moved on, and the journey continued for many nights and days; and, from the way my grandmother talked about the long journey, it fits the description of far New Mexico territory, where the journey ended. After being brought there, my grandmother was told to herd sheep with a young boy, and there she spent two years. By that time she had learned to speak the Mexican language fluently.

This is the rest of the story as my grandmother told it:

"One day I was told to move the sheep up to the mountain and that a boy would help me. Once there, the boy would return and then bring food to me now and then. The boy brought food at least four times. Then I decided to run away; so, early the next morning, I told the two smart sheep dogs who understood the language to bring in the sheep that evening, and I took off on foot and ran all day and all night. After three days I came to a mountain and climbed it. I found a stream and drank some water. Just then I heard a noise above me, and two Mexican riders appeared on the mountain. I saw two more on an open field. One of them shouted to the others that I was there, and I was recaptured and brought back to the camp.

"I spent two more years there, which made four years altogether. Possibly the *Diné* were residing at Fort Sumner during that time. A beautiful white husky horse was brought, and I was told to use it to herd sheep. I was told that the boy would bring my food, and this time I was to take the sheep to another mountain. The mountain was curved so that it had a big valley. Every morning, as soon as I let the sheep out of the corral, I would race the white horse through the valley until it got used to running long distances. At the end of each run I would groom the horse and feed it hay.

"I had decided to run away on horseback. Once my mind was made up, I again instructed the dogs to bring in the sheep that evening, and early the following morning I prepared to leave, taking four ears of dry corn for food. I raced off on the horse at high speed and rode all day and all night. The following day and night I continued riding, and, at dawn on the third morning, I was exhausted and I felt so tired that I was falling asleep in the saddle. I unsaddled the horse and left the home-made Mexican saddle hanging on a branch with a thick saddle pad to cover it. I used the rough rope to hobble the horse and took the other rope off the horse's neck. I fell asleep immediately. I don't know how long I slept, but when I awoke I found the horse missing. With haste I went looking for him, but he was nowhere in sight. I tracked him and found that he had run off in the direction from which I had come. I finally gave up the search, and I returned to where I had left the saddle. I took the long rope, wrapped it around my waist and started walking. I walked all day and all night.

"Finally, on the third night, when walking in pitch darkness, I stopped and stood still, sensing danger. I picked up a small rock and threw it ahead of me. I didn't hear it hit the ground; so I knew there was a big canyon there. At this instant an owl hooted nearby, and I said to the owl, '*Shicheií* (My Grandfather), where is the path down to the bottom of this canyon? Can you lead me down?'

"The owl flew off and hooted again some distance away. When I caught up with him I found him sitting on an old stump near the edge of the canyon. Right then I knew there was a way down for me, and I advanced closer to the edge. There were a lot of yucca and large cedar trees growing at the edge. I gathered some dry bark and made a fire so that I could look down to see where the path was. I found myself looking into a narrow hole that appeared to lead all the way to the bottom. I started edging my way down slowly. I took a torch for light and guidance. Some places I needed to use my rope, and I would place it around a solid rock and let myself down with the other end. Some places I had a difficult time, but most of the places I got down pretty easily, and soon I was at the bottom of the canyon.

"Once at the bottom, I threw the rope away and started walking as fast as I could, running a short distance at times. Far off I could see a mountain, very dim, and I aimed for that mountain. By the time I reached it and climbed to the top, it was getting dark. I

The girl would race the horse through the valley daily to train it to run long distances.

came upon a wide stream, and, after satisfying my thirst, I filled my Mexican-made jug with fresh water. While I was resting by the stream I heard the howl of a wolf from the direction where I had just come, and I knew he was on my trail. I ran toward some giant cedar trees nearby, and I climbed into one of them. I had with me a long, sharp knife with a needle point, and this was ready in my hand. Before long, I heard the splashing of water, and two wolves appeared, running fast toward me. They passed me and went over the hill, but, before long, they tracked me back to the tree. Their sense of smell helped them find me. They growled and ran back and forth, trying to get to me. This went on for a long time, but finally, toward daybreak, they gave up and left. They didn't return; so, at sunup, I climbed down and headed for another mountain in the distance.

"By that time I had for food just two ears of dry corn. I finally reached the mountain and found a big valley. As I headed down the valley I saw at a distance ahead of me what at first I thought was a black horse, but as I came near I saw that it was a bear. When the bear saw me it ran toward the mountain. I came upon the carcass of a deer which the bear had killed. The bear had eaten part of the abdomen. I said to the *shash* (bear) '*Shicheíí* (My Grandfather), I'm going to have a feast with this fresh meat,' and I cut off the hind legs and took them with me.

"I started my journey again, heading for another mountain. After reaching it my drinking water was gone. I built a fire and cooked some of the deer meat. After satisfying my hunger I continued my journey, but I became very exhausted after walking several miles. It seemed that I couldn't walk any farther because of suffering from thirst; so I sat under a big cedar tree to rest. Soon a dove made a sound nearby, and it occurred to me that a dove usually makes its habitat near a water hole. When it flew off, I followed at some distance. Then I saw it in a tree from which it flew away again. It made its usual sound as it flew, finally alighting in an area where there were more trees. Then, when I climbed over the top of a huge rock, there before me was a big lake, and on the shore was the dove. I took a long drink and filled my jug with water.

"I spent the night by the lake, and, the next morning, I went on again. Far off in the distance, very indistinct on the horizon, was another mountain, and I headed straight for it. Later, I learned that this was one of the *Lók'ai'jígai* (Lukachukai) Mountains. I found afterward that I was at a place called *Tóhááli* (Toadlena, New Mexico).

"I finally reached the mountain, passed over it and came out to *Tójish'á* (Wheatfields). I had been barely struggling homeward, but, when I discovered I actually was in my homeland, I got excited and practically skipped along because it had been four years since I had been captured and taken away by force.

"I came to *Tséhilį́* (Tsaile). From there I was on a horse trail that led alongside the mountain all the way to *Tsézhin Náshjíní* (Black Round Cliffs). Just before *Tsézhin Náshjíní* I got a drink of water from a small stream. Then I walked toward the west and came upon footprints and noticed that the wild cacti which grew in the area had been chopped and collected. As I walked along some tall bushes a man appeared just ahead of me. He saw me right away, and he shouted to others about the visitor. 'It's a woman coming,' he said.

"People came running to see who it might be. *Ashkíí*, too, came, and he shouted, 'It's my mother! My mother!' A man ran out of a hogan and stopped the crowd from rushing up to me. He told them not to touch me – that certain ceremonial songs would have to be conducted before I could be allowed to enter the hogan. I was ordered to stay out and wait under the shade of a cedar tree. From inside the hogan I heard the songs begin, and, after a while, a medicine man came out singing and walked toward me. He went around me counter-clockwise four times; then he told me to go with him into the hogan.

"The medicine man had also ordered the people not to shed a tear over me. An all-night ceremony was performed, starting with songs, prayers, a bath with holy water and drying with holy cornmeal. After that I spent four holy days and nights in the hogan. Then I was allowed to return to my home in *Tsézhin Náshjíní.*"

This is the end of my grandmother's story as it was told to me long ago.

People came rushing out to see who it might be.

Curly Tso

Seventy-eight years old and living in Page, Ariz., Curly Tso is a retired stockman whose grandfather, one of those who escaped the Long Walk, told him this story which relates to the period just before and during the tragic "Walk." It recounts in vivid style several events of the period. Mr. Tso is of the *Tł'izíłaní* (Many Goats) clan.

I WILL TELL YOU A STORY that happened a long time ago. A journey started from *Tsé'ani'į́įhí* (Rock Is a Thief – north of Cow Springs). My grandfather, named *Atsidíík'áak'éhé* (Wounded Hammering or Wounded Silversmith), was the leader of six men who set out. They were on horseback, traveling west and north toward Salt Lake. My grandfather used to make the trip annually because he was a silversmith and made horse bridles which were traded for things like deer hides, buffalo hides, etc. The things that had been made and were to be traded were packed on a horse. I have forgotten the names of the men except for two – my grandfather, *Atsidíík'áak'éhé*, and another man named *Łį́į́'yilchį́įh Biyáázh* (Horse Smell's Son).

The journey continued for several days, and the men traveled through what now is called *Wí'ishbiil* (Richfield) – where a massacre was to take place on the return trip. It took them nine days to arrive in Salt Lake, from where they went into *Nóóda'í* (Ute) territory where the trading usually was done. This time, the trading took two days, and, among other things, a rifle was purchased. Then the men started back and soon got to Salt Lake where preparations were made for the long journey home.

On their way to Salt Lake, they had spent the night at a place where there was an old homestead that looked like a cowboy ranch. There were three houses made of lumber, and four or five hay piles several feet high. There was a little rock ranch house a short distance from the rest of the houses. The six men spent the night in it.

Returning from Salt Lake, they decided to spend another night in the old rock house before they continued the next day. Arriving there, they found things stacked in one corner. They were called potatoes, but the Navajos didn't know what they were called at the time. A fire was built inside the house in a fireplace, and they cooked some potatoes. By that time, the sun had gone down, and it was getting dark. All of a sudden, a group of White Men rode up. They had rifles fastened to their saddles. One of the White Men got off his horse and came over. Of course, he and the Navajos didn't understand each other's language, but they tried to communicate the best way they could by signs. When the Navajos had arrived earlier, they had noticed that the lumber houses and all the hay stacks had burned to the ground, and they couldn't figure out what had caused it. What probably had happened was that on the morning they had left on their way to Salt Lake, they had been careless about putting out the fire, and the wind probably had come up and had blown the ashes into the hay and had set the whole place on fire and burned it to the ground.

It was hard to understand what all was said by signs. Five other White Men (besides the one that came over) had stopped some distance away and were building a fire, and it appeared that they were preparing to spend the night there. In the meantime, my grandfather and his men were trying to figure out how the hay and the houses had burned, and why the White Men were there, and it was concluded that they intended to kill the Navajos because each had a rifle. But, at the same time, they didn't appear hostile. My grandfather said that he had a feeling that the White Men were there to kill them and that perhaps they were to blame for what had happened to the hay and houses; but there was no way they would know for sure whether they had caused the fire. Even if they did, it was accidental. But, just the same, it could be said that it was done deliberately. One of the other Navajos said that the White Men appeared friendly, and he didn't think they were there to cause the Navajos any harm. By that time the White Men were sitting around the fire with their rifles beside them, handy.

Because it was late at night, the rest of the Navajos had gone to sleep while my grandfather stayed up. Somehow, he didn't trust the men outside. He looked out at intervals through a small hole to see what they were doing. They were still lying around the fire and appeared to be sleeping.

Finally, at daybreak, he placed more wood on the fire that had kept going all night. At daylight, the White Men began to practice target shooting, using an old stump.

Again that morning there was a difference of opinion among the Navajos, debating as to what they should do. Most of them agreed that the men outside would not do them any harm, but *Atsidíík'áak'-éhé* still objected, saying the safest thing to do would be to stay inside the rock house because the bullets wouldn't come through it. They were safe there, and they could stay until dark, when they could make a run for it. Most of the men wouldn't listen. They kept saying the White Men appeared friendly; and, in spite of *Atsidíík'-áak'éhé's* objection, two of them went outside to join in target practice. *Atsidíík'áak'éhé* wouldn't step out because he had a suspicious feeling that the White Men were there for an evil purpose.

Soon, one of the White Men gave a gun to one of the Navajos to try his effectiveness. The practice went on for some time, when, all of a sudden, there were other shots, and one of the Navajo men fell over with a moaning sound. Almost at the same time, the other Navajo man fell over. Both had been shot to death. One of the White Men headed toward the house, hurriedly, carrying a rifle.

Atsidíík'áak'éhé was trying to get the gun ready that had been purchased in Salt Lake, but he accidently broke it; so he had his bow and arrows ready, aiming at the White Man who, by now, was running straight for a white horse that was tied to a pole close to the house. The Navajos' horses were tied, too, but quite a distance from the house. There were the rest of the White Men's horses, also, but they all had been hobbled and let out to graze the previous evening, and now they were half a mile away.

Just as the White Man started to mount the white horse, *Atsidíík'áak'éhé* hit him with an arrow, and the man fell to the ground, moaning. The rest of the White Men rushed over and carried him away. *Atsidíík'áak'éhé* wanted to shoot another one, but he didn't have a chance right then. They placed the wounded man down at a distance and tried to take the arrow out, as my grandfather observed through the hole.

The white horse was feared now by both the Whites and the Navajos. No one tried to run and mount it; so there it stood. It was decided then that each Navajo would take a chance and run for the White Men's horses some distance away. Each man picked a horse to get away on. Once more *Atsidíík'áak'éhé* tried to persuade them to wait until dark, but they wouldn't listen. Their minds were made up; they were anxious to get out and try their luck. The first man ran for one of the horses, was wounded before he jumped on it, rode away at high speed, but was falling from side to side in the saddle. The White Men took shots at him as he rode away over the hill.

The second man ran out to take his chance as soon as the shots rang out, knowing that it took time to reload the rifles. While the White Men were busy reloading, he made his escape, headed in the same direction as the first man and rode away like lightning. However, two or three shots were fired, and he was hit.

Finally, the third man attempted to escape, following the other two in the same manner. He was wounded just as he jumped in the saddle.

So now, three men had escaped but all of them were wounded. One man was left unhurt, and that was *Atsidíík'áak'éhé.* He made up his mind to stay there until evening. Perhaps, then, he would have an opportunity to escape without getting killed or wounded; so, while waiting for darkness, he sharpened his long hunting knife and his arrows.

Looking through the small hole in the wall of the house, he could see their (the Navajos') horses grazing, and he knew they were good fast horses, and he hated the thought of losing them. They were especially trained for long journeys, and they were tame. He wished he could escape on one, but that seemed impossible. He didn't trust the White Men's horses because they looked too fat and probably couldn't run for more than a mile. Such thoughts were going through his mind as he watched the white horse and wondered how fast it could run. It stood there all day; no one tried to go near it.

The White Man who had been wounded earlier that morning was still alive, although he appeared to be suffering, lying with a blanket over him near the fire. Finally evening came, and it was time to prepare to escape. From observation through the small hole, he could see that one of the men was out gathering the horses and driving them in from the field. They started to saddle up.

The Navajos' horses were too far out of his way to take a chance for his escape. He knew, if he tried, he never would get out alive. The only one would have to be the fat white horse.

It was obvious that the White Men were getting restless, for they had been pacing back and forth around the fire; and it was quite cold. While they were busy with their horses, *Atsidíík'áak'éhé* rushed out and jumped on the white horse. Just as he took off at high speed, he felt something warm penetrating into his back and through his lower abdomen. It didn't hurt at first, but he knew that he had been shot in the back. He thought that at any moment he would go unconscious and fall off the horse; so, as fast as he could, while riding, he wrapped a deer hide tightly around his abdomen – a hide that he happened to have on him. He sped off in the direction of the others. It wasn't long until he reached the last man that had taken off, and he was slumped over in the saddle on the horse. He was wounded in the shoulder, and part of his arm had been shot loose. It was dangling from his side. *Atsidíík'áak'éhé* rode up beside the man

As the storyteller's grandfather rode away on a white horse in the darkness a rifle ball hit him in the back.

and asked him if he would be able to make it. He replied, "I'll never be a complete man any more. You do what you can to get away." *Atsidíík'áak'éhé* said that he was wounded himself and that he might not be able to get home. The wounded man dragged himself off his horse and told *Atsidíík'áak'éhé* to shoot the horse with his bow and arrow.

When he started to fix his arrow, my grandfather became aware of his wounds which felt sort of numb, but the pain was bearable. The deer hide tightly wrapped around his waist supported him.

He left the dead horse and the wounded man behind and rode off, heading in the direction of home. It was full moon, and the night was clear. By that time, though, the white horse was slowing down from physical exertion.

As he rode some miles farther, he came upon another wounded Navajo who was slowly walking, leading his horse by the rein. The man told *Atsidíík'áak'éhé* to travel on and not to bother with him for he would only be a burden. He was wounded badly and didn't think he could make it very far. He said, "Just shoot the White Men's horse and ride on." *Atsidíík'áak'éhé* told him that he was wounded himself but was trying to get away the best he could.

After shooting the horse, he rode on and before long he reached the third man who appeared to be suffering badly from his wounds.

He was sitting against a bush, while the horse was grazing nearby. Again, he pierced the horse with an arrow and rode on.

Soon he came to a winding road through volcanic rocks, and, as he traveled upward, he was thinking that if only the rest of the men had listened and taken his advice, perhaps they all would have been alive now.

As he reached the top of the hill, the white horse was very exhausted and couldn't seem to go any farther. *Atsidíík'áak'éhé* knew he wasn't getting anywhere, and that from the back the White Men were on his trail and riding fast to catch up with him. His best bet would be to walk. As soon as he reached the top, he pierced the horse in the chest, left it staggering behind. Then he started walking as, over in the east, dark clouds were shifting fast toward his direction. Before long it started snowing. He had heard several gun shots and he knew the wounded men were dead. Probably he was the only survivor, and how long he could stay alive was a question; but he felt all right. He wasn't bleeding. He started looking for a place to hide from the men who were on his trail. His tracks were mostly covered with snow by now. As he walked along he looked for a shelter. Soon he came to a place where there were some large rocks, and he noticed a lot of debris piled against one rock, looking like the home of rodents. He dug out some of the debris, crawled inside where there was enough room for him, and that was where he spent the night. During the night he heard horses' hoofs approaching in his direction. The White Men passed by, and it wasn't long before they returned. By that time, it was snowing very hard. There was at least half a foot on the ground.

After the White Men had gone back, assuming that they had given up their search for him, *Asidíík'áak'éhé* fell asleep. He was exhausted.

The next morning, he rose at sunup and looked in all directions. All he could see was snow covering the land and mountains. It was knee deep.

His stomach had grown to an enormous size. It had swollen during the night. He walked to the edge of the ridge and looked east to where the fighting had taken place. He could see smoke rising from the ranch, and he started walking the other way.

On this side of *Wí'ishbiil* (Richfield), close to the mountains, is where these events took place. Even the white people call it the *Hodóogání* (Massacre Area).

Atsidíík'áak'éhé continued his journey on foot for several miles, using a stick to support himself. As he came over a little hill, he discovered that the snow was not nearly as deep, and, from there, walking was much easier.

Finally, he came to an area where there were flat volcanic rocks, and some of them were hollowed out like bowls. He built a fire and put some hard stones in the fire. Soon the stones were red hot. Then he placed the stones in a rock bowl along with plenty of snow. While the stones were heating, he had gathered sagebrush, chopped it into fine pieces, and now he placed it in the bowl.

When he was ready to drink the sagebrush juice, he unwrapped the deer hide from his waist, and he found that a mass of blood had caked up around his waist. He drank the juice, as much as he could hold, and, soon after, all the blood that had accumulated internally, or which had bled internally from the stomach wound, started discharging through his rectum like water. He discovered that the bullet had gone into his back, missing his spine by about an inch, and it had come out below his right rib cage.

After the discharge of blood, he was relieved and felt better. His stomach had flattened out, and he continued his journey because he felt like walking. It was toward evening by that time, and he was thinking of a place to stop when he arrived at a woody area. There was plenty of firewood, and there he spent the night.

As he continued his journey toward the east, one day he came upon a particular herb used as medicine. His journey took him 24 days, and, at the end of those days, he reached *Ch'ááyáhii* (Under Arm), and in this vicinity was where his relatives were to meet him, as the story goes.

During the days that he traveled homeward, he didn't eat, but he had plenty of his herb medicine. He said later that the medicine saved his life. He had become so thin that he was practically just a skeleton. The medicine was called *déétjáád* (wild plants). It had been used by Navajo medicine men.

He had dreamed of this medicine one night when he was in severe pain. In his dream he was told the direction in which this herb grew and for him to take plenty of it because he was to nourish his body with it in place of food. He was a medicine man himself, singing the *Iináají* (Life-Way ceremony). Naturally, he had followed his dream instructions the next morning, and he had found the herb. He gathered plenty, and he started applying it to his wound and drinking tea made from it. As he drank, and during the process of applying it to his wound, he sang some of his sacred songs.

He felt better then – good enough to travel, and, soon, he came to *Tódáá'ni'deetiin* (Trail Crossing Edge of Water) where he crossed the river, using sticks to support himself. He had been using one from the beginning of his journey. Now he prepared another so that two sticks could support and balance his weight as he crossed the river. He was glad when he got across safely.

He gathered some dry driftwood along the river bank and built a fire so he could dry himself. At that time, there were no such things as matches. *Atsidíík'áak'éhé* carried two special little sticks which he used to start fires. They were small enough to fit into his hat, and he carried them all the time.

By the time he was dry, it was near sunset. He started walking again because he had to cross the rest of the canyon before it got dark. After arriving at the other side, he gathered some salt weeds for a fire. The charcoal from this greasewood usually burns for a long time. He drank some of his medicine and sat by the fire all night with arms folded. Once in a while he would stir the charcoal.

He continued his journey the next day through *Séíbikóóh* (Sandy Wash) and *Tsé'íí'áhí* (Standing Rock), following a horse trail. He remembered a hogan not too far from where he was, and he thought it would be the best place to spend the night. When he arrived, he gathered wood, built a fire and spent the night there.

By that time, the six men were missed at home, and the relatives began to wonder. They talked to one another about it because the day they usually returned had passed. The relatives were worried. That was at *Tsé'ani'į́įhí* (the Rock That Steals), near Black Mountain.

Certain medicine men, at the time, specialized in a healing ceremonial called *Íísts'ą́ą́'* (Listening Ceremony). We don't hear of this ceremonial any more, just what now is called *Déést'į́į́'* (Looking Through Crystal Rock ceremony – Vision-Way) which is popular and performed by a lot of medicine men. The relatives decided that a medicine man should be brought to perform in order to find out what had happened to the men who should have returned several days before. This was done, and the medicine man reported his findings, saying, "It's no use. All I hear are flies buzzing around, except for one man. He's nearly making it back."

Preparations were made right away to go and meet this man, and a group of Navajos, including the medicine man, left. It was early in a morning when this group was traveling across from where the hogan was, and one of the men saw smoke rising from it. He said, "Why is there smoke, no one lives there now. Let us find out."

When they reached it, they entered and found *Atsidíík'áak'éhé.* He glanced among them, immediately fainted, and it was quite a while before he came to. Right away, preparation was made to perform a ceremony over him, which lasted the rest of the day and

Members of his band found *Atsidíík'áak'éhé* badly wounded, thin, exhausted and almost starved in an abandoned hogan.

night. He related his story as to what had happened to them and that he was the only survivor. The next day they left for home. They packed him on the extra horse that had been brought for him and left. About the *Íísts'ąą'*, I don't exactly know how it was performed, but, from what I have heard, a medicine man, while performing his ceremony, usually left the hogan, and, a short distance away, he would sit for a long time singing, with his eyes closed – more like he was in meditation.

Upon returning home, some well-known medicine men who specialized in the *Iináají* (Life-Way) were brought in, along with certain kinds of plants used in performing the ceremonial to get the patient well. It was a particular medicine man who performed over him and completely healed him. After he was well again and back in good health, he couldn't get out of his mind what had happened. He wanted to go back to get even. That was all he thought of.

He went around to different families, mostly families and relatives of the five who had been killed. Several men volunteered to go with him; so six Navajos left, heading toward the area where the incident had taken place. When they reached *Dził Binii' Łigaii* (White Face Mountain), they came upon sheep tracks, and, not far away, they found a sheepherder's camp. There was a tent, and sheep were grazing nearby, but they didn't see anyone around. They rode to the tent. *Atsidíík'áak'éhé* got off his horse and rapidly walked up to the front of the tent and found that two White Men, two women and two boys were inside the tent. They were startled when he appeared at the door, and they stared at him. Without any hesitation he pulled his gun and shot the two men first and then he shot the two women. The two boys ran out and headed away in terror. They caught the boys right away. The six men discussed what they should do with them. Some said they should take them as captives. Others disagreed, but, *Atsidíík'áak'éhé* said, "No! They shall be killed right here and now." He had no mercy on them.

"Now," he said, "I am satisfied. We shall leave for home immediately." They traveled all night and finally arrived upon a herd of wild cattle wandering around in a canyon. They gathered the cattle together and started driving. On the third day, arriving at *Tooh* (river, San Juan River) toward evening, the cattle were driven across the river without any difficulty. It took another day and a half to reach *Ch'ááyáhii* (Under Arm) where some Navajos were living. Some cattle were distributed, and slaughtering and feasting took place at every home. Then the six men went on home, where there was more feasting among the relatives. There, *Atsidíík'áak'éhé* said, "Now, I really am satisfied; I'm even for what was done to me."

Eventually, all the cattle were gone, even though they were eaten sparingly by families and relatives.

It was several years after my grandfather's adventure that another event started to take place, as it was told by my grandfather. Word got around that the government soldiers (White Men) had settled near *Na'nízhoozhí* (Gallup, New Mexico). At about the same time, the *Kiis'áanii* (Hopi People) started waging war upon the Navajos, and killing us. It seemed like all hate and bitterness had been unleashed against the Navajo people as the rest of the Indian tribes allied with each other against them. Such tribes as *Kiis'áanii*, *Naakaii* (Mexicans) and *Nóóda'í* (Ute Indians), as well as the *Bilagáana* (White People) became enemies of the Navajo people. However, straight west, down in *Tsinaa'eeł Dahsi'ą́* (Lee's Ferry or Boat Placed Above), was a place where a lot of people survived from the enemies. The place is very rugged, and it is down in the canyon with many hiding areas where no enemy is likely to go unless he is familiar with the area.

During the expectation of enemies, a large settlement of Navajos had moved down there, some coming after making narrow escapes from the enemies. Others came alone after the rest of their families had been taken captive or had been killed. The enemies had come among them to raid, taking most of their livestock such as sheep and horses.

To the north, down in *Tł'ohts'ósítah* (Narrow Grass, between Tuba City and Black Butte) is another area where a lot of Navajo people escaped from the enemies. This place is located across the big canyon where there is only one entrance into another canyon, and within that canyon is a large area surrounded and protected by cliffs. A large settlement of Navajos managed to hide and survive from the enemies there. From all directions came the enemies, and it seemed like there was no really safe place to hide. People were fleeing here and there.

It was to this canyon where *Atsidíík'áak'éhé* took his people, and he was the leader of the large settlement until after *Hwééldi* (Fort Sumner). Right after the movement down there, *Atsidíík'áak'éhé* gathered all the young warriors, and he started training them in different ways to attack an enemy from a horse. In Navajo, it was called *deezlá* (preparing a person for warrior). This training went on daily. *Atsidíík'áak'éhé*, along with his father-in-law, named *Dahghaa'í Dahsikáád* (Spread Mustache), trained these warriors to be ready in case of enemy attack, but no enemies ever found their way down there.

It was learned that the white soldiers were scouting around, rounding up the people and herding them to *Tséhootsooí* (Fort Defiance). The scouts were government soldiers, riding in several different groups. It was horrible the way they treated our people. Some old handicapped people, and children who couldn't make the journey, were shot on the spot, and their bodies were left behind for crows and coyotes to eat.

All these people were forced in from different directions and herded to *Tséhootsooí* like bunches of wild cattle, and from there they were moved to *Hwééldi*. Of course, the people who moved down into the rugged canyons, who included my ancestors, managed to survive down there, and they never experienced the tragic treatment by the white leaders as well as by other tribes. The soldiers went out as far as Navajo Mountain in the north, as far as *DziłŁijiin* (Black Mountain) toward the west and to *Tónaneesdizí* (Tuba City) farther west.

A majority of the Navajos didn't know the reason why they were being rounded up, and different stories went around among the people. There were reasons like: The government in Washington had ordered that all Navajos be rounded up and bunched together at *Tséhootsooí* and then taken to *Hwééldi* where they would be put to death eventually — killing them by means of subjecting them to different diseases, starvation and exposure, as well as using every other possible way to kill all of them. The government's reason seemed to be that the white people, coming this way, needed more land, and Navajos were scattered out too far and lived on some of the best lands; so, in order to give the white people the land, plans were made by the government to kill most of the Navajos and send the rest to *Halgai Hatéél* (Wide Plains or Oklahoma), or, perhaps, to round them up and force them to live close together like the Hopis.

Personally, I often wondered, after I became aware of white men's laws, why our ancestors were treated so unjustly. White Men make and preach about all kinds of laws, laws that protect individual rights; and where were these laws then? At the time, the Navajo people were ignorant of the fact that if an individual does something wrong that individual is punished according to the laws for his wrong doings, but the laws do not say to place blame and have innocent people suffer the consequences; and such was the case that the Navajo people went through.

On the journey to *Hwééldi* (Fort Sumner) the people had to walk. There were a few wagons to haul some personal belongings, but the trip was made on foot. People were shot down on the spot if they complained about being tired or sick, or if they stopped to help someone. If a woman became in labor with a baby, she was killed. There was absolutely no mercy.

A few years ago I had a chance to go to *Wááshindoon* (Washington), but I missed my ride and didn't make it. A group of elderly people was appointed to go there to give testimony concerning the horrible events that our ancestors went through. The terrible way our people were treated is what I wanted to talk about. Of course, back then, my remembering was still good, but, today, because of my poor health and old age, my remembering is fading out. My plan was to make a statement in front of the government officials. I wanted to ask for compensation for the injustice done to our ancestors.

Before the "Long Walk," a man named *'Ahidigishií* (Hand or Finger Signal) became the enemy of his own tribe and went raiding upon them. With him traveled several men and women. They were a tough gang, and he was the leader.

As they traveled, if they happened to come upon someone herding sheep, they would help themselves, butcher one of the sheep and have a feast. This band was feared by the people. What I am to tell you happened, for example, when a certain family was moving to *Tséhootsooí* (Fort Defiance), right after the order was issued for all Navajos to go there and that those who refused to go voluntarily would be shot on the spot. The family was slowly moving toward *Tséhootsooí* from north of *Tónaneesdizí* (Tuba City). Near *Dziłdiłhiłii* (Shadow Mountain) there is a certain canyon, and up this canyon is where the family was moving. Ahead, around a bend, is where *'Ahidigishii* and his gang were hiding, waiting to grab one of the sheep. Since *Hastiin Łtsoí Ts'ósí* (Yellow Slim Man) was driving the sheep, along with one of his kinsman, the gang didn't bother them, but, right behind, two children were riding a big fat mare, with some bundles of belongings packed on. *'Ahidigishii* waited until the mare came along, then threw the children off and took the horse, which they killed right over a hill. The children went running up to the two herders, telling what had happened.

In the meantime, the rest of the family had gone ahead because the sheep were slow, and it was pretty hot. Plans had been made about where to camp for the night. Toward evening, one of the men left the camp to go and help bring the sheep in. When he met *Hastiin Łtsoí Ts'ósí* he was informed of what had happened; and it was decided to kill *'Ahidigishii*. Two men left to go back to do it. One man took a rifle, and the other had bow and arrows.

As the two men came over the rim of the canyon, they saw smoke rising from the area where the gang was having a feast. As soon as they saw the two men, *'Ahidigishii* departed from his band and hastily headed toward a small hill not far away. He sat on a small rock and started aiming his bow and arrows in different directions, acting very fearful. The two men rode up to him without fear, and *Hastiin Łtsoí Ts'ósí* said to him, " *'Ahidigishii*! Why did you kill our horse?" He turned his nose up in the air and wouldn't speak a word. *Hastiin Łtsoí Ts'ósí* got off his horse, walked up close to him and struck him on the side of his head with the rifle butt. He slumped to the side, and *Hastiin Łtsoí Ts'ósí* shot him right there and left his body. His band disappeared quickly. That is how *'Ahidigishii* was killed. I never found out who he was, where he originally was from nor what clan he was, but he was killed by my great-grandfather named *Hastiin Łtsoí Ts'ósí*.

People like *'Ahidigishii* made enemies all over, involving the whole Navajo tribe. His gang went raiding other tribes. It was a few people like him who aroused other tribes and made enemies against the Navajos. He made innocent people suffer and pay with their lives.

What actually happened to the people while they were confined at *Hwéeldi* I don't know because my ancestors never went there, but I have heard a lot of stories about what happened. According to the stories, as I remember, it was said that a lot of people died soon after their arrival at *Hwéeldi*. This resulted from not eating the proper food, starvation, disease, poor living conditions and exposure.

Some elderly Navajos hesitate to talk about the past now. They'll merely make remarks like, "Why should we talk about such a thing? It's in the past and it's better just to forget it. It was bad, but we survived somehow and came back to our land."

Agreements finally were made between the Navajos and the government. The Navajos were forced to give up their children to the government so that they could get the White Men's education, which also caused resentment between the Navajos and some white people who worked for the government.

There was an incident which caused a disturbance among the people during the period after the return from *Hwéeldi* when a well-known Navajo was killed by a White Man over his daughter and whether she could be forced to stay in school. It happened out toward the northwest part of the Reservation.

The man was named *Tádídíínį́* (Corn Pollen) of the *Tsínaajinii* (Extended Dark Trees) clan. His daughter still is alive today. She had been going to the Tuba City Boarding School of the Bureau of Indian Affairs and had run off several times and walked home – about 70 miles away. After she had run off the last time, she was at home with her parents when two policemen came to take her back, but she refused. The father also refused to let his daughter go, saying, "I refuse to let her go. Suppose she runs off again and freezes somewhere. I won't permit her to go back because of what might happen to her."

One of the policemen said, "Don't say that. We must take her back to school. Bring in the horse and saddle up for her."

"No!" was the answer from *Tádídíínį́*. There was a strong argument between the father and the policemen, and finally the policemen left.

Upon their return to Tuba City, they reported to *Naat'áani Ałts'óozí* (Slim Leader – the Indian Agent) who, it turned out, was responsible for the killing that took place later. *Naat'áani Ałts'óozí* ordered the police to go back and bring the man himself; so, right away, they departed and went to *Séí Haagai* (White Sand) where *Tádídíínį́* lived. He had expected them for days. He was ready for his visitors. He didn't know what was coming, but he suspected danger, and he had hid a gun not far from his place called *Tsédees'ah* (Pointed Rock). He thought that his visitors were due to appear any day; his horse was ready, and he was on the lookout from a hill. He could see riders coming his way at a distance. He had a small revolver hidden on him in case of danger, but he had no intention of using it unless it became necessary.

He thought to himself: "It's my daughter. One way or the other, if she wants to be here, she can stay. I'll win out on this point."

He was sure they would permit him to keep his daughter.

This time there were four Navajo policemen. The order from *Naat'áani Alts'oozí* was to handcuff *Tádídíiní* and bring him in. The father settled himself in a hogan, awaiting his visitors. One of the policemen said, "We've come for you." He replied, "Is that right? I am not about to go with you."

"*Naat'áani* has strictly ordered that you come back with us," answered a policeman. And *Tádídíiní* said, "That doesn't matter; it's my decision as to what I should do."

Siláo Bidii (Belly Policeman) at that moment went up to him. Others followed and grabbed *Tádídíiní* and handcuffed him. His horse was there, but he said he would rather walk because he was a man of great speed and endurance.

At that time the Kaibito Trading Post was under construction, and there were quite a few people there, including some of *Tádídíiní's* relatives. People watched as he approached the post, handcuffed, with policemen right behind him. He said, "I am being led by force, against my will. Cut this thing off me," referring to the handcuffs. *Tsínaajinii Yázhé* (Little Black Extended Tree) brought an axe, chopped the chains away and *Tádídíiní* turned and started walking away up the canyon. The policemen looked after him, but made no attempt to stop him. They just left.

"I shall send some white policemen this time," said *Naat'áani* when he heard what had happened. "I want the man brought in, also the man who chopped off the handcuffs." *Siláo Bidii* was appointed to lead the group to *Tádídíiní*. After a night camp, they were seen riding above the trading post early in the morning.

Tádídíiní had left his hogan to visit some relatives who lived nearby and to tell his family to move to another hogan some miles away because he was expecting visitors any day.

When the police arrived they found no one at the hogan where *Tádídíiní* supposedly lived. They saw hogans some distance away where *Tádídíiní* was visiting, but the police didn't know that. They decided to go there to inquire about *Tádídíiní*. Without being noticed, they arrived, and one of the policemen got off his horse and went right up to the hogan and pulled up the blanket that was used to cover the door. He looked around at the people who were inside, and he recognized the man they were hunting. He shouted, "There you are, *Tádídíiní*. Let's go." He told his companions that *Tádídíiní* was there, and he walked right in without any hesitation. He grabbed *Tádídíiní*. There were three White Men and one Navajo policeman.

As he went forward to handcuff his victim, *Tádídíiní* resisted, and the men got into a fight. The rest of the people in the hogan rushed outside. *Tádídíiní* threw the policeman to the back of the hogan, face down, drew his revolver and triggered it twice, but it just clicked. Somehow, the safety thing on the revolver was locked. A man in the doorway had a long rifle aimed at him, and he shot him. *Tádídíiní* fell forward. The policeman got up saying, "Now, it's better with *Tádídíiní* dead." They got on their horses and rode off at high speed.

It was some miles to *Tádídíiní's* hogan, and one of his relatives took off to notify the family and also his brother, *Hastiin Yidlóhí* (Mr. Laughter). When his brother learned what had happened to *Tádídíiní* he became furious and rode off after the policemen. It was late, however, when he got the message, and the policemen were well on their way because they suspected danger. It was said that one of the policemen stopped at the trading post long enough to purchase a few things to eat.

In the meantime, *Hastiin Yidlóhí* was tracking the men rapidly. Somewhere above *Dziłnanaashtł'iizh* (Crooked Mountain) it got dark; so he decided to spend the night at a family's place. His aim now was to go straight to Tuba City and kill that *Naat'áani* who was responsible for the death of his brother.

Upon his arrival in Tuba City, he went straight to *Naat'áani's* home with his revolver, but it was deserted. A man told him that *Naat'áani* had gone to Flagstaff in his car. (A few people had cars at this time.) It was hopeless to do anything else; so he returned home the following day.

Several days later the people who witnessed the shooting were collected and hauled to Tuba City for a hearing. They testified as to what had happened.

Some investigators came out from Washington to examine the body. It had been left inside the hogan, but the door was boarded up. After about 10 days they came for the body and took it to Tuba. It was in the winter; so it still was fresh.

Another hearing was held, and the people who witnessed the killing were given $600 apiece – for what I don't know. So that is how a man named *Tádídíiní* paid his life for his daughter.

Betty Shorthair

Betty Shorthair, 65 years old, lives at Sweetwater, Ariz., where she is a well-known medicine woman. Her story of Navajo tragedies was told to her by a grandmother.

A CERTAIN NAVAJO MAN DROVE SOME HORSES to Shiprock from Sweetwater, and he was killed by the *Nóóda'í* (Utes), along with all the horses that he herded.

The man was a member of the *Bitáanii* (Under His Cover) clan. After that incident a war began. Because the *Nóóda'í* (Utes) were killing them, the *Diné* wandered just about everywhere, trying to find safety. The Utes also would bring their horses into the *Diné* cornfields to eat the corn. With the corn gone, the only source of food for the *Diné* was the seeds of grass and other plants; and some of the *Diné* starved to death.

My deceased grandmother, my mother and one of my aunts went over to *Tséyi'* (Canyon de Chelly) at that time to pick cactus fruits to eat. They had learned that there were a lot of such fruits at *Tséyi'*. The three of them carried their belongings, and when they got there they saw what had happened. When it was still summer it had been said, "The soldiers will journey to us." Shortly after that it was said, "The soldiers have journeyed into *Shash Bitoo'* (Bear Springs – Fort Wingate)."

There was an elderly lady by the name of *Aszdaan Tsii Báhí* (Gray-Haired Lady) who had a home in a cave atop the cliff where the *Diné* were to move in. On account of this they carried their belongings on their backs to where the elderly lady had another home; and, as they were bedding for the night, my mother's sister said, "We will run over there; we will also hide in the cave." Even though the others said "no" to her, the three of them started for the cave. As they were running along, they saw something moving among the sage bushes; so they quickly sat down until the figures had passed. My mother said, "I guess those are the soldiers that were said

The Utes would ride their horses into the Navajos' cornfields and let the animals eat the crops.

to come. No wonder their clothes are blue." After she raised up, she said, "We will cross here. I don't think they will move fast; the ones that are carrying the food, I guess, are still far behind."

So she started running again, and the other two ran after her. The three of them went down *Tséhadeesk'i* (Layer Rock Trail), then around and up another hill. By that time it was late afternoon. When they got to the top of the hill my mother said, "We will spend the night over there. They say there are a lot of *Diné* there." While they were walking along they saw many Navajos camping in an arroyo, and there were a lot of fires. Some *Diné* were grinding grass seeds, others were making corn meal. Looking the other way they saw an *alch'i'adeez'á* (male hogan), with smoke coming out of the top. My aunt said, "We will bed for the night over there at the hogan, where it won't be too cold." It was in the month of December, for there was snow on the ground. Room was made for them as they entered the hogan. In the hogan there were some pumpkins and corn. The family had lived there for a long time. There was a woman about to give birth who later was killed by the soldiers, and a man and a little girl. The three women were provided with space inside the hogan, and they were seated to tell each other stories.

My mother said later, "I awoke sometime before dawn and was just lying there awake when day broke." When the fire was being built at daybreak, my grandmother said, "Go outside to look where we came from, my daughter. I will grind some grass seeds and make hot mush cereal for you; then we will leave again." When my mother went outside there was sunlight appearing atop the mountains. A man came up, and they knew him. He was called *Hastiin Łtsoí* (Mr. Yellow Man) because he always herded seven goats. Right behind him something appeared in blue, and it made a sound, like yelling. Another one came up, and another, until four of them were there, and still she hadn't told the other Navajos. She just looked at them. She started to run back when the fifth one came up to where the others were, and she shouted, "Something in blue has come up from where we came up, my mother." That was all she said. The girl was in a state of shock at the surprise attack because she never had seen a soldier before.

Then all of the *Diné* left in a hurry, even those that were grinding the grass seeds, and they went down the cliff on a ladder made of spruce logs and yucca plants. I don't know what they were going to do there. Instead, they should have run in a different direction. Some went to a dismal cave on the canyon cliff where there was a hideout, but she just stood there, and the man returned, grabbed her by both ears, shook her and said, "What's happened to you, my grandchild? Not many of us are left here. All of the others have gone down the cliff into the cave. The *Bilagáana* (White Men) came below us. Just give it a try and start running."

While the girl was in a state of shock the *Diné* fled away from her. When she started to leave she couldn't run, she just walked. The man who had grabbed her was carrying a rifle back to where the other Navajos had fled down the cliff. As she was walking along a younger man met her and said, "My dearest young sister," and he took her over his shoulder and started down the cliff with her. The girl's sister (my aunt) was standing below the cliff. The man told my mother to take hold of his bow; then she took hold of it and started down the cliff. "When you reach the bottom, let go of the bow," he said to her. After they both reached the canyon floor, he started back up the cliff, and he called to the others from the top of the cliff, "Run as fast as you can and keep on running and running. Some of you are just walking along. Don't just stand there; keep moving. I'm going back," I guess he went back to where he was going to get killed. So they all started running, and they could hear the sounds of guns shooting. I guess the White Men came with *biinájiihí* (gun powder) meant for the Navajos. All day the sound of the guns went on.

Two girls who went into a cave in the cliff were shot down, and they were hanging out from the cliff. As my mother's group was running along, there was a woman walking toward them with blood flowing from her hip. She had been shot by the soldiers. It was late afternoon. Another lady was walking along, and they caught up with her. There were many footprints, and still the noise of the guns continued. Then they found a ladder going up the cliff, like the White Man's ladder, made out of spruce with poles going horizontally on top of each other and with chopped ropes made out of yucca that were hanging down beside the ladder. They used those to help climb up the ladder to the top of the cliff. When they reached the top a few Navajo survivors were sitting around. The number is unknown. All of the others had been killed. My mother's mother wasn't there, and my mother kept crying, "I think they killed my mother." She and her sister were sitting among the groups. A little way off a lady kept coming out of a shelter and telling everybody, "Don't be walking around over here, stay over there." The two girls spent the night there.

At midnight they heard someone talking. It sounded like their mother. Then the voice said, "I wonder if all of my children are killed or if one survived." Then she came near them. Something called *chi'di* (tanned buffalo hide) was wrapped around her

Three women ran to Layer Rock Trail when they saw the soldiers.

shoulders, and she was carrying a small bag of rye, also a small grinding stone inside her bag. The story that my mother used to tell me was very scary and unbelievable. While the woman was standing there with the bag on her back, the soldiers were still shooting at the men as they were gathering the empty bullet shells. Still she was standing there, with some of the other Navajos trying to push her aside. The soldiers were shooting at her and the two men beside her. The men were called *Kęshiini'biye'* (Cane Son) and *Choo'yiní* (Hunchback). They were the only three who had survived in the cave on the cliff.

At dusk, someone spoke. It was a White Man who was with the Enemy Navajos. Then one of the Enemy Navajo said, "Tomorrow all of you will gather at Chinle — all that have survived; and from there you will go to *Tséhootsooí* (Fort Defiance). The White Man said, "I wonder if one of the *Diné* survived." Not one of the *Diné* spoke. After the White Man and the Enemy Navajos left for Chinle, darkness appeared, and the Navajos came out and started following them.

When daybreak came the Navajos agreed, "We will now surrender at Chinle where we were told to go, all of us that survived." After daybreak they left for Chinle, where peace was offered. My ancestors were the first to surrender, and they were held as captives. They were given rations, such as bacon, white flour and coffee — just enough for each individual Navajo. Some made a mistake with the coffee beans, thinking they were regular beans. They tried boiling the coffee beans instead of regular beans. I guess they didn't know the use of the coffee beans. Some fried the bacon, and ate it with the coffee beans; then some of them had upset stomachs.

Those who surrendered were started on a walk to Fort Defiance, but it was bitter cold and they stopped at a house where they lay on the floor. Some died of hunger there. It is not known how long the remainder stayed there. At Fort Defiance they were given rations again which made many Navajos sick and killed some.

When they left Fort Defiance, ox wagons carried their food, and they followed on foot all the way to Fort Sumner, where they spent four years. For rations they received the same things that they had got while they were at Fort Defiance, such as the flour and coffee; and they were assembled in adobe buildings to receive those rations and to be accounted for. My mother told me that two Navajo leaders by the names of *Bi'éé' Łichíí'ii* (Red Clothes – Kit Carson) and *Ma'a'zísí* [no English translation] used to give out rations. Another Navajo by the name of *Ch'il Haajiní* (Manuelito) [literally, a Plant Extended] also was their leader who talked to, and encouraged, the Navajos while confined at Fort Sumner; and another man called *'Ahidigishii* (Finger, or Hand, Signal) as well as *Bihą́ą́na* [no English translation, taken from Spanish], were leaders, too.

The *Diné* gradually tried to convince the soldiers that they should be set free, and, finally, their talks seemed to be getting to look better. The Navajos said, "Now we will not shoot any more arrows, you will put your guns down, and we will put our bows and arrows down." After two years, however, the Navajos still were saying among themselves, "Those of you that make bows and arrows, keep on making them; those of you that make spears, keep on making them. Somewhere in the future we think that the White Men will harm us again. If they put us in confinement another time they will kill us all."

That was the way they talked, and, for that reason, things were not better. The two men who gave out rations talked for them again, "No! Not one will be killed." With births and more people coming in, the population at Fort Sumner had increased. If they still had been on their own land they all would have died of hunger, and they were saved from other tribes and from wild beasts as well, such as mountain lions and wolves. It was promised that the Navajos would not be harmed again if they put down all weapons and also the White Men put down their guns. After two more years, the Navajos and White Men made an agreement. And the *Diné* promised to put their children in schools so that they would be leaders in the future. The treaty was approved, and from that time they were free to go back to their homeland. They walked back to Fort Defiance, and rations were given to them, along with one sheep, two sheep or even three sheep. Big families were given, I guess, two or three sheep, and the Navajos began to live their old lives again. The goats they could get from the lands of the *Naakaii* (Mexicans) with something that they had for exchange. They were also given iron hoes, shovels, picks and axes, and they were told to work with those tools on the land they once had. At Fort Defiance a meeting was held about the children that were to be put in school, and it was there that the first twelve children began to be educated. Now all of the *hastoí* (menfolks) who were put in school back then are gone. My grandmother used to tell me about the rations, sheep, tools and children.

I can remember only a few of those first children, like *Béésh Łigai'íí'iní* (Who Prepares Silver), *Béésh Łigaiiłi'iníats'osiigii* (Slim Prepares Silver), *Hastiin Bilagáana* (Mr. White Man), *Jeetinn* (Jay King), *Ch'il Haajiní* (Manuelito) and *Hastiin Adiits'a'ii* (Mr. Interpreter – Chee Dodge).

Because of our menfolk talking for us at Fort Sumner, we were on the right way of living again, and, also, we now have children in school. As some leave the twelfth grade, others are just starting to school. A great many have attended since the agreement was made.

With the farm tools that were given to them they cultivated small corn patches back on their lands; and, after another year, they were issued plows, even though there were no horses to move them. There were two men by the name of *Adiildiłí* (One Who Plays Stick Game) and *Chą́ąyiyiishíní* (One Who Kills Belly). Someone called *Gáamalii* (Mormon) was the only man who had horses, as I was told. Then the two men said, "We will build a house and we will perform a sacred ceremonial called *Hozhǫǫjí* (Beauty Way)." A few of the women made a saddle blanket from the sheep's wool that was given to them, some wove the black; others the white, and they carried it to the Beauty Way ceremonial, which was held all night. They sang after they were washed with yucca root soap and after they were dried with ground corn flour, in the way that the Navajos do to a sick patient. A special sacred ritual was done all night for the bridle, rein, saddle blanket, saddle and rope; and, on account of the Beauty Way ceremony, we once again had horses.

After the ceremony, they brought back two horses – one from the man called *Gáamalii* who was paid something for an exchange. Later, the horses and sheep and goats over-grazed the land. My mother used to tell me that we shouldn't mistreat or hate our horses because our deceased grandfathers did the sacred ceremony for them.

When I tell my grandchildren about the Long Walk, they don't believe me. I tell them that they wouldn't be as they are today if their ancestors hadn't gone through the confinement and even died of hunger. Yes, some starved to death, even young people, and others came back and died of old age.

I am the only one left of our family. My sister, my brother, my mother and my grandmother all are gone. My father used to be called *Hastiin Ba'alíłéé* (Mr. Depended Man). He was a member of the *Tábąąha* (Water's Edge People) clan.

Yasdesbah Silversmith

Yádeesbaa' Silversmith

At the age of 90 *Yádeesbaa'* Silversmith still herds sheep near her home at Lukachukai, Ariz. Her story of escape from Fort Sumner was handed down by a grandmother. She is of the *Ashįįhí* (Salt People) clan.

THE JOURNEY TO FORT SUMNER began because of a terrible war. That was what my grandmother told my mother, and she passed the story on to me. My mother was probably a young child at the time of the Long Walk. There is a place called *Dleesh Bii Tó* (White Clay Spring), a little way southeast of here. From there on up this way there used to be farms. One day as some of the *Diné* were roasting corn in a pit, all of a sudden a loud noise was heard from the direction of a place called *Ałch'inaa'ahí* (Points Come Together). The noise resembled thunder crashing. Our people were always on the alert, as it was a fearful time. Other people sleeping on the hill also heard the noise. Then someone yelled from the top of a hill, as men did in those days. As the man was yelling, horses' hoofs were heard. The Utes were approaching fast. They attacked the people who had been sleeping and killed a lot of them. Some *Diné* fled up the hill where, on the very top, stood a man named *Ałts'áálį́* (Branch of the Wash) who saw the shooting and killing taking place down below. He saw a lot of our people killed.

Later, the Utes came together at *Dleesh Bii Tó* where there were some corn patches. The raiders put their horses into the corn patches and let them eat the corn. Someone called *Tsii'bálígaii* (Grayhair) almost annihilated these Navajos by bringing in his raiders. *Tsii'bálígaii*, as I was told, was a Ute.

There really is a lot to this story, but I'll tell you just a portion of it. As the *Diné* fled, my grandmother ran off with a baby. She ran up the hill called *Kídzii'báhá* (Open Space to Mountain). On the top,

Navajos were sleeping on a hill when they heard a noise and someone yelling.

she and the baby sneaked under a very thick bush, and the bullets went over their heads. The two hid in the bush for some time; then the child spoke, "My Mother, there are no more *Nóóda'í* (Utes)."

Soon, the two came out from under the bush. Sure enough, there were no Utes, but they could hear shooting way off somewhere. My grandmother, carrying the baby on her back, walked for some time. Then she came across a baby in a cradle. It seemed to have cried to death, his or her head was just hanging down. My grandmother looked at the baby, but she could do nothing. She went on, and my grandfather found her by tracking her down. By that time the enemies had moved to the *Díwózhiibii'tó* (Upper Greasewood) area. Shooting could be heard there. How many *Diné* were killed we don't know.

Anyway, that war went on for two or three years, I think. I don't know for sure. During the fearful period, the *Diné* fled everywhere. There were no permanent homes or places for the *Diné* to stay. They depended on *Tlohdééh'* (seeds of grass) for food. Corn was scarce. The *Diné* depended on deer hunting, too.

One day the *Diné* were told to meet at what is the present-day Fort Defiance, Arizona. It was said, "*Diné* with peaceful minds will be issued rations." Who passed out the information, I don't know. I myself have heard no one mention that. Anyway, some *Diné* walked there, and bacon was issued to them, along with other rations, like white flour and coffee in bean form. Some people tried to boil the beans. Then, one day, a Navajo man that understood Mexican came by, and he told the *Diné* the proper way to use coffee. He explained to the *Diné* that the coffee was first ground into a fine powder; then a small amount was put into boiling water. After the coffee was boiled, the grounds were separated from the liquid and the liquid was drunk. Sugar powder also was a lot different from what the Navajos had known. It used to be dropped into the coffee. It probably was in a ball shape. The *Diné* didn't know how to cook bacon, either. They boiled it and ate it. As a result, a great number of *Diné* died of dysentery.

All this happened at Fort Defiance. The *Diné* continued to come in for rations, and, pretty soon, there were a lot of people. As the number increased tremendously, they were moved on to Fort Sumner in New Mexico territory. Most *Diné* walked the whole way. Only a few were taken in wagons. The journey took many days and nights. Another thing, on that journey most *Diné* ran low on food supplies. Some ran out and were starving. Then, at Fort Sumner, it was even worse. There was famine, even though rations were given out.

Back here, the *Diné* who survived had to eat almost anything they could find — like cactus and horses and sheep killed by the Mexicans or the Utes. The heads, feet and skins used to be eaten. Deer meat was pretty tasty when it could be found.

At Fort Sumner our people spent four years of a miserable life. In spite of that, religious ceremonies were practiced. Squaw Dances and singing ceremonies were held. As the Squaw Dance required horses, and horses were scarce, the *Diné* would put long sticks between their legs and pretend they were riding real horses. Our people even went on a rattle-carrying ceremony in that manner.

Although they were supposed to be protected, other Indians raided the Navajos. I don't remember; it was either Oklahoma Indians or the Mescaleros that attacked at Fort Sumner.

A wood called *nááztání* (mesquite) was used for firewood when it could be found. It was hard to burn, especially when wet. But, at least, it burned and gave some heat to our ancestors. As for water, there was plenty. A river flowed nearby.

For four years our people kept asking that they be sent back to their own country. One of our leaders was Manuelito, and he was one of the men who requested constantly that they be sent back. Finally, at the end of those years, they were freed. It was said that the bad people were to be separated from the good people. Whether that was done, I don't know. Before Fort Sumner, some people had been peaceful, but a minority were wild and caused trouble for the rest by stealing other Indians' and White Men's sheep and horses. When other Indian tribes got tired of the Navajos' stealing, they started raiding, with the intention of killing off the *Diné* – completely wiping them out. That was when our people were taken to Fort Sumner.

As for my ancestors, even though they had heard that they might be free to leave some time, they decided to run away from Fort Sumner. So my mother, carrying the child that she had picked up back in the homeland while being attacked by the Utes, also was carrying another baby which she had given birth to at Fort Sumner. Later, a man named *Hastiin Háhołáhí* (Mr. Noisy) helped her carry the older one. While he was carrying the little girl, he went under a tree, and a branch whipped the baby's eyes. Her eyes became watery, and tears rolled down her cheeks. She was treated with all kinds of medicine, but it didn't help; her eyes just turned white. So my grandmother had white eyes. I saw and knew her.

Somewhere on their way back, the man who became my grandfather stepped on a big cactus needle, and it stuck into his foot – the bottom of it. He tried to pull it out but was unsuccessful. Soon his foot swelled big. Later, he put a bandage on the foot. Inside the bandage, right on the sore, he put dried pitch gum to suck out the cactus needle. The people spent five days on a mountain. At the end of four days my grandfather undid the bandage. His foot was pretty sore, with pus coming out. As more of the pus was squeezed out the cactus needle finally came out, too. The next day the people started walking again. My grandfather barely could walk. He hopped most of the way, following the people who walked mostly in the washes.

Once, when they came out of a wash, they saw something moving in the distance, and they saw that there were three elks. My grandfather had a rifle (a front-loading muzzle), with only one bullet. He said, "I'll hop ahead of you people. When I get close enough, I'll take a shot at one of the elks. I might hit one. Also, I want you to stay behind me. If I shoot one, I want someone to run over and get the elk's arms (front legs) between his horns so he can't get up and run off."

So my grandfather went ahead of the people, who quietly moved along some distance behind him. Then, all of a sudden, the people heard the gunshot, and one of the elks fell over. Quickly my grandmother put the baby that she was carrying on the ground and started running. She was afraid the elk would get up and run off. She did exactly what my grandfather had said to do. She got hold of the elk's two arms and put them between his horns as my grandfather hopped on one leg to the elk. As the elk was still kicking, my grandfather gave it a number of butt strokes on the forehead with his gun until the animal was dead. (My grandmother told my mother this story, and my mother passed it on to me.) The people then dragged the elk down into the wash where they butchered it. Then a big fire was built. All night the people fried or roasted the elk's meat. Bones were chopped up and ground to little pieces. The skin was taken off neatly and saved. Finally, the meat was distributed among the people.

Then they went on. Soon, however, they ran out of drinking water. All this time they had been taking just enough water to keep their mouths wet. They just had been going on and on, in the general right direction and hoping they would reach their old homes. By now they were too far away from the mountains, and one person was just hopping slowly. It had taken a long time to get as far as they were. When they ran out of water the children started crying with thirst. It was after dark of a certain day, and the older people were very

The storyteller's grandfather shot an elk while his little band was escaping from Fort Sumner (Bosque Redondo).

thirsty, too. Off in the distance, on the mountains, were snow and ice. My grandfather asked the other man to go with him for ice, but he refused. So my grandfather went alone, even though he hardly could walk. All he took with him was a little knife and a water bag of elk skin. Sometime during the night he made it to where the ice and snow were. He broke up some ice and put it into the bag. Then he started back. On his way he heard all kinds of noises here and there, but he kept on going, praying every now and then. Just before daybreak, he reached the thirsty people. My grandfather used to say, "When I got back in the morning, the people were about to die of thirst. And the worst one in the bunch was the man I had asked to go with me. When I started giving water to the people, he was the last man to drink. I let him suffer for a while. I told him, 'I asked you to go back with me, but you refused; so you don't need to drink'. Finally, I gave him some water."

After drinking, the people started walking in the wash again. All the way they kept walking in washes, past several mesas. By now, nine days had passed since they had taken off from Fort Sumner. They passed another large mesa. Somewhere along the way they crossed a river where the people drank plenty of water and my grandfather refilled his water bag. The walking continued. In 10 more days they reached Fort Defiance. My grandfather used to say, "We ran away a year before the people were freed from Fort Sumner."

I have not heard it said that they were missed; besides, lots of other people ran away, too. Many of them had run away earlier. When my grandfather and his people reached Fort Defiance, a lot of Navajos were around there. When various groups got to Fort Defiance they were issued food.

About the whole bad period from before the Long Walk until they got settled back in their homeland, my ancestors said, "We suffered from everything, especially hunger. We ate just about all the birds there were, also bears and porcupines. Crows were about the only bird that couldn't be eaten. Some people tried it, but they said the meat was so bitter they couldn't swallow it. My grandfather used to say, "My stories are dirty." One time I asked him, "What are you going to tell us about that time?" He said, "One time, when we were real hungry we found a hogan. The people who had lived there probably had moved out a few days earlier. When we went in we saw something stuck between hogan posts. It looked as though the people had killed their horse for food and had left a piece of sore horsemeat. Even though the meat was full of sores, we boiled it and ate it. We thought it was going to kill us right away, but I am still living today. Just outside the hogan was a bunch of crows hopping around."

One day my grandfather did die for good. Before that, he almost had died a few times. Then, one night while he was staying at his granddaughter's place, he walked off a cliff.

He had taken his people from Fort Sumner back here to Lukachukai, Arizona. To conclude, five people were involved in the story – my grandfather, my grandmother, her two children and one other man named *Háhołáhí.*

Ason Attakai

Asdzą́ą́ Adika'i

Mrs. *Adika'i*, at the age of approximately 95, is confined to bed in her home at Piñon, Ariz. Her story about the Fort Sumner years came from her paternal grandfather.

BEFORE THE *DINÉ* HAD WAR WITH OTHER TRIBES, there had been peace. Then the troubles started, resulting in the *Diné* being driven to *Hwéeldi* (Fort Sumner). Some *Diné* escaped capture and stayed here. While at *Hwéeldi*, the *Diné* lived in shelters made out of some kind of sharp bushes called *náázťání* or mesquite. Mesquite roots also were used for firewood. Cows were killed, and the hides were given to the *Diné* to make huts or shelters. One of my ancestors (my grandfather on my father's side) used to collect hides and was named after his work. He was called *Hastiin Akałii*, or Mr. Hide. Some of the *Diné* cried at *Hwéeldi*, saying they wanted to be at certain places back in their homeland.

One day, after four years, the *Diné* were told to assemble. They thought they were going to be issued another ration, but when they got together they were told to prepare their food to take along with them because within four days they would start back to their own country. When the *Diné* heard the news, they said, "We hope you are telling the truth and mean it. We want to go back to our country." Many *Diné* were crying. Four days later they started their journey back. Their belongings were put into huge wagons that were pulled by eight teams of oxen or steers. They returned to *Tséhootsooí* (Fort Defiance).

Before the Long Walk my ancestors started to Fort Defiance from around *Łóó' Háálį́* (Fish Point — northeast of Black Mountain Trading Post at southern point of Black Mountain) and *Shą́ą́ Tóhí* (Sunnyside Spring — below western edge of Black Mountain, northeast of Cow Springs). There were two points then, but one slid or caved in. Now, only one point remains.

I don't know exactly how the journey started and proceeded. Not many people knew or told all of the details. I do know that the *Diné* had all kinds of hardships on the way to *Hwééldi*. Some of them wore their shoes out getting there.

After the *Diné* got back to Fort Defiance and spent a few nights there, they were real anxious to return to their own homes. I don't know how many days it took them to get back here to the Fish Point and Sunnyside Spring areas from Fort Defiance.

It is said that not all of the *Diné* went to *Hwééldi*. Those who didn't survived on sources of food like yucca and prickly pear fruits and other cactus fruits. I knew a man of the *Kinyąą'áanii* clan (Towering House Clan) who said he didn't go to *Hwééldi* (Fort Sumner). He died of old age a long time ago.

I can remember food being distributed to the *Diné.* It was called commodity food. I heard of sheep being issued to them after returning to Fort Defiance. In the beginning of food distribution, a greenish-colored coffee and yellow sugar cubes were given to the *Diné.* When they would hear of commodity food distributing they would go on horseback, leading an extra horse. They went all the way to Fort Defiance. My late father and my late uncle on my mother's side used to go over there. He lived at *Tahchii* (Red Hill). He was called *Atsidii* (Silversmith). Another of my grandfathers from down below at a place called *Tódik'ǫǫz* (Salt Water) took people over to Fort Defiance. They called him *Hastiin Łtsoí* (Yellow Man).

Many women at first didn't know how to cook those foods. One time my great-grandmother mixed flour with burned juniper ashes and put it into hot boiling water like making corn mush. But soon it just boiled over. She tried to stir it and put more water in, but she couldn't make it. That's when my late mother came in and said, "That isn't the way it's done or eaten." Then she showed my great-grandmother what to do with the flour. Some would put flour in a tin can and heat it until it turned yellowish color. Coffee beans would be roasted, too, and were eaten with flour. That's how the Navajos lived at the time when they first went to Fort Defiance. Only a few of the *Diné* knew how to use those things which later were to become our main foods.

Before the journey to Fort Defiance and Fort Sumner, the *Diné* lived in remote areas. It was a fearful time. The enemies never got to the top of *Łóó' Háálį́* (Fish Point). The *Diné* always had to flee from enemies. Corn patches were destroyed, and horses hardly ate much when the *Diné* were being attacked. When horses heard sounds of approaching enemies they would take off toward home with their heads high. Hardly anybody slept. All the *Diné* did was make bows and arrows. The enemies had guns and lances that could be stuck through you. The *Diné* had only their bows and arrows.

Navajo women made mush of juniper ashes mixed with corn meal.

Akinabh Burbank

Ałk'inanibaa' Burbank

Mrs. Burbank of Valley Store, Ariz., at the venerable age of 90 lives quietly with her family. Her Long Walk and Fort Sumner accounts came from her various grandparents. She is of the *Táchii'nii* (Red Streak Running Into the Water) clan.

THE NAVAJOS WERE HERDED TO FORT SUMNER because of events that took place in and around the *Tséyi'* (Canyon De Chelly) area. It was in the fall, when it was about to snow, that a frightened feeling settled among the Navajo people – a feeling of danger from enemies. The *Nóóda'í* (Utes) were expected. They were the enemies that the Navajos had encountered from time to time, raiding back and forth; but now they were moving into our territory to search for us and kill us all.

Just below the place called *Lidbáásiláhí* (Smoke Signal Hills) there is a big erosion where the people moved into caves to hide from the enemies. However, some Navajos who had been taken captive showed the enemies the hiding places of our people. After they moved into the caves, the Navajos watched for the enemies in different directions and at considerable distances. Some miles to the northwest, along the edge of *Tłó'yíí'chíí'í* (Red Clay Ridge, southwest of *Ch'ínílí* – Chinle) there was an old trail that led north. Along that trail appeared white covered wagons moving in the direction of the caves, but the people didn't know what they were because they never had seen such things. They tried to figure out what was coming, some thinking they were big snow balls rolling along the trail. From a distance they probably did look like snowballs.

The Navajos waited and watched as the caravan moved along the valley and finally came to *Dził'ghą́ąhas Kai'í* (Apache Trail) toward sunset; and the people with the wagons made camp at *Hóótsohgii* (now Thunderbird Ranch). (By that time the Navajos had recognized the things as wagons and the people as Mexicans and white soldiers.)

The people did not sleep. They were observing what was going on at the enemy camp where tents were pitched and the enemies settled for the night. The next morning the intruders started moving around early. They were bringing in their horses and saddling up. Then they started moving on horseback toward the cliffs where the people were hiding. Before long, the enemies confronted the people who were hiding in the caves to which the captives had led them. Otherwise, the enemies never could have found them. The enemies opened rifle fire on the people in the caves, while the people fought back with bows and arrows. Some people were shot; some were falling off the cliff.

Then firing ceased for a while. An enemy party had moved and was coming down from above. The man named *Bitł'ízhííyę́ę* (His Bladder) had led the enemies down to where the people were. After more dreadful fighting, dead people were lying here and there, and many wounded were crawling around. Some fell from the cliff, including men, women, children and babies.

After the fight, the leader of the enemy party observed the tragic scene, and it frightened him. He broke down and wept, saying, "What a terrible thing we have done to these people!"

The enemies then left and went back to their camp at *Hóótsohgii*. They did not continue the attack against the few survivors. The commander still regretted what they had done to the people; so he told two captives to go back with a white flag, talk with the leader of the Navajos and persuade the people that they should not fight any more.

The two captives, doing as they were told, went up the hill toward the caves and soon a few people gathered there. The captives delivered the message, which went something like this: "From here on we will not kill any more people or harm them in any way. I invite them to our camp and they are welcome." Three men, all of the *Mą'ii' Deeshgiizhnii* (Coyote Pass) clan, and one other man went to the enemy camp, along with the captives who escorted them. When they arrived they found tents prepared in rows side by side; and, just as the Navajos approached, soldiers sprang up with their guns pointed toward them. The captives led the four visiting Navajos toward a large tent where the leader was waiting. When the Navajos and the enemy leader confronted each other they exchanged greetings. Once more the leader of the enemy broke down and cried over the tragic event he had caused. (If he was such a cry-baby, why was he waging war out here?)

The Navajos went out of the canyon to the camp and saw rows of tents and many soldiers.

White covered wagons appeared on the canyon trail, moving toward the caves.

An agreement with the leader was made that they would not fight any more. It was the white officer's idea.

During the discussion the troops sat around while the leader was talking, saying how sorry they were for what they had done to these people. The officer explained to the few Navajos who were present that in Fort Defiance they could get free food, but that, from there, he did not know what the future held for them.

The Navajos had explained how they were suffering and dying from hunger, mostly because of attacks by enemies.

Of course, there had to be interpreters for the officer, and they were Navajos who had been captured some time before and who had learned the English language. The visitors were given food and cigarettes, the type that were rolled with tobacco. Then the leader said, "Take this food and cook it so that you and your families can eat plenty. After a good meal, come again."

The Navajos departed and returned to the caves with the food and bearing the message about the cease-fire. They told the rest of the people not to be afraid and not to hide because the enemies would leave and the band, at its convenience, could move to Fort Defiance where it would be supplied with food.

The following day the Navajos returned to the enemy camp where they were given white flags signifying peace. The officer said, "Take these flags and go among the people wherever they live and tell them to move to Fort Defiance where they will be provided with plenty of food."

The Navajo messengers left with the white flags, going in different directions, locating people and telling them about going to Fort Defiance. The news was spread widely, some of the men going as far as Gray Mountain where Navajos were picking piñon nuts.

My great-grandmother was among those gathering nuts. My great-grandfather, *Tótsohniineez* (Tall Bigwater) whom I never saw, was a head man there.

One day my great-grandfather came running to where the people were working, saying that he saw something strange moving toward them in the distance. The people gathered together, trying to figure out what it could be. While the rest of the people ran for shelter, my great-grandfather stayed behind to confront what now appeared to be a Navajo man carrying a white flag. He became impatient waiting for this man; so he went forward to meet with him. He was pretty curious about the flag.

The messenger explained how an agreement had been made between the White Men and the Navajos not to fight any more. He also explained how he was sent by the leader of the enemy to spread the message and for them to move to Fort Defiance for supplies of food. He explained, "I have food with me now to show and prove to you that the enemy wants peace and they have given us food. If you go to Fort Defiance you will be cared for and will have plenty to eat."

The next day, the people decided that they would go to Fort Defiance, and they prepared to leave within another day. They were happy and excited to know that the enemies wanted peace.

The nuts that had been picked were forgotten. They were dumped and covered with greasewood. Just when everyone was busy and almost ready to leave, my grandmother got in labor with a baby, and it was my mother who was about to be born. Because of the baby coming, the family was left behind, including my grandmother, grandfather, their three boys and the baby (my mother) that was now born. A shelter was made of cedar branches to provide a place for the mother and baby.

It was a month later before the family was able to follow the rest of the group to Fort Defiance. On the day of the move, the family packed horses with family possessions, and each had a horse to ride. The family owned 15 goats, one sheep and some horses, and all were driven on the journey. It was a slow trip, even though the group headed straight toward Fort Defiance from Gray Mountain through *Tsézhinbii'* (Dilcon, Arizona). Spring had come when the family finally arrived. They found a large number of people living on the slope of a steep hill. Smoke was rising from each camp. The families were living outdoors, and the weather had been cold. There was a happy reunion with the rest of the relatives, and my great-grandfather was recognized and greeted by other people because he was a head man.

Meetings were held among small groups, discussing how each family had made the journey, what might happen, the enemies' desire for peace, how the Navajos seemed to trust the words of the white leaders, etc. At the same time, plans were being made among the white leaders about how to solve the problems of the Navajos, now that a large number of them were living there and some still coming in. It was decided (or had been decided before) that the Navajos should be moved to Fort Sumner where they would be much safer from enemies like the *Naałání* (Comanches), *Nóóda'í* (Utes), *Dziłghą'í* (Apaches), *Báyóódzin* (Paiutes) and *Kiis'áanii* (Hopis) than they would be here on their own land where they often were in conflict with these enemies. The White Men said, "They don't seem to have a chance of survival here; so the best place will be Fort Sumner."

The plans, and the reasons why the Navajos should be moved to Fort Sumner, were explained to the people, and, again, food, care and protection were promised by the white leaders. The people assumed that everything was going well and that they should follow orders. The final decision was to herd the Navajos to Fort Sumner. The trees were getting green in the spring when the Navajos made their move, and, finally, there was a day when they arrived in Fort Sumner and were confined.

By the end of four years at Fort Sumner my mother was more than four years old. The Navajos were pretty restless and yearned to go to their homeland in spite of the free food that was provided for them. It was planting season, and the people from *Tséyi'* (Canyon de Chelly) were the ones who had the strongest urge to go back. They kept wondering how their orchards of fruit were – or they were worrying about it being time to plant again.

The Navajos confronted the white leaders, saying they wanted to go back to their own land because they were lonesome. Now that the Navajos were lonesome for their homeland, the white leaders had to figure what kind of an agreement should be made to send the Navajos back to their homeland. It was decided to take weapons away from the Navajos and adopt a policy for the Navajos never to carry or use bows and arrows and guns any more. It was said among the white leaders that there had to be definite policies set up because, as the Navajos increased, the younger generation would tend to go on warpaths, and there had to be a complete stop to the fighting.

Once more, the head men and the white leaders got together to discuss the release from Fort Sumner, provided that the Navajos would follow and abide by certain policies that would be set up by the White Men.

During the confinement at Fort Sumner a lot of people perished from diarrhea because of the change in diet and the poor quality of the food. Also, various diseases had spread, and the people couldn't tolerate the situation any longer. That was another big reason why they wanted to go home.

When the Navajos arrived at Fort Sumner no other people were living there. Our people had to dig trenches and holes in the ground to be used as shelters. Some cows were slaughtered, and the hides were used for shade and windbreaks. After the bushes and small trees had been cut and burned, the people had to dig *nááztání* (mesquite roots) for firewood. The women wore woven wool dresses called *biił*. (They still wore that kind of dress even at the time when I was growing up and old enough to notice things.) The men's clothing

At Fort Sumner the people had to live in trenches and holes, with hides and brush for cover and windbreaks.

usually was made of deer hides obtained from hunting. After skinning an animal the hide was softened and dyed blue or yellow. These hides made nice clothing. Some were worn like a *chiléého* (vest). As a little girl I saw this type of clothing.

While at Fort Sumner, twice the enemy *Naałání* (Comanches) attacked the Navajos. It even happened the night before they were to leave. The soldiers came to the rescue and told the *Naałání Dine'é* (Comanche people) not to fight; and the enemies left.

After all this trouble and suffering, the Navajos were released, but, before the departure, the white officers said, "From now on all the children that you rear are ours. Send these children to us so that we can send them to school to get educated. You now will go on your way."

After the long trip back to Fort Defiance, with most of the people walking, sheep were given to the families, as well as some food. The sheep had been promised, as part of the treaty, before the Navajos had left *Hwééldi* (Fort Sumner), and at Fort Defiance they received their sheep. Then the White Men told the people, "Now you are on your own, go your way; now that you have some sheep, take care of them."

With these words the Navajos were released, and they scattered in different directions toward their old homes.

My great-grandfather died about four years after the return from Fort Sumner.

As I said, the people had agreed that their children would be educated by the White Man, and the result is evident today.

Also, this land is not our land. The Navajos had to surrender their children and their land so that they could come back to the land. At least, that is the way our parents and grandparents have told of history and events.

The Navajos started sending their children to school about five years after Fort Sumner. First, only a few boys went, some becoming spokesmen for the people later; but, as time went on, these men died off. I don't believe there is one alive today.

Some of these first students were *Siláo Álts'ìhí* (Small Policeman), *'Ołta'í'tsoh* (Big School Boy) and *Hastiin T'áá'sáhí* (Man by Himself). Although it was long ago, I still can remember when those boys were in school. I assume that education was forced upon the children of all Indian tribes – not only the Navajos.

Going back to the return to Fort Defiance, for transportation the Navajos managed to obtain some horses and a few old wagons, probably junk that the White Men did not want. A small number of good ones were provided by the white leaders.

Some people were not able to find any kind of transportation, and, after getting out of Fort Sumner and walking for days, they couldn't go any farther; so they settled along the way and there the descendants still live. These people represented several clans. Some called each other *Tsédee'aałhi* (Chewing Stones) but of the same *Mą'ii' Deeshgiizhnii* (Coyote Pass) clan.

My great-grandfather and great-grandmother were among the first people to arrive back from Fort Sumner. Surprisingly, they discovered some people living on *Dził Łijiin* (Black Mountain). They were living peacefully. It seems that, while most Navajos were herded to Fort Sumner, some had managed to hide and survive.

About that education after the return, children from each family were sent to school at different times, like a certain family would not send all its children at once, although they might all be of school age. Often, to prevent their being sent to school, parents would hide their children. I suppose that each family had its reason for wanting to keep children at home, like needing them to herd sheep and to help around the hogans. The Navajo police would come around to hogans, urging parents to send their children to school. They would say something like, "Send your children to school. It is good for them, and you have to abide by the agreements that were set up."

I suppose it was hard for some parents to understand these policies and agreements that had been made between their own leaders and the White Men. Now, you don't find any children at home. In those former days it seemed that children would go to school whenever they felt like going. Some would just quit, especially the girls, as soon as they could find husbands.

After all the sad events, and just when life seemed to settle down and go at a smooth pace, bottles (liquor) came crashing into the midst of the people. It affected a lot of them badly, driving them crazy and killing off men and women. This is happening among us still today, but no one seems to be doing anything about the terrible situation.

One wonders why people cannot tell each other to lock up the stuff or do away with it. Liquor is one of the things that is making the future uncertain.

John Smith

Mr. Smith, more than 70 years old, is a medicine man who lives at Piñon, Ariz. His narrative came from a grandfather. He was born into the *Mą'ii' Deeshgiizhnii* (Coyote Pass – Jemez) clan.

PRIOR TO BEING TAKEN to Fort Sumner, the *Diné* were gathered at Fort Defiance. From there, small children were put into wagons pulled by big steers and taken to Fort Sumner. Most Navajos walked the long distance.

Before being rounded up at Fort Defiance, some *Diné* had said, "We are on the warpath." As a result, the *Diné* made all other Indian tribes their enemies – *Nóóda'i* (Utes), *Naałání* (Comanches) *Dziłghą'í* (Apaches), even the *Kiis'áanii* (Hopis) who had lived close to us. So there was danger from everywhere in every direction, according to my late grandfather *Tł'aasání* (Old Seat or Old Lefter).

As I said before, the *Diné* walked into Fort Defiance of their own free will. They did not all come in at the same time but in groups over a long period. About the Long Walk, White Men drove the wagons full of children through Albuquerque, New Mexico, and then on to Fort Sumner, crossing at least one dangerous river. At Fort Sumner, the *Diné* discovered sweet potatoes, which they would dig out, cook any old way and eat. As the years passed, they discussed what the commanding officer, *Haskééjínaat'áá'* (War Chief), would say to them about returning to their homelands. The *Diné* had talked about it among themselves, and that is how the *Mą'ii' Bizéé'nast'ą́* (Put Bead in Coyote's Mouth) ceremony took place. I still have the bead with me which was used in the ceremony at that time. My ancestor got that white shell bead from *Hwééldi* (Fort Sumner).

In the ceremony, the *Diné* made a circle; then a coyote was turned loose in that circle. The *Diné* wondered which direction the coyote would go when he got out of the circle, and it went in our direction – that is, toward what is now our Reservation. Maybe that meant that our people were to return back to their own land.

The next day, when the *Diné* gathered again, a white shell bead was put under a tongue, and a ceremonial prayer was said with it to the commanding officer. After that, the *Diné* were informed that they could start for their homeland within four days. The news got around fast, and the people were saying, "We are to return to our land." Women and men started crying from happiness, saying they were lonely and homesick. Being in confinement was like being in jail, they would say.

To go back, some of the *Diné* had stock with them which they had driven to *Hwééldi.* The sheep were grazed across the river from the confined area. For years before the Fort Sumner trip, the Navajos had had many horses in their land, but the *Nóóda'í* (Utes) had stolen them. A Ute leader by the name of Whitehair or Grayhair had made an agreement with *Haskééjínaat'áá'* (Commanding Officer – War Chief) that he was going to keep what he had taken, like horses, *Diné* males and females, even children. "I'm going to keep all these," said *Nóóda'í Tsii'bálígaii* (Grayhair Ute), the Ute leader. Permission was granted; so *Nóóda'í Tsii'bálígaii* had his gun made shorter. As soon as he had zeroed the weapon he went on the warpath to attack the Navajos. He made his attacks at night, often during the full moon when it would be like daylight. Even though the *Diné* expected the *Nóóda'í* to come, still many Navajos were killed.

This attacking took place before the *Diné* were taken to Fort Sumner. The Utes were all well armed with guns; so many *Diné*, with only bows and arrows, were killed. In this connection, two *Diné* men by the name of *Haskénazhni'iin* (Mean Youngster) and *Naakaii Yázhí* (Little Mexican) were on a trip to a place called *Ashįįhí* or Salt. While there one man's father was killed. His father's name was *Haskénazhni'iin*, too. His father's brother had been killed, too. They called him *Jaanééz Yázhí*, or Little Mule. The enemy would rope the tops of forked-stick hogans and bring them down to the ground, destroying them. That was when one of these men, the father of young *Haskénazhni'iin*, was shot down coming out of his hogan. Afterward, the *Nóóda'í* went up the mountain, which now is called *Nóóda'í Tsii'bálígaii* (Grayhair Ute). It was late winter when this incident took place, and it was snowing hard.

To come back to Fort Sumner, four days after the Navajos' release had been discussed, the *Diné* were being brought back to their homeland – most of them going on foot. Others hunted game, running here and there, while traveling back. Probably some even killed deer because it was said that lots of deer were around at that time. That's how *Diné* fed their children and brought them back. The

Diné had problems. After their release from *Hwééldi*, they talked about how they were going to survive, what food to live on after they returned to their homelands, and how to continue living on into future generations. All of these problems they had discussed among themselves at night.

A big problem was the need for horses. All the horses which had belonged to the *Diné* had been captured by the *Nóóda'í*, also the *Naałání* (Comanches). *Wááshindoon* (the U.S. Government) had encouraged this. The government had given permission to *Nóóda'í Tsii'bálígaii* (Grayhair Ute). As told before, he was the one that killed almost all of the *Diné*. The *Diné* had been warned not to make weapons any more, like bows and arrows, for the purpose of war against other tribes which were *'ąná'í* (enemies). We *Diné* haven't done anything wrong yet, but our children are being taken and drafted into the armed forces by *Wááshindoon*. I, myself, almost went into the armed forces. My *tsíiyéeł* or *chunga* (hair knot) was the reason that I didn't go. When they had me in Phoenix for my physical examination they wanted to cut my *tsíiyéeł* off, but I told them "no." These army men wanted to know why I said that to them. "It represents dark rain showers, and my whiskers were put there by *Mą'ii'* (Coyote)," I said. "It's a sound statement," the White Man said, stepping back.

The enemies, especially the Utes, would rope the top of a forked-stick hogan, pull it down and kill those living there.

Casamira Baca

Mr. Baca, of the Alamo section of the Navajo Reservation in New Mexico, was 100 years old when he recounted the following story which he heard from his late mother. His main clan, on his mother's side, is *Tó'baazhní'ázhí* (Two Came to the Water People), and he was born for the *Ashįįhí* (Salt People) clan on his father's side.

I WILL TELL ABOUT SOME EVENTS that my late mother told me a long time ago.

Years back, during the fearful times of enemy attacks, during the Long Walk to *Hwééldi* and after the return, was when the people scattered to the wide parts of the Navajo area. From *Hwééldi* most went back to their own homeland, but some went in other directions in search of food.

Before the Long Walk, the people raided back and forth with other tribes and the Mexicans, all of whom were their enemies. Such tribes were *Kiis'áanii* (Hopi), *Nóóda'í* (Ute), *Naałání* (Comanche), *Naasht'ézhí* (Zuni) and *Dziłghą'í* (Apache) – all of these tribes joined and became friends and fought the Navajo people. There was no safe place; the people were continually on the run. They would move about, searching for hiding places, carrying what little possessions they had, including their children. It was a time of fear and unrest.

So it was that the people settled here near Alamo. Some miles distant from here is a place called *Sigooláa* (Socorro). Between here and there is a place called *Bééshhaagééd* (present-day Magdalena). At Magdalena there was a copper mine where some Mexicans were working, and some of these Mexicans used to go into Navajo territory to raid and kill. So the people used to flee south from the enemies, all the way to *Mandoosah* (Quemado – in west-central New Mexico, southwest of Magdalena), also to areas around *Tséłł'-áahalchíí'* (Cave With Round Red Rock), where there were rock caves in which the people lived while hiding. Also, over toward the north, was *Tsįįdeezhlí* (Tree Wash Start), and Navajos used to flee there and beyond to a place where there was a huge mountain called *Dził Dátsáah* (Round Top Mountain), which ranges down toward *Dził Diłhił* (Dark Mountain). There are also other mountains over to the southwest called *Nǫǫdá'haaz'éíí* (Magdalena Mountains). In all of these regions they would hide. They are near and south of the Navajo Alamo Reservation, northeast of Quemado.

My late uncle was named *Juan Dejoo*, his father was named *Chico*. It was during the time mentioned above that this certain incident took place. *Chico's* wife had just borne a baby when they were attacked suddenly by a few Negroes. Evidently the Negroes were friendly with the Apaches, and, together, they were attacking the Navajos. *Chico* stayed by his wives and his family to protect them. He had two wives. Some neighbors fled to seek shelter. A Negro leader riding a black horse came to close range and took a shot at *Chico*, and the bullet hit and wounded him in the groin. With an old-time musket, when *Chico* got a chance, he managed to shoot the Negro right in the back; and, with a loud cry, he took off on his horse at high speed, and others followed him. The Negro man was the leader of that small band. Some distance away he fell off the horse. The others dismounted and gathered around him. They put him across the saddle and took him away at sundown.

That evening, when *Chico's* pain from the wound subsided, his relatives put him on a horse, and he started traveling with his family towards *Ashįįhí* (Salt Lake, N.M.). Somewhere along the way, the wound got very severe, and he said to his family, "My children, go travel on. I am in much pain and can't go any farther. I will catch up with you if I don't die. I will climb to the peak of *Nǫǫdá'haaz'éíí* (Magdalena Mountains) and spend several days here. I will catch up with you when I'm well. Stay hidden in the daytime and travel at night and go through places where you won't be likely to be seen by the enemies."

While the family traveled on, *Chico* barely made it to the peak of the mountain where he spent four days nursing his wounds with different kinds of plant medicine which helped him get well. The others went on to *Ashįįhí* and then to *Tsįįdadéesgaaí* (White Tree Extended Out). Beyond that place the family caught up with the rest of the relatives who had fled ahead of them. After *Chico* got well, he rejoined the group at *Dził Nineez* (Tall Mountain). From there, they moved across the valley to *Tsé Beeheedzéd* (Frighten Rock – near El Morro) where they encountered more enemies, which kept the group moving here and there. Finally, the family and relatives reached *Tsé'ałk'ézgish* (Twisted Rock), but they had to keep moving, with no rest. Another mountain range called *Są' Siłtsǫǫz* (Old Age Clay), ran through the area, and the people moved to it. At *Tsétsóóshádzoh* (Nearer Canyon Marks – in the same area) the people settled for a while, but, one evening, there was another surprise attack by *Naasht'ézhí* (Zunis). There were muzzle-loading rifles fired by both sides, and, then, a mass attack.

A man by the name of *Tsóósí* (Tsosie) pretended to be of the *Ashįįhí* (Salt) clan. He was a Mexican who had been captured as a little boy and raised by *Hastiin Náshdóí* (Mr. Bobcat) of the *Naakaii Dine'é* (Mexican People) clan. During this attack, he was shouting and encouraging the Navajos to fight with all their might. After the battle was over, the Navajos had slain most of the enemies and discovered two of their men killed. Because they had killed a mass of Zunis, the Navajo people were hated by them. This is how the story goes.

My late mother was of the *Tó'baazhní'azhí* (Two Came to Water) clan, married to the *Ashįįhí* (Salt) clan. My late father was named *Hastiin Łtsoí* (Yellow Man) – in Mexican, Malyanna. Both died in their old age. I am of the *Tó'baazhní'azhí* clan and related to the *Ashįįhí* clan. I now am one hundred years old.

Casamira Baca of the Alamo area in New Mexico was 100 years old when he recounted his story in 1972.

Charley Sandoval

At the age of 72, Mr. Sandoval lives at Cañoncito, N.M., where he is a medicine man and livestock owner. His story came from a grandmother and a grandfather. He was born into the *Tábąąha* (Edge of Water) clan.

MY NAME IS CHARLEY SANDOVAL. The place where I live is called *Tóhajiileeh* (Cañoncito). Long ago, my late grandmother and grandfather on my father's side used to tell this story. Both of them went on the journey to *Hwééldi* (Fort Sumner).

It was the *Diné's* own fault to be rounded up. The *Diné*, using bows and arrows, had been having war with other tribes. That was the reason why they were rounded up by the military army from *Shash Bitoo'* (Fort Wingate) and driven to Fort Sumner. There the *Diné* spent five years. They cried for their own country while staying there.

So the *Diné* promised to give up all their bad habits, and then they were released to go back to their homeland. They traveled and traveled. They spent one night south of here at a place called *Tóbii'* (Into Water). My grandmother used to tell that they got back to *Tóhajiileeh*, while the others continued to Fort Wingate and then to *Tséhootsooí* (Fort Defiance). From there the *Diné* parted and went in different directions to where they had come from.

On the journey to Fort Sumner, one Navajo man was ahead, leading, and the rest just followed. The Army escorted and watched closely so that nobody escaped. I never was told about the number of people who made the journey, but they traveled on foot. The women carried their babies on their backs. The route went through Albuquerque and from there to Fort Sumner. It was quite a long way from here. There were trees, mountains and a number of houses. Some distance away from the houses the *Diné* were kept prisoners. As I was told the story, the place was not fenced.

The *Diné* were cared for with rations, but they didn't know how to cook the things. There were green coffee beans and flour, but the *Diné* didn't know how to make tortillas with the flour. There was bacon, too. Cooking had to be demonstrated to them. Back here, the *Diné* survived on plants such as *haasch'ééd̨ą́ą́* (wild berries), *chiiłchin* (sumac plants), *tłohdééh* (seeds of grass), *nimaasí* (wild potatoes) and *hasgaan* (yucca fruit). These were the *Diné's* main foods during that time. At Fort Sumner the *Diné* did no planting. As I have heard it said, no ceremonies or chants took place either.

After a while, the *Diné* pleaded to go back to their country and said they were lonely for it. Also, they promised not to harm any more people. That is why they were allowed to return. It was at that time that this place was given a name. There was a big deep hole, and, at the bottom, was a spring. There was no way that a person could get down there. The *Diné* used to carry with them some sort of *tóshjee'* (water jug). They tied a braided, narrow yucca leaf rope to a jug to bring up water with; but the jug would not sink in the water. It just floated on top. So the *Diné* tied a stone to the bottom of the jug to make it sink down. That is how they fished out their water. And that's the reason this place is called *Tóhajiileeh* (Cañoncito). It was named after the *Diné* had journeyed back from Fort Sumner. That is how my ancestors told their stories.

The *Diné* used a narrow rope made of braided yucca leaves to lower a jug to the water. When the jug just floated on the surface they tied a stone to it to make it sink.

Francis Toledo

Francis Toledo, 68, is a livestock owner at Torreon, N.M. This is an account of bitter experiences as told by one of his grandmothers. He is of the *Tódich'íinii* (Bitter Water) clan.

THIS PLACE IS CALLED *YA'NÍÍLZHIIN* (TORREON), New Mexico. It has been named like that for a long while now. I am of the *Tódich'íínii* (Bitter Water) clan.

My late grandmother said she could remember, when she was about the age of fourteen, that the *Diné* began to flee from enemies. They had been told by *Hastiin Ch'il Haajiní* (Manuelito), not to take off one by one. They were rounded up by Manuelito and started on a journey to *Ch'oshgai* (Tohatchi Mountains) because of the attacks from every direction by other tribes like the Pueblos, as well as the Mexicans. The enemies traveled in groups on horseback, and there would be as many as *naakidineeznádiin* (two hundred) of them.

At that particular time the snow was deep, and that's when this story took place. After much struggle, many *Diné* had survived, but some were captured and taken as captives to other places by the enemies. Probably some old men and women had been killed, too.

So Manuelito led his people to the base of the Tohatchi Mountains. There, he told the *Diné* to capture eagles for their feathers and to gather lots of feathers, to make two bows each, and spears. "We will not be killed poorly; we will be considered dangerous," Manuelito said.

The *Diné* did what they had been told. Each man had two bows and lots of arrows. Then Manuelito told them to hunt deer and not to lose a single piece of ligament (sinew) because they were used to grease and make bows. This man – Manuelito – was telling them the truth. He was the leader of his people, who then moved to the top of *Ch'oshgai* (Tohatchi Mountains) where they captured eagles every day. The *Diné* had gathered many feathers by that time. They made bows during the night.

When spring came, Manuelito told his people to make poison arrows. Snake blood was used, and the poison was put on the points of arrows. When the *Diné* were being attacked, they used their poison arrows. When an enemy was hit by one of the arrows his body would become swollen, and he would not live long. That is why the *Diné* were considered dangerous.

Then they moved to a place called *Noodahaas'eíí* (Rope Ladder). I don't know exactly where it is, but near it is a place called *Ashįįhí* (Salt Lake, New Mexico). Within two years the *Diné* were moving around there still being attacked from every direction. But the enemies were unsuccessful in conquering the *Diné.* At that time the enemies began to fear them because of their poisoned arrows. Some *Diné* who had been taken captive escaped; and one of the women came back and said that enemies who had been hit by poisoned arrows died. Their whole bodies had become swollen before they died. That is the reason why the enemies feared them.

The captured *Diné* kept coming back, one after another, and the enemies said, "The Navajos are no good; all of them are going to be annihilated." The reason why the trouble had started was that many of the *Diné* were bad. They were told by their leaders not to do anything bad, but, still, they took off to where the Mexicans were herding sheep, killed some of them and raided their sheep. The *Diné* also raided the Pueblos of their cattle and drove them home. A man by the name of *Chą́ą́téé łí* (Wide Belly) of the *Mą'ii' Deeshgiizhnii* (Coyote Pass) clan got angry. I guess he must have spoken English, because at that time the military moved into Santa Fe, and Wide Belly went over there and said, "All these damned Navajos are going to be annihilated. I am going to travel around that way, and I'll return from the northern direction. A limit of time will be set, and the *Diné* will be killed."

He was asked, "What if they kill us?" And he answered, "They won't kill us all." Then the commanding officer asked how many years he would fight the Navajos, and he asked the commanding officer to loan him rifles – that he was going to fight the *Diné* for five years. [Wide Belly had been in trouble with his own Navajos and had turned against his people. He was called a *Diné 'Anáʼí* (Enemy Navajo).]

That was before the Navajos had heard of the annihilation, and, after that, they got angry. The military had only some old rifles that were not much good and which took time to load. They were called "*bii'ná'jíhí*" (front-loading muzzle). They required lots of gun powder and buck shot. Wide Belly told the commanding officer to help him with the supplies, and he left on his journey. He traveled to the Pueblo territory, talking to them and also to the Mexicans, the *Nóóda'í* (different tribes of Utes) and the *Beehaí* (Jicarilla Apaches).

The *Diné* fought with these enemies for two or three years, and then they were saved by the White Men from *Yootó* (Santa Fe). After that fighting was over, the *Diné* were taken to a place called *Hwééldi* (Fort Sumner). I think that two White Men came from Santa Fe and went around carrying a red flag. They told the *Diné* that they (the *Diné)* must go to Fort Sumner. Two *Diné* were made leaders to lead the others to *Hwééldi.* The *Diné* reached Fort Sumner, about two hundred miles from Albuquerque. They were given rations; also cows were killed for them, and shoes and blankets were provided, as well as pots and pans.

From back here, the *Diné* journeyed to that place, one group after another. My grandmother used to tell that many of them went.

The *Diné* spent three years at Fort Sumner before they returned to their land. At the end of their stay, these two men (white) showed up again. They said, "Back at Fort Defiance, merchandise has been brought in for you people. Go back there. No fighting is going on now."

At Santa Fe the commanding officer gave an order that if anyone killed another Navajo he would be thrown into jail. So the *Diné* journeyed back from Fort Sumner to Fort Defiance. There they were seen dressed in jeans and other decent clothes and were given shoes. The women received clothes, also needles and thread — things which were issued by two white women going around.

During life at *Hwééldi*, the *Diné* pleaded for their freedom, and they were taught military discipline. Manuelito then said that they would do their pleading in Washington, and a commanding officer there wrote an order to take with them to Washington. At that time a railroad was being built close by *Sisnaajíní* (Blanca Peak). Two women also went on a trip. One of the women's names was *Asdzą́ą́ Tł'ogi* (Hairy Lady). I don't remember the other one's name. Anyway, the women were clever at making speeches. For days and days they traveled until they reached their destination, where they pleaded with the peace commission. The *Diné* didn't know how to speak English nor understand it, and I think a man by the name of *Tsóósí* (Tsosie) was interpreting for them. He might have been a Mexican or a *Diné.* The peace commissioner then asked the *Diné* if they would set down their bows and arrows. They were asked this one by one. They talked like this: WHITE OFFICIAL: So you put your bows and arrows aside, right? *DINÉ:* Right! WHITE OFFICIAL: You set your spears aside? *DINÉ:* Yes, we will set them aside! WHITE OFFICIAL: You have got over your angriness? *DINÉ:* Yes, we are not angry any more. WHITE OFFICIAL: Are you going to help me in the future? *DINÉ:* Yes, we'll help you. WHITE

OFFICIAL: Are you going to let your children go to school? *DINÉ:* Yes, we will put them in school. WHITE OFFICIAL: They are going to be educated? *DINÉ:* Yes! WHITE OFFICIAL: Okay, thank you!

Those things are being done these days, like our young boys being drafted into the armed forces. Also almost all of our young generation are educated to some extent.

The *Diné* returned from Washington and were released from Fort Sumner. Children and food were put on the wagons. A great multitude journeyed over hill after hill, some on foot, some on horses, others in the wagons. When they reached Fort Wingate many were in a hurry and started taking off, saying, "We're lonely for our beloved country." But they were told not to take off until they got to Fort Defiance where rations could be issued to them.

At Fort Defiance, besides the other things, the men received hoes and axes and were told to work with them. They were told to go back to your lands but to return within 14 days. The White Men also said to return within 14 days. The White Men also said they didn't know how long things would be issued. Fourteen days later, the *Diné* reported to Fort Defiance again, and two sheep were given to each person, from babies born the night before to old people, even though there was a large number of Navajos. They were told that sheep would be issued just one more time; so the *Diné* received one sheep to each person the second time.

After all this had taken place, Mauelito said to his people, "We will build hogans, so our population will increase rapidly from this day on."

So *Diné* gathered together and put on a ceremonial chant to sacrifice *nitł'iz* (precious stones). The ceremony was held for about four days, and that is the reason why our population has increased rapidly up to these days. If it had not been for the ceremony it wouldn't have been like this.

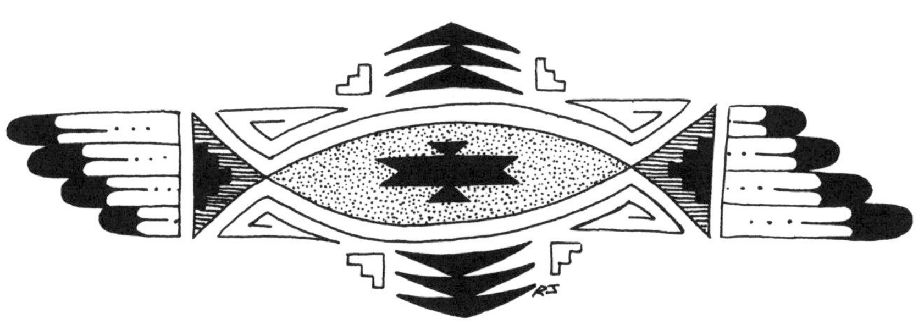

Florence Charley

A housewife in her sixties, Florence Charley lives at Chinle, Ariz. Her Long Walk account came to her from a great-grandmother. She is of the *Tábąąha* (Edge of Water People) clan.

THERE IS NOBODY AROUND who knows the true story of the Navajos' "Long Walk." No man or woman knows exactly what took place during that time. We just repeat as closely as we can remember what our ancestors told us.

My great-grandmother said that she had gone on the Long Walk. The reason for being taken to *Hwéeldi* (Fort Sumner) was that the *Diné* were stealing from *'aná'í* (other tribes), Mexicans and White Men; and they were caught sometimes in stealing livestock. My great-grandmother used to tell her story this way: There was extreme hardship in those days. People didn't eat anything like what we eat these days. They lived, or survived, on other kinds of foods, such as prickly pear fruits or juniper blueberries. The *Diné* ate just about anything. That was before they went to *Hwéeldi.*

Some of the Navajos were called thieves, and quite a few of them lived in *Tséyi'* (Canyon de Chelly) up in the rocks. There still are signs of ashes in those rocks where they lived. When the *Diné* heard that the *'aná'í* (enemies) were on their way, they hid on the cliffs up in the walls of *Tséyi'*, and there's a place called *Ak'eha'į* (Do Their Way) and also *Tsébiiníjíjáhí* (*Diné* Fled in the Rock) where the *Diné* went. That's when they were attacked by the soldiers. Most of them were killed, but some were captured and evacuated out of the Canyon by the Army and were informed that they were to be driven way off somewhere to a place called *Hwéeldi.* They had hardly any clothing, not like jeans and shoes like today; and, in that way, they were driven out. Also, the few who survived didn't have anything on hand to cook with, like pots or kettles. (Pots were made of mud-clay, and I don't know what was boiled in them — probably juniper blueberries or prickly pear fruit. Rabbits would be caught at times and rabbit stew would be prepared.)

According to my great-grandmother, when the journey to Fort Sumner began the *Diné* had hardly anything to comfort them or to keep warm, like blankets. Women carried their babies on their backs and walked all the way hundreds of miles. They didn't know where they were headed. Finally, the *Diné* reached their destination, but they were to shed many tears during their stay at *Hwéeldi.* The rations that were given out were unfamiliar to them and made them sick, and many died of the food. It took some time for them to get used to it.

Four years were spent at that place. The sister of my great-grandmother was about to give birth to a baby when the *Diné* were told that they could return to their homeland. Many of them had been crying *"Tséyi'"* and pleading to be sent back to Canyon de Chelly. The *Diné* had discussed the matter among themselves, and they pledged to compel their children to go to school. So they were released and journeyed back home. The government (or *Wááshindoon*) is still holding on to the Navajos' children, but they had made a promise at *Hwéeldi*, agreeing to let the children attend school, and they continued with it in future generations.

On their way back from *Hwéeldi* the *Diné* had been informed that they would receive rations. Also, sheep were given out to them, and some corn. They got back to *Tséhootsooí* (Fort Defiance), and from there they went to where they used to live – their homelands.

Two of my grandparents also made the Long Walk, and they used to tell about it. They both died of old age. They were not captured. They just went with the others. About the schools, the *Diné* had been ordered to enroll their children, but it has been said that some people tried to hide them. Some *Diné* and White Men went around to people's homes telling them to let their children attend school. Those who refused or disobeyed the rules, their children were taken away from them by force. So, some Navajos kept their children from going to school, and that's the reason lots of them did not attend school and are uneducated like myself.

My deceased grandmother didn't want me to attend school. She wanted me to herd sheep instead. One of the main reasons why lots of children were out of school was sheep herding; and the *Diné* used to train their children in their own way for making a living, such as carding wool, weaving rugs and grinding with grinding stones. Also, there were horses and cows to be cared for. Those were the reasons why the *Diné* kept their children from going to school.

After the return from Fort Sumner, there were extreme hardships; but it has been said that the Navajos had leaders who gradually improved things. When my grandmother passed away, my grandfather told me it was no use for me to herd sheep; so he let me go to school. That was in Chinle. The education level went up to about eighth or tenth grade, but school was a lot different then from what it is today. Even to speak our own language was forbidden to us, and we used to get up real early in the morning, line up and march around like military armies do. We had no kind of activity like dances and those things. There was no vocational training like today, but we had a little working experience like cooking, sewing and doing laundry work; and that's how we went to school. I had to quit school because of an illness.

Children were taken by force to be placed in far-off boarding schools.

Frank Goldtooth

Frank *Béésh Biwoo'ii*

Ninety-year-old *Hastį́į́* Frank *Béésh Biwoo'ii* chiefly rests in bed at his home in Tuba City, Ariz. His discussion of the Long Walk and Fort Sumner derives from stories told by a grandmother. His clan is the *Tódich'iinii* (Bitter Water People).

I AM AN OLD MAN, with no teeth, although I am still called *Béésh Biwoo'ii* (Goldtooth). Having no teeth hinders me from talking clearly.

I am asked to tell stories of historical events of our ancestors, and some of them, related to me by my forefathers, are clear in my mind. Who would think that some day in the future we would be asked to repeat the stories that our ancestors handed down by word of mouth? Who would think that all kinds of research about past events would be done? In the past, who was to know what was to come? Now, we are being rediscovered through our past history. The question remains: Why is our history to be rediscovered by going back to search for the events that took place regarding our ancestors over a hundred years ago?

The journey to *Hwééldi* (Fort Sumner) included my grandparents on both sides. Those are the people who told me of the events that took place at that time.

It has been said that the reason why the people were marched to *Hwééldi* was because, as we were told over and over, they had been stealing. We were no stealers. We were branded as being a bunch of thieves because they couldn't find any other excuse to make us march to *Hwééldi.* The main reason why we were herded there was because of the rise of enemies, such as the *Nóóda'í* (Utes). Enemies and Navajos started raiding each other back and forth. Many Indian tribes joined together and fought against the Navajo people. Another group that became our enemy was the *Naakaii* (Mexicans). Also, a lot of Navajo men joined these others to fight against their own people – which I believe is still going on today through employment. These traitors led the enemies in hunting down the Navajos who were trying to hide but were scouted down and slaughtered. This rise of enemies made the Navajos scatter into large areas. Close relatives were separated; families were separated as they sought shelter wherever possible. A man named *Biighaan Diłí* (Big Backbone) was one who helped the *Kiis'áanii* (Hopis) and the *Naakaii* scout for the Navajo people. They helped to chase the people out of their hiding places, then killed them or took them as captives to be sold as slaves. The *Kiis'áanii* tribe had no livestock of its own. Their only source of meat was rabbits, which they hunted on the mesas. After other tribes rose against the Navajos, the Hopis joined the fight, taking our livestock. These people who were our close neighbors, and who had been for years and years, became our enemies. When these other tribes became extreme in fighting the Navajos, something called the government stepped in to help us, to take us away from the enemies, to take us to a place called *Hwéeldi.* We were in the hands of the government, and our order was to march to *Hwéeldi* where we would be safe from our enemies.

During the confinement at *Hwéeldi*, some enemies came to raid, killing and kidnapping and taking what little the Navajos owned in trying to survive. Some of our people at *Hwéeldi* were angry because they said it was not right that we should be there – a place where there was nothing, people just dying off from starvation, different kinds of disease, exposure, etc. A lot of deaths resulted from a change of diet, being forced to eat food that was unfamiliar to them.

After four years at *Hwéeldi*, the people finally were released after pleading with the white leaders to let them go back to their own land.

I want to say here that a lot of people managed to avoid the march to *Hwéeldi.* They hid in rugged areas, cliff dwellings and other places where enemies were not likely to find them.

Some Navajos even went into the territory of the *Chíshí* (Chiricahua Apaches) where they became allied with that tribe until the "Long Walk" people had returned from *Hwéeldi.* My grandmother was one of those who went among the *Chíshí* during that time. She returned after the others came back from *Hwéeldi.*

Her journey to the *Chíshí* began from *Dził Łibaii* (Gray Mountain). It was made on foot, with the people carrying packs on their backs, no different from the people who walked to *Hwéeldi.* Upon their arrival they were accepted into the tribe, and they found

Storyteller's grandmother brought home fat goats given to her by Apaches.

that the Apaches were engaged in war with the white soldiers who were trying to round up those people just as they did the Navajos. That warfare still was going on when my grandmother returned home. She brought back with her some big fat goats which had been given to her as a gift from the tribe. The goats multiplied through the years until recently, during Stock Reduction, when they were taken away from us by force. That is the way my grandmother talked about her living with the *Chíshí* for almost four years.

When the people from *Hwééldi* returned to their land they were told that there was a boundary line, something like a circle, in which we were to live and that outside of that line we were not permitted to make our living. We could go outside these boundary lines only when we went to trade with other Indians, Mexicans or White Men. The agreements that were made then with the government did not include the *Kiis'áanii* (Hopis); also, the land that was set aside for us then did not include the *Kiis'áanii* land.

We now live within our four great sacred mountains, where our *Diyin Dine'é* (Holy People) want us to live, but most of the mountains themselves were taken away from us by the white people. Today, we hear that some of the land that was given to us to live on belongs to the *Kiis'áanii* and that they have the authority over it. What became of the agreements? What became of the documents that show that this is our land, even before our march to *Hwééldi* and even before the White Man came.

Today, we have no land to call our own, our words are not respected and they are not heard in *Wááshindoon* (Washington). What is to become of us and our children?

What right do the *Kiis'áanii* have that they claim almost our whole Reservation. After all, our ancestors suffered for it and they paid with their lives.

Part of La Plata Mountains in southwestern Colorado, northwest of Durango and northeast of Cortez. The photo was taken from approximately the southwest. They are the Navajos' sacred mountains of the north, named *Dibé Nitsaa'* (Big Sheep). They also are called the Obsidian Mountains. The Navajos refer to the colors of the four main sacred mountains (and directions) as Dawn, or White Shell (east); Blue Bead, or Turquoise (south); Abalone Shell, or Yellow (west), and Obsidian, or Black (north).

Mount Taylor – *Tsoodził* – in northwest New Mexico about halfway between Gallup and Albuquerque, some 15 miles northeast of Grants. Known as Blue Bead or Turquoise Mountain, it is the Navajos' sacred mountain of the south. Its elevation is 11,389 feet. The photo is from approximately the southwest.

Blanca Peak, the Navajos' sacred mountain of the east, in south-central Colorado, about 20 miles northeast of Alamosa and 15 miles north of Fort Garland. It has an elevation of 14,390 feet. The view is to the east-northeast. The Navajos call the mountain *Sisnaajíní* (Blackened Belt, which is visible in the photo). It also is known to them as Dawn, or White Shell, Mountain.

The San Francisco Peaks, which start only a few miles north of Flagstaff in north-central Arizona, are the Navajos' sacred mountains of the west. Mt. Humphrey, at 12,670 feet, is the highest in the state. The mountains are called *Dook'o'oosłííd* (High Top Melted Off) and are known as the Abalone Shell Mountains. The photo was taken from approximately the northeast.

Henry Zah

A former Tribal Councilman, Mr. Zah, about 70 years old, lives at Smoke Signal, Ariz. His story was told to him by a grandmother and a grandfather. His main clan is *Táchii'nii* (Red Streak Extending Into the Water People).

NAVAJOS KNOW JUST WHAT they have heard about *Hwéeldi.* They don't know the exact story. The old people of that time are all gone; so stories are hard to get.

More than a hundred years ago, we, the *Diné*, didn't have single strong leaders, and we lived like being on two paths or two separate ways, fighting and having war with other tribes that lived in neighboring territories. For that reason, *Wááshindoon* (the United States government) took us to Fort Sumner a little over a hundred years ago. It was because of our own angriness. Old men and women folks told of it that way – the ones who took the journey. Those people went through all kinds of hardships traveling to *Hwéeldi.* Our ancestors used to tell their stories this way: It was for a reason that the *Diné* were taken to *Hwéeldi.* We *Diné* had sharp weapons on hand.

My great-grandmother's name was *Asdzą́ą́ Táchii'nii* (Red Streak Extending Into the Water Lady), and my great-grandfather's name was *Naalnishí* (Worker). Their mother went on the Long Walk. She was of the *Tódich'íínii* (Bitter Water) clan. After they returned, they got back their lands which we now call the Navajo Reservation.

Before the return, a meeting was called between the commanding officers, the peace commissioner and the Navajo leaders or head men. The *Diné* pleaded with these officers, and a peace treaty agreement was settled between them. The *Diné* were told to put down their weapons, like bows and arrows; and the head men had agreed to do it. They were told, "From today on into future generations you will not get hold of these weapons again nor harm any more people, and you will return to your country without your stealing habits."

All these agreements the *Diné* had to go by after they were released at the end of four years. Numerous Navajos had died of starvation and sickness.

When they got back to Fort Defiance, the *Diné* were issued rations, as well as livestock like sheep, goats and horses; and some even got cows, one head per person. One sheep also was given to men who were heads of families. (My late grandfather told the story that way.) Some Navajos got from two to five head of sheep. They were issued according to the number of families. Rams also were issued with the sheep, and the *Diné* were told to take care of the sheep so that they would increase in the future, and they were told that the sheep were useful in many ways, from the hoofs on up; also, that wool would bring money and money would buy clothes. It was explained that the women would weave rugs with the wool and sell the rugs for money and that the sheep would provide mutton to eat and to keep you healthy.

Later, the government took away much of our stock when it increased too much, after the government had warned the *Diné* about the conditions of the land. This had been warned when the sheep were given. The *Diné* had increased their livestock, and it was thought of as if the sheep still belonged to *Wááshindoon.* Some *Diné* are still living on the offspring of the stock that *Wááshindoon* had given to them; some lost all their stock and don't have any now. There are some people who are serious about making a living. They are the ones who have livestock.

About educating the Navajos, there was a young boy around Fort Defiance who seemed to be the only one that spoke English; so he became the interpreter. When officials came from *Wááshindoon* he was there to interpret for them. He was known as *Hastiin Adiits'a'ii* (Chee Dodge – Mr. Interpreter, Mr. Hearing Who Understands). When the *Diné* journeyed back from Fort Sumner to Fort Defiance he was the interpreter, too, especially with officials who arrived from *Wááshindoon* to discuss things about education. The officials told the *Diné* to have some kind of education among themselves and to carry it on for their children into future generations. They said that some of the children might have high education, and, in return, they might help the *Diné* with it because the *Diné* might live better lives and their parents might live in good homes when education was completed from bottom to top. It would be something good and valuable.

That was the kind of advice the officials gave the *Diné*, and, for that reason, education has been taking place up to today. When education first got started, there were very few schools, and they were small. The government had promised there would be 30 *'ólta'í* (students) in a class, with a qualified and experienced teacher. The agreement was made. I don't know if this is being done to date. There are just a few schools around here, but, from the beginning of education to these days, it has been going on; so I believe that it is true.

During the Fort Sumner days, *Diné* head man *Hastiin Ch'il Haajiní* (Manuelito – a Plant Extended) had taught his people the same ideas. He told them that education is a ladder to future success. He was of the *Tótsohnii* (Big Water) clan. He was one of the real leaders at Fort Sumner, and he was one who pleaded for us to be released and returned to our country.

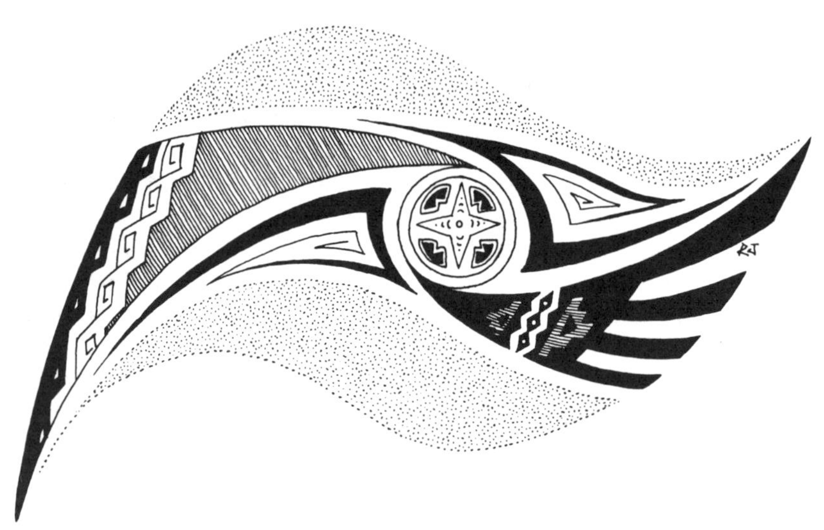

George Littlesalt

George *Ashįįhíyázhí*

George *Ashįįhíyázhí*, 70, of Navajo Mountain, is a livestock owner who heard many stories of his people's history from his paternal grandmother. He is of the *Kinłichíi'nii* (Red House People) clan.

AT *TSÉHOOTSOOÍ* (Fort Defiance, Arizona), where some of the Navajos lived, the piñon nuts had ripened. It was the fall season, and there had been lots of nuts on the evergreen trees that are called piñons. Then the people learned that the nuts were falling far north at *Dził Ashdlá'ii* (La Sal Mountains); so they moved up there; and they picked the little nuts and lived with some of the *Nóóda'í* (Ute) Tribes that they used to know before they went to the La Sals, located in the southeastern part of Utah.

When they arrived they built two houses, one for them to live in, and one for them to store their belongings in. They were brushy huts that were made out of cedar or piñon trees, used to stay in at night; and they could safely bring their bags of nuts to where they had built the two houses. At that time piñon nuts were not sold to the traders. They were picked to be eaten as food. The only corn patches that they had were down toward Fort Defiance. If the corn did not ripen in the fall, the people depended on the nuts for food. They also used to have horses, but it was a lot of work taking care of them and not having them run away. The horses kept trying to go back to where they were driven from.

They were picking piñon nuts, while trying to keep their horses near, when some Navajos came up and said, "Where are the suspected enemies?" And they were told, "*Yá át'ééh* (Hello)! No enemies, no enemies. Don't say that there are suspected enemies; there aren't any enemies." They continued to pick nuts. Just then, another man came running up and said, "There are many suspected enemies a little way off from here."

As soon as they heard it they all resaddled their horses, and just as they started back to where they came from, one little boy said, "The place that we had our belongings, we have forgotten the little puppy."

One of my late grandfathers by the name of *Disjégi* [no English translation] left with some of the Navajos from where they had been camping. He and another man were riding a big white horse, with a bag of piñon nuts between them. Sometimes they would walk, leading the horse. After a while, my grandfather rode back to where they had their horses, even though he had heard that there were enemies. The horses were scattered but he caught one; and a lot of enemies, all dressed in red, could be seen from a far distance. He tried to hide behind a tree, but they already had seen him, and some of the *Nóóda'í* started to chase him on their horses. He outran them on his horse, and he went over quite a few hills. When he came to the top of one hill and looked back toward the enemies, they also were on a distant hill. Then he left, with the *Nóóda'í* far behind, and rode across a sandy area on his white horse.

He caught up with a man who was running, and the man said, "It has become rough for me; the enemies are after me." Then the man approached my grandfather beside the horse, and my grandfather grabbed the man's hair, and jerked him in the back of him on the white horse. They went on until it was almost dawn, when they slept for just a few moments. Then they started out again toward *'Ooljéétó* (Oljetoh or Moon Water).

About 20 days later word of mouth came around that some of the *Naakaii* were scouting along near *Naakaii Betóh* (Mexican Waters, Arizona), and they heard about enemies over by *Dziłna'otłiizh* (Teec Nos Pos Mountain), up near where Arizona, New Mexico, Utah and Colorado come together today. Another place that the Mexicans were moving was at *Denihootso* (Dennehotso, Arizona). There were a wagon train and pack horses, and they were driving horses that they had stolen from other people. Some of them had left the wagon train and gone off in a different direction toward *'Ooljéétó.*

The coming of the enemies was heard of by the Navajos, and they started with their livestock toward the highland areas where they would not be reached by the Mexicans who just traveled on the lower ground and couldn't get to the Navajos. The Mexicans said it was no use trying to chase the tribe called Navajos. Today that place is named *Naakaii Kíhoniiłkaadi* (Mexicans Chased Navajos up the Hill). After the Mexicans left, the Navajos checked to see if they really had gone; then they continued toward the region beyond *Naatsis'aan* (Navajo Mountain), right to the gorge area where they

A Navajo man ran up and said, "Many suspected enemies are a litttle way off from here."

had made a settlement. There were corn patches down in the gorge. The Mexicans left some of their people at the Colorado River, and the rest continued into the canyon. There the *Nóóda'í* killed some Paiutes while they were picking piñons. Two Paiutes who were killed were called *Chaa'* (Beaver) and *Hastiin Shiyiishí* (Bend Man). A Navajo man called *Hastiin Biighanii* (Mr. Backbone) was against his fellow Navajos, and he knew a lot about them. He was out with the *Nóóda'í* looking for the Navajos. Long before, when the *Nóóda'í* had taken away the livestock of various tribes, he had become a friend of the *Nóóda'í*.

One of the Navajos started back to the top of Black Mountain from near Navajo Mountain, and he packed as food a bag of corn and some piñon nuts. He had another man with him, and it took a long time to reach the top of the mountain. Up there, as they were riding along, suddenly they saw a Ute who was holding his front-loading muzzle rifle as he followed the horses' tracks to see how many Navajos had passed by. He was counting the footprints of the horses. He had a big blue-colored horse, and he was a big man. When the Ute saw them he started to chase them. The Navajos started down the mountain through a very rugged and rocky area. When they reached the foot of the mountain the Ute aimed his rifle from the top, with the bullet meant for one of the men. Instead, it missed him and hit the horse's hip; and the horse dropped and died.

The two Navajos came upon the Navajo camp while they were being chased. The Navajos screamed, and the sheep which were scattered about were afraid, and they formed into a close group. Because of the noise and the rifle shooting, one of the Navajos called *Asdzą́ní* (Real Woman), a member of the *Kinłichíi'nii* (Red House People) clan, just stood there in the midst of her flocks. There were more Utes, and they started after other Navajos, some of whom went westward, while some continued through the back of *Dził Łijiin* (Black Mountain) and into a small canyon that is located a little way beyond. The Navajos went upward until they had gotten to the top of the trail, even though it was very rough. At that time trails were not worked on. One of the Navajos went back down the trail for some reason. His name was *Hastiin Bigodii* (Mr. His Knee), and he was a member of the *Tódich'íínii* (Bitter Water People) clan. The *Nóóda'í* started after *Hastiin Bigodii*, and he turned back up the trail. While the horses were being driven up, the Navajos started to flee again from the enemies. *Bigodii* had put a buffalo hide under him on the horse – a hide that is called *chį'di* (buffalo hide). Just as he jumped on his horse and was about to start out, the hide slid to the ground from under him; so he jumped off, went back to pick the hide up, threw it over his shoulder, and, as he started to run, the noises were approaching in the midst of the oak trees. When he reached the top of the trail, he was wounded by a bullet in his left knee.

The enemies continued to head toward where the Navajos were driving the horses, but two Navajo men sneaked back without the enemies noticing them, and they saw Utes following the herd of horses. Just a little way off, some Navajos were driving more horses, and a shot was heard at a distance. It was an enemy who wasn't sitting on his horse; he was on the side of it, holding on as he was shooting at the Navajos. The horses scattered.

The Navajos went after the horses to get the herd back together, and they went up the canyon ridge, even though it was very hard to climb. The Navajos then went after the other horses and brought them back down to the floor of the canyon where the enemies had left off. The Navajos who had fled returned and started butchering their sheep – the good fat ones and the non-reproductive ones – because, before the enemies' attack, the Navajos had planned to have a sacred nine-day ceremonial called the *Azniidáá'* (Fire Dance) for a lady named *Saanii Yázhí*, who was a member of the *Ashįįhí* (Salt People) clan, because the lady had been a *yisnaah* (slave).

As some of the Navajo men were chopping wood the enemies attacked them again. Soon everyone knew about the attack, and some of the Navajos started to leave by horse and on foot. They were yelling at each other back and forth across the canyon, saying, "Don't let them back out; we will destroy all the trails, and we will make them stay down there. We will destroy every possible trail that we know of." Then the enemies said, "That is enough. We will return all of your sheep; give us another chance; this will be all." And they were given a chance by the Navajos. The woman who was standing in the midst of the sheep yelled, "Back up! We want to come back up. The sheep that are killed we will make into food, and we will journey back." So the enemies were given a chance and were freed.

Some of the Navajos that were on the other side of the canyon went to *Dził Łibaii* (Gray Mountain) and on to *Béegashiibito* (Cow Springs, Arizona). Somewhere in the vicinity of Cow Springs, as two Navajos were wandering around, and just a little way from them, two enemies were sitting on their horses. As soon as the Navajos saw the enemies, they said, "Those are not Navajos"; and they hid from them until they went out of sight. It became dark as they stayed in the brush, and it was dark when they came out. They went back up the trail, and they saw enemies moving to *Tónehelį́įh* (Tonalea, Arizona) and on to a place called *Tó'ałchiní* (Wild Water or Smell Water — near

Settlements were made down in the gorges, and patches of corn were grown.

Tuba City, Arizona). They were Utes, as well as Pueblo *Kiis'áanii* (Hopis).

At Tuba City, where there was a place with lots of bushes, the Navajos came to hide from the enemies. It was called *Bąąh Tó* (Bread Spring). A man named *Hastiin Łtsoí Ts'ózí* (Mr. Flat Yellow Man) a member of the *Tł'izíłaní* (Many Goats) clan, which is the same as the *Kinłichíi'nii* (Red House People) clan, went back to see where the enemies were. Just as he reached the top of a hill, the enemies saw him, and they started chasing him on their horses. However, his horse fell down on him. At that time the Navajos had woven rugs that were used as blankets on the horses' backs. The horse ran away and went toward a place called *T'iisyaakin* (House Under the Cottonwood Tree). The Navajo's tied hair got loosened. The men did not have short hair then. A man who was a member of the *Naakaii Dine'é* (Mexican People) clan rode up when he was running after his horse, and the enemies were approaching just a little way off. The enemies then separated into two groups. The Navajo's horse stopped and was caught, and the other Navajos who were hiding slipped off toward *Ba'adiwaí* (Bodaway, Arizona). The enemies then left to beyond the Gray Mountain area.

Then the Navajos asked a very sacred medicine man named *Dahghaa'í Sání* (my grandfather, Old Whisker) to come where the other Navajos were, and another medicine man who was a member of the *Lok'áá' Dine'é* (Reed People) clan named *Sǫ' Yinił'įníí* (Who Watches the Star). Those two went to the place called *Tó'ałchiní* (Smell Water), and there they asked for water (snow); and it started snowing. Off in the distance some people were cold and their hands were freezing as they walked along; and another Navajo did a more sacred ceremony, and he then drove some horses to where the Navajos were walking in the snow. He was a member of the *Naakaii Dine'é* (Mexican People) clan. Then the Navajos fled up Gray Mountain to where they hoped to have the *Azniidáá'* (Fire Dance) they had planned. They said, "We will leave here, and we will go up Gray Mountain. We don't think that the enemies will come there; and we will sing." And there they did perform the Fire Dance in a brushy circular enclosed place made from cedar and piñon trees.

A Navajo man by the name of *Béésh Łigai Yits'idii* (Mr. Silversmith), my late father's father (he used to call himself my grandfather, but he did not tell me his clan) said this about the Fire Dance that was performed back then: "This Fire Dance didn't happen only a few years ago because at the exact place where the fire was built a spruce tree has grown up, and it is so big now."

At the place now called Page, Arizona, was where my ancestors used to live. One of them was a member of the *Kinłichíi'nii* (Red House People) clan. He was one of my late grandfathers whose name was *Dahghaa'í Sání* (Old Whisker). Two of my menfolks were born there also. They were *Bilá Yázhí* (Short Finger) and my late father. Just a little way from Page they would go out to hunt for food that they were in need of, such as mountain sheep. At that time the mountain sheep used to run in that area. Even though they had sheep of their own, they wouldn't kill them; they just liked to hunt.

Near there someone burned a porcupine, and then he put out the fire; and right across from where he was there was a group of *Báyóódzin* (Paiutes) that was wandering around on horses. One of the Paiutes saw the smoke and was wondering how he could cross the canyon because there was much water flowing in it. Just a little way down the stream he came to a place where there were a lot of pebbles below the water; and he came to where he saw the smoke, even though he was afraid to look around. Then he went back across to where the others were, and he brought them across. It was then that they met my late grandfather, *Dahghaa'í Sání*, who understood the Paiute language. (The languages of the Utes and the Paiutes were different.) So he talked with the Paiutes, and they asked him to become a friend of theirs. Their only food was lizards and milk. There was plenty of milk because they milked the sheep and goats. There were lots of grasses that were higher than the sheep.

One of my ancestors used to call the milk and the hot mushy cereal which was made from it "*géeso*." When one of my brothers who went to school somewhere was told about the milk and the hot cereal, he wondered what they meant by "*géeso*," and he asked one of the men, "What do you mean by '*géeso*'?You mean the '*géeso*' for the car?" And the man just laughed.

A lady came to the Navajo group who was a Paiute; also an enemy man whose cheek was branded with a circle. Another man had a wounded arm which had been hurt at the time when the Navajos and the enemies had fought at Navajo Mountain.

The Navajos used to have small corn patches, even though they just planted it any old way; and an enemy man was put in charge of the house because he had joined the Navajos and also because he was drinking the goat's milk as well as the milk of the sheep. Just a little way from there a small corn patch had been planted at another man's place. He was called *Ch'ah'niteel* (Sombrero, or Big Round Hat), as well as Bob Begay. This corn patch was along the fertile wet area beside the river, and there was where they put the one with the branded cheek in charge of the house. There were many homes, and there were sheep at about every home, which made a good living for all the Navajos.

There was a Navajo named *Yidééz* (Burned of Skin), who was cleaning his rifle (the front-loading muzzle kind), and, just as he was about to load it he put the powder too near the fire – the powder caught a spark and it burned him just like a gas which is dangerous to us today. Then he was given the name *Deez.* His father was called *Hastiin Deeschiinii* (Mr. Red Streak People), and later the burned man was known as *Yidééz* (Burned) *Deeschiinii Begay.* There weren't any clothes then like we have today; so one of the Navajo men made pants out of a goatskin which wasn't even tanned.

The enemies went as far as San Francisco Peak, scattering the Navajos' sheep and goats.

Another Navajo man used to imagine things in his mind. He thought that he saw Hopis who were singing against the Navajos. He had been beaten up by a bear near *Tséhootsooí* (Fort Defiance). He used to tell his people that a certain way was safe and that another way wasn't safe. That was the way he was protecting his people from fear of the enemies. He also used to hear warning sounds. He went out at night and sat a certain distance from his home; then he warned his people against any enemies or others who weren't friendly.

There were nine Navajo homes in one group that weren't harmed by the enemies. They were just by-passed. Food was scarce because of fear of the enemies. The Navajos' main source of food was the meat of the sheep. Finally, after several years, all the Navajos were driven away by the enemies to *Hwééldi* (Fort Sumner, New Mexico). The enemies scouted to see if any Navajos had been left behind. They went to Gap, Arizona, and a little way off from Gap where some more Navajos were caught and driven to *Hwééldi.* Some of them, however, ran away and went toward *Dook'o'ooslííd* (San Francisco Peak), where more Navajos were hiding. Still the enemies went toward San Francisco Peak and scattered the Navajos' sheep and goats. Some of the goats somehow ran away from the herd and went on to a cliff.

Some of the Navajos crawled into a hole to hide, and there they spent two days without any of them coming out. Then, one of them who was brave enough came out of the hole and looked to see if any enemies were still around. As he was looking, goats cried out from a distance, and he went over to where he heard them, and, true, they were on a cliff. The cliff was very smooth to get up; so he went to a stream where there was lots of driftwood, and he brought some back. He made a pathway with it to the cliff by putting one wood atop another and piling it all with rocks. Then the goats came down from the cliff.

The name of the Navajo man I can't recall. At that time the name was mentioned to me, but, as we all know, we menfolks often forget, even though we are told quite a few times.

Anyway, they chased the sheep and the goats from the canyon to *Dziłdiłhiłii* (Shadow Mountains) and onward to *Ba'adiwaí* (Bodaway) and then to Coppermine. They only herded the sheep that were ewes, and the goats; and they went like this for two years.

At *Leechíí'* (Lechee), Arizona, (in the Tuba City area) the Navajos who came from the Shadow Mountains met with some Navajos that weren't caught by the enemies. My late grandfather, a member of the *Táchii'nii* (Red Streak Extending Into the Water People), used to work with silver. He and another man went to the top of Navajo Mountain, but, first, they spent a night at the foot of the mountain before they went up the next day. There they performed an unknown sacred ceremony, and they asked for the Navajos to return from Fort Sumner.

A certain Navajo at Fort Sumner was really brave, and no one could beat him in what he would say; and he argued with a White Man who came from *Wááshindoon* (Washington, D.C.). A sacred Navajo prayer was used to have the Navajos that were in confinement freed to return to what is now the Reservation. The talk kept on for eight days, and they finally agreed that the Navajos would be let free.

My late ancestor said it was ten years that the Navajos spent at Fort Sumner, but another man told me it was four years.

They returned first in the month of June when all the native grass had ripened. It was to Fort Defiance, Arizona, that they first came, and quickly the word spread by mouth to all Reservation areas. The Navajos that were herding the sheep without the rams then came to an elderly Navajo man who had rams, and from that time there were many more rams.

After the confined Navajos returned from the camp at Fort Sumner there was freedom everywhere. Those who had been hiding from the enemies came out of their hideouts, and today some of the others hate us. The family I came from are all deceased.

The gorge where some Navajos hid didn't have a name for a long time. It was about where the Paiutes crossed – now Lee's Ferry, Arizona. There were many piñon nuts in the area just a little way off. The Navajos would wander around for nuts, and they were like nomads. They would move to a certain place and stay there for a few days picking nuts. After that they would be gone again.

A Paiute man had two wives, and, at a place where they had made a camp, the Navajos said among themselves that a Paiute woman was about to give birth. Some of the menfolks went to where the woman was. As they were approaching the woman, one of the Paiutes met them and told them to stay away. As they stood there, and as they looked to where the woman was about to give birth, one of the Paiutes was standing on the woman's womb trying to push the baby out. The Navajos tried to enter the brush corral, saying that wasn't the right way to treat a woman about to have a baby; but, still, they were pushed aside. Then the woman gave birth; and soon the second wife went into labor.

So, on one night two women gave birth for one man.

Near the Colorado River both the Navajos and the Paiutes cleared much of the land and made their cornfields. The soil was very wet and fertile, and many members of both tribes used it.

Today the Paiutes claim that the land is theirs and that the Navajos were not the first ones to live there – that the Paiutes were the first to occupy it a long time before any enemies came around. The Paiutes are treating us just like the Hopis are doing, claiming that the land is theirs.

Here at Navajo Mountain we live our own separate ways. I guess the Navajos from other parts of the Reservation think of us as people who live peacefully and quietly. But that isn't quite right. We just ignore each other up here.

Robert Longsalt

A medicine man at Navajo Mountain, Robert Longsalt, 89, here relates stories told by his grandfather and other forebears. His main clan is *Ashįįhí* (Salt People).

THIS DIDN'T HAPPEN RECENTLY. I mean the Navajos being driven to Fort Sumner. Due to the rugged areas around here (Inscription House), some Navajos hid out in such places as *Nii'tsį́'ii* (Raw Face – in Navajo Canyon) and *Ch'ááyáhii* (Under Arm – in Navajo Canyon); also the opposite side of what is now Page Dam and down the canyons toward this way. A good number of Navajo families lived in those areas. My grandfather, named *Dahghaa'í* (Whisker) was one of them. Other men were *Késhgolíi* (Short Toes), *Dahghaa'í Láni* (Many Whiskers) and *Bik'a'ísání* (Old Arrow).

At a place near here (Inscription House) some Navajos did some farming. They lived on whatever they could get off their farmlands. I wonder if some Navajos really spent four years at Fort Sumner. It was said that my grandfather used to pray from the top of *Naatsis'aan* (Navajo Mountain). Finally, the Navajos were marched back to their homeland, and it appears that many got together in this area.

It was said that, earlier, there were wars in the Chinle and Canyon de Chelly areas. That was where most battles were fought between the Navajos and the Utes, Apaches, Mexicans and even the Paiutes. All these other Indian tribes were our enemies. The Navajos fled everywhere, wandering all over the place. Lots of our people were killed; in return, we killed a lot of their men.

The Navajos' guns were bad. It took quite a while to reload them. They were called *bii'ná'jíhí* (muskets). To reload a *bii'ná'jíhí*, a Navajo first poured the gun powder into the muzzle of the gun; then he packed down the powder and a lead ball with a piece of rod or a stick. Now it's real easy to reload guns. There was nothing like modern guns then. So the Navajos had a real hard time using them. Besides guns, there were our bows and arrows, which were our menfolks' most effective weapons. Arrows in their container were attached to a person behind his back. Men would run out onto a battlefield and never would get shot or killed. These were the Navajos who held back or drove back the enemies.

This is the way my ancestors and my grandfather told their stories. My grandfather's name was *Ashiiké Łání* (Many Boys). He was of the *Bitáanii* (Under His Cover) clan. This is his story.

To load the old-fashioned guns that occasionally could be obtained by the Navajos, powder was poured into the muzzle; then, with a bullet and wadding, everything was packed down with a metal rod or a stick.

Ernest Nelson

A former Chapter president and a medicine man, Ernest Nelson, 64, of Shonto, Ariz., here tells a story as related to him by his maternal grandmother. He is of the *Kinłichii'nii* (Red House People) clan.

IN THE TUBA CITY AREA only the *Nóóda'í* (Utes) raided us, according to one of my ancestors. The Utes scouted for us, and warriors were brought into our territory.

Over there on the top of *Dził Ninéez* (Tall Mountain) some men held a meeting about the Utes who had moved into our territory to annihilate us. The Navajos just said something to them, and they turned back and moved away.

Later, the *Naałání* (Comanches) came in against us.

Here at what is now *Shą́ą́tó* (Shonto) School, up toward the end of the present fences, there is a little red hill. From the top of that hill, says my ancestor, the Utes attacked the Navajos one day just before dawn. As our people fled, three men were killed.

As they fled, they ran along where the power line is now, and all the way to the edge of the canyon, then down into the canyon, with the women carrying their small children on their backs. Three men were old, and they crawled under the cliff to conceal themselves. As the Comanches came by, all three of these men were killed. The remainder continued through the canyon; and, as the people were fleeing over the hill between the Mesas, two more women were shot. Just where the forest begins, another lady was shot to death while carrying a baby on her back.

My late grandfather's name was *Dahghaa'í Daksikáád* (Spread Mustache), and he was the head of the family there. Once, when they heard rifle shots, they rode away on their horses; and, as the enemies were following, my late grandfather drew a line in front of them, and the Comanches just started back. Afterward, below us here, just at the edge of the canyon, many of the Comanches were killed with arrows. The Navajos did not have guns. The rest of the Comanches departed to where they had come from. Then, after the Comanches had fled, the soldiers came. They were white soldiers, and they just shot over the Navajos' heads and rounded them up. They said, "All of you will go to *Hwééldi* (Fort Sumner), where you will settle down." And, the Navajos were herded to Fort Sumner, New Mexico. That was about one hundred and eight years ago.

Almost all of them had to walk the whole way – maybe three hundred miles or more. The women folks and the men folks carried most of the children, and when they got tired others would take turns. There were some wagons to haul food, old people and little children. The soldiers and Mexicans rode horses. The Navajos were just provided small amounts of food that they ate with water that they carried with them.

At Fort Sumner the Navajos suffered from many needs. They were given rations only on Sundays when they were herded into adobe buildings where the rations were passed out by soldiers who guarded them. The soldiers shot any Navajos who would leave the ration line. That was their order. The people also were issued some poor clothing, like pants, shoes and shirts for the men.

They tried to plant crops, but nothing would grow right.

A lady was shot to death while carrying a baby on her back in a cradleboard.

Bows and arrows had to be used to fight the Comanches because the Navajos had no rifles at the time.

My own ancestors didn't go on the long walk. They lived along *Naatsis'aan* (Navajo Mountain) just before many Navajos were driven to Fort Sumner. When enemies came for them they fled down into the canyon gorge behind Navajo Mountain.

After the rest of the Navajos were taken to Fort Sumner my ancestors came out of the canyon and went toward what now is Page, Arizona, where they spent about two years. For two more years they hid in that area of canyons, hearing by word of mouth that the Navajos would not return from Fort Sumner. Then, after four years, news came around that the Navajos had returned. It was said that the soldiers and the Navajos had agreed to put away their weapons and that the Navajos were to be free. It was said that many Navajos had returned to the *Ch'ínílí* (Chinle, Arizona) area. Some of the Navajos who had hidden here journeyed toward Chinle, and there they joined the others that had returned from Fort Sumner. From that time their friendship was refounded.

Those who had stayed here used to live at such places as *Ba'ázchiní* (Paiute Canyon) and *Ch'ááyáhii* (Under Arm – in Navajo Canyon). The *Báyóódzin* (Paiutes) were scouting at that time from the area of Salt Lake, Utah, or from somewhere else, saying that all of the Navajos were to be killed.

At Salt Lake the Paiutes and the Utes were issued rifles by the government to go out and scout for the Navajos. That was the way they treated the Navajos. At the place called *Ch'ááyáhii* the Navajos shot one of the Paiutes that was a second lieutenant in his underarm with an arrow. That is how the place got its name *Báyóódzin Bi' Ch'ááyá Biishíní* (Paiute Killed by Wound Under His Arm). At the place called *Ch'ááyáhii*, where the Navajos had fled from the Paiutes, there was a *Gáamalii* (Mormon) who was in charge of the Paiutes. He was saying that all of the Navajos must be killed, and that the land then would belong to the Mormons – and to the Paiutes and Utes as well. He put the Paiutes in there, and said to them, "If you will kill all of the Navajos the land will be your own." There the Mormon was killed with an arrow, and his rifle fell from his hand. Then one of the Paiutes was shot in the cheek by a Navajo. That is how the place got its name of *Nii'tsį́'íí* (Raw Face – in Navajo Canyon). And that is where they shot off a second Mormon's little finger when the Navajos wounded him. After the Paiutes fled from him he lived in a cave, and that place is called *Biláyázhí* (His Short Finger – in Navajo Canyon) because one of his little fingers was shot off. That is south of Navajo Mountain.

The Mormon stayed there until his hand was healed; then he asked the Navajos if he could go back to where he came from. He said, "I want to return to my land"; so they just let him free, and he went to his own land.

Two of the Paiutes used to visit the Navajo homes, selling deerskin. Once they went to a Navajo home at dusk where they were to spend the night as there were two houses adjoining each other. One went to each house; and that night, when one of them was asleep, a Navajo lady gave birth to a baby. The Navajos teased him at the time about giving him a special name. Finally, they called him *Ba'ázchiní* (Paiute Canyon) because a lady gave birth in the house he slept in.

Another area that is known as Bodaway, Arizona, was in the land of the Paiutes. A Paiute by the name of *Ba'adiwai* (Bodaway) used to live there, or so they say. In the back areas of Bodaway there are lots of plants that are yucca-like and that have tall grayish-like things sticking up from the centers. They grow around Gray Mountain, onward to San Francisco Peak and in other places, too. The seeds were eaten because they could be baked underground, and they were delicious.

At that time some Navajos lived with the Paiutes at Red Rock and Cedar Ridge, Arizona. They all ate those plants. In Navajo they are called *noodal báhí* (soap weeds), and in Paiute it is called *ba'gaaí*. The Navajos and the Paiutes used to say that they were going to where there were lots of *ba'gaaí*, and somehow they missed the pronunciation and called it "ba' ah doway," and that is how Bodaway got its name.

A few Navajos used to say that Bodaway was once the land of the Paiute Indians. The Paiutes said it wasn't their land; it was just given the name because both tribes missed the pronunciation.

The Navajos ate just about anything, like grass seeds, sumac berries and some other seeds, as well as that soap weed that I have mentioned about Bodaway; also currant berries. Our late ancestors ate these native foods, and they were almost the only sources.

Here at my home is where I spend my summer months. A little way off from here, at the place called *Ashį́įhí Yazh Bikǫ́ǫh* (Littlesalt Canyon) is where I spend my winter months. A place a little way off from here toward the windmill is called *Łį́į' Bighaní* (First Horse Corral). I call all of this place around here *Łį́į' Bighaní* because the horses are of great wealth to us.

I belong to the *Kinłichíi nii* (Red House People Clan), and it was the tribe of the Hopis that we descended from, as it is said. I am related to the *Tódich'íinii* (Bitter Water People Clan).

Clifford Beck, Sr.

Mr. Beck, of Piñon, Ariz., is a former Tribal Councilman and a member of the grazing committee. He is 67 years of age. The following brief discussion derives from stories told by his elders. His clan on his mother's side is *Ashįįhí* (Salt People), and, on his father's side, it is *Kinyąą'áanii* (Towering House People).

MY NAME IS CLIFFORD BECK, SR. I belong to the clan *Ashįįhí* (Salt People), and *Kinyąą'áanii* (Towering House People) is my father's. I was born in mid-March in the year 1905. Now I am 67 years of age. My late father's name was *Kinyąą'áanii'diil* (Big Towering House), and my late mother's name was *Asdzą́ Ashįįhí* (Salt Clan Woman). Both are deceased. I am not an educated man.

Menfolks and womenfolks of long ago told that it was known the *Diné* had been living around here as far back as 250 years ago in these mountains – Black Mountain, Gray Mountain, Navajo Mountain and White Ash Mountain. Back in those days the *Diné* started having war with other tribes, like the *Nóóda'í* (Utes), *Dziłghą'í* (Apaches) and *Chísí* (Mescaleros). The fighting took place between 250 and 100 years ago. The *Diné* lived in these mountains because so many enemies were around, and the *Diné* could hide in various areas. Then *Wááshindoon* (the United States government) found there was war going on around here; so an order was given for the *Diné* to be driven to *Hwéeldi* (Fort Sumner). Navajos from the Black Mountain area went to Fort Defiance first. Some went on their own free will; others had to be scouted for and were taken in as captives.

A man by the name of *Hastiin Kintsiil* (Mr. Ruins), from *Kintsiili* (Ruins – on top of Black Mountain) told me one time that he had fled around in these areas and had not been to Fort Sumner. A woman by the name of *Asdzą́ Bináa'ádiní* (Woman Blind), was from a place called *Tódáádí't'áá* (Lid on Water Hole), located eight miles north of Piñon, from where she left on her journey to Fort Sumner. After her return, she went back to *Tódáádí't'áá*. Another woman of the salt clan named *Saanii Yázhí* (Little Elderly Woman) was from Black Mountain also, and she was captured by the *Nóóda'í* (Utes) and was taken back to *Tonts'osíkóóh* (Mancos Creek, Colorado). She spent several days there; then she escaped. She was my grandmother. She fled across the *Tooh* (San Juan River) and then traveled to *Tséyi'* (Canyon de Chelly) and later came back to Black Mountain. She didn't go to *Hwééldi.*

The girl fled across the San Juan River.

John Tom

John Tom, of Many Farms, Ariz., is a medicine man – about 75 years old. His account of Fort Sumner events was told to him by his mother. His clan is *Kinyąą'áanii* (Towering House People).

ABOUT 115 YEARS AGO the wars between the Navajos and other Indian tribes began. Trouble started at Mount Taylor when two boys were killed by the Navajos. From that spot trouble quickly spread throughout what now is roughly the Navajo Reservation. It was because of the fighting between the Navajos and other Indians that our ancestors were taken to Fort Sumner (Bosque Redondo) in what then was the eastern part of the territory of New Mexico.

According to my mother's story, she was three years old when she was taken to Fort Sumner, and she spent three years there with her family.

When the Navajo people were set free from that captivity, two Navajo leaders were in charge of moving-out operations. The two were *Ch'il Haajiní* (Manuelito) and a man named *Dibéyázhí* (Lamb). Lamb was a man of great knowledge of religion and ceremonies. A few days prior to the Treaty of 1868, four Navajo leaders came to see him, saying that the conditions at Fort Sumner were getting real bad and that they had heard all Navajo people were going to be killed starting in four days. The leaders wanted the old man's opinions on the situation. *Dibéyázhí* (Lamb) said, "Whoever they are, they don't have the authority to do that. Early tomorrow morning I want some people to find and bring back two baby coyotes."

So, early the next morning, people started looking for the two coyotes. It did not take long to find them; and, as the old man had requested, the coyotes were brought back, one male and one female. Then the old man conducted a ceremony – *Mą'ii' Bizéé'nast'ą́* (Put Bead in Coyote's Mouth) – for the four Navajo leaders, using the two baby coyotes in his ceremony. The four leaders then were blessed with the power of the coyotes. After the ceremony the four leaders went to see the man in charge at Fort Sumner. Again, they asked to be set free.

They said, "What are you going to do with us next? You brought us here, and we are suffering very much from everything now. Besides that, we are very homesick and want to go back to our land very much."

The man replied, "All right, you people will be free to go back four days from now."

Two coyotes were brought in – one male and one female.

You see, it was according to Lamb's will and ceremony that our people were freed from Fort Sumner. A day after they left, the old man died of old age. It took 16 days for the people to move from Fort Sumner back to Fort Wingate, both of which are in what is now New Mexico.

My grandfather on my father's side was born at Fort Wingate. It was said that he was born early in the morning while the United States soldiers were in formation; so he was named *Siláo* (Soldier). My grandfather also was known or called by another name – *Hastiin Ntł'aaí* (Mr. Lefthander). My grandfather learned his singing ceremonies and stories from the men that learned their ceremonies and stories from the old man, *Dibéyázhí* (Lamb). I learned a small

After the Coyote Ceremony four leaders went to see the man in charge at Fort Sumner.

Before leaving Fort Sumner the tribal leaders signed a treaty (of 1868) with the U.S. government.

portion of my grandfather's ceremonies, and I know some of his old stories. The ceremonies and the stories I know are my life. They guide and protect me every day and night.

It was said that when our people were freed from Fort Sumner they signed a treaty with the United States government. One provision of the treaty of 1868 concerned education. The treaty says that Navajo children will be educated by the white people and Navajo parents shall not interfere with whites educating their Navajo children. Navajo people agreed to the treaty and were set free. As schools got under way, however, some Navajo parents did not like the idea; so there were a number of cases of trouble over "white" education in various parts of the Navajo Reservation. One well-known incident occurred at Round Rock, Arizona. There an agent named Shipley was thrown out after his life had been in danger. Four people defended Shipley – three men and one woman. The three men were *Hastiin Welá* (Mr. Walla), *Béésh łigai'íí'íní* (Who Prepares the Silver) and *Chaalátsoh* (Big Charley), and the lady was Hosteen Walla's wife. All three men who defended Agent Shipley were hired later by the school.

The first school was started at Fort Defiance, Arizona. At that time there were only three buildings in Fort Defiance. I saw it with my own eyes.

In coming back from Fort Sumner most of our people traveled on foot. There was hardly any livestock. Sometime after they got back sheep, goats, horses, wagons, hoes and other tools were given out by the government. So you see that many of the sheep, goats and horses that some of us have today really came, in the first place, from the white people.

Tom Jim

Tom Jim of Rock Point, Ariz., is a medicine man who heard the story of the Long Walk and the tragedy of Bosque Redondo (Fort Sumner) from his father. He is 75 years old. His clan is *Ashįįhí* (Salt People).

A LONG TIME AGO the *Diné* (the People, the Navajos) lived here as we had originated, and the stories that have been told and passed down from our ancestors are what I will talk about.

My late father, *Deeschiinii* [his clan] *Atsidii* (Silversmith) traveled to Fort Sumner on the Long Walk. Among the thousands of others was a man known as *Dził Haabas Biye'* (Roundtop Mountain's Son) who used to talk about the journey. These men told me the stories. My name in Navajo is *Deeschiinii Ats'idii Biye'* (Etsitty's Son, *Deeschiinii* – Red Streak People – clan).

I will talk mostly about the stories that my father told me about the Long Walk. At that time we lived here, using as food certain kinds of plants, such as *tł'ohdeentł'ízí* (a kind of grass seeds), *chiiłchin* (sumac), *neeshch'íí'* (piñon nuts), *hasgaan* (yucca fruit) and *haasch'ééd ą́ą́* (wild chokeberry). *Naadą́ą́'* (corn) usually was planted annually. These were gathered and stored to last through the winter months.

Some sheep and horses were owned by families, and meat was obtained from them. This is how the people survived through many years, but the time came when the Navajos gained enemies among other tribes. It is said that four or five men would travel in a small band to raid some tribe named *Nóóda'í* (Utes) and the *Naakaii* (Mexicans), and this brought the conflict between the tribes and with the Mexicans. Soon the *Nóóda'í* Tribe came into the Navajo territory on raids. Then other tribes became our enemies, and they traveled around in bands to take sheep and horses away from the Navajos, as well as our women and children.

Small fights would occur between the tribes here and there. The Navajos fought with bows and arrows, while the enemies had guns.

Soon, other tribes joined to fight the Navajos. The *Nóóda'í* (Utes), *Naałání* (Comanches) and the *Naakaii* (Mexicans) became allies, and they all scouted and raided in Navajoland. Many of the Navajo people became very discouraged because of these conflicts between them and their enemies.

It came to the point that the White Men said, "Let us gather or round up all the Navajos into one place." So the Navajos were rounded up and assembled at Fort Defiance.

There, wagons, with oxen pulling them, were provided to haul some food and belongings; and the journey was made to Fort Sumner. However, not all the people went on this journey. A lot of them managed to hide.

Finally, at Fort Sumner, many of the Navajos spent as long as four years, with other groups constantly arriving. After the four years, there were speeches and talks made by some White Men, saying, "From here on you will not take up any more weapons. Now there will be peace. You will place your children in school and let them learn, and after they have learned English, they will in turn help you."

This is some of what was said, and it was agreed with the Navajos that they would abide by the agreements.

While confined at Fort Sumner, conditions and surroundings were very poor. Small amounts of food were issued, sometimes not enough to survive on, and a lot of people died of starvation. Firewood was another major problem because it was very scarce and hard to get. However, the time came to leave Fort Sumner and to return to Fort Defiance. For two years, even though they moved on to their own areas, they received government food and items from the White Men.

While there, some Navajo men were made deputies and later became leaders of the Tribe. Some of these leaders were given large wagons when they left Fort Defiance. The people scattered and started moving toward their old homes, going in different directions. Once back home, the people settled and real Navajo life resumed.

In the meantime, *Hastiin Adiits'a'ii* (Henry Chee Dodge) was educated in the White Man's way, and he worked hard to save enough money to set up a trading post at *Bisdootl'izh Deez'áhí* (Round Rock) where the people could trade. Before long, the sheep had increased, and the people were able to obtain enough wool to trade at 10 cents a pound. Prices of food were very low then. For instance, a 50-pound sack of flour was $1.50. Coffee was 20 cents a pound. Compared with prices today, it seems unbelievable that once they were so low.

The people continued to gather plants for food after their return. *Tł'ohdeentł'ízí* (grass seeds) were ground with corn and fixed in a variety of ways, making delicious meals. A lot of us were raised on those kinds of food.

Eventually those plants began to disappear, but, at the same time, livestock such as horses, cows and sheep had increased to large numbers. There was plenty of rain and plenty of grass in those days. Livestock became the main source of income for the Navajo people; and, because of the tremendous increase, the Navajos were faced with another problem in the 1930s and were forced to go through another catastrophe.

From Fort Defiance the people scattered and moved toward their old homesteads. A few leaders had been given wagons.

Robert Etsitty

Robert *Ats'idii*

This gentleman, at 80, is Vice President of his Chapter, living at Crownpoint, N.M. He says that Navajo historical accounts were passed down to him by his forefathers and other elders. *Táchii'nii* (Red Streak Extending Into the Water) is his main clan on his mother's side. He was born for the *Naakaii Dine'é* (Mexican People) on his father's side.

I AM FROM CROWNPOINT, New Mexico. I am of the *Táchii'nii* (Red Streak Extending Into the Water People) on my mother's side and *Naakaii Dine'é* (the Mexican clan) on my father's side. My children are of the *Bitáanii* (Under His Cover) clan. I am a Chapter officer – vice president. The journey to Fort Sumner and stories pertaining to the confinement there is what I am asked to tell. *Diné* on various parts of the Navajo Reservation are being interviewed.

A number of people have been visited. Some gave real good information; others did not. As for me, I'll tell you what I have heard, even though it is brief. Why history happened the way it did, I don't know. When I began to understand things as a child, I noticed that the late Navajo men and late Navajo women had owned valuables and were wealthy. They had lots of sheep, cattle, horses and donkeys. I also noticed that water wasn't scarce then. There were grasses of many varieties which sheep, horses and cattle could graze on.

As I said before, the late Navajo men and women were prosperous on account of their animals and grazing land. Then the *Diné 'Ana'í* (Enemy Navajos – Navajos who had become enemies of their own people) started to contact one another in some way and made plans that caused trouble. Some young Navajos who were treated badly – like *yisnaah* (slaves) – by the older wealthy people turned against those prosperous Navajos. Among them were lots of sheepherders for the Anglos (white owners of sheep). Many cattle and horses were owned and cared for by those ranchers; and there were Mexican sheep owners. Probably with the idea of causing trouble for the wealthy *Diné*, the trouble-making Navajos said, "Those *Diné* with lots of livestock are not going to continue to enjoy the privilege of making a good living by raising livestock."

That is the way I heard the story. It was the plan of the *yisnaahnáháłingo* (treated like slaves). I guess the Navajo young people who might be called *Diné 'Ana'í* (Against the Navajos or Enemy Navajos) held meetings, made plans and then started to raid the White Men's and Mexicans' sheep, killing the herders and taking the flocks to Navajo lands. They also killed cattlemen and drove their cattle back here; and they killed ranchers and brought back bands of horses.

That is what the *Diné 'Ana'í* did. They were the ones that caused all the trouble. Someone named *Naakaii Bichaaniiteeł* (Mexican, His Belly Is Wide) had two sons who were sheepherders and cattlemen. One day they were raided and killed by the *Diné 'Ana'í*. At that point *Naakaii Bichaaniiteeł* sent a message to Washington, D.C., requesting, "Let us have the Army to help us, we really are having trouble with *Diné 'Ana'í* (Enemy Navajos)." He probably wrote up a report in that manner. His request was probably acknowledged. Accordingly, the *Naakaii* (Mexicans), *Naałání* (Comanches) and *Nóóda'í* (Utes) – our main enemies – scouted us all the way up here on to the Navajo land.

Then there were the Apaches who worked against us. As a result, many of our late menfolks, late womenfolks and late boys and girls were rounded up and driven to Fort Sumner. The *Diné* were being cared for, or, rather, they were taken care of. Even though they were taken care of, they suffered many things. Food was provided for them, but still the *Diné* suffered sickness and epidemic as a result of eating the foods that they were not acquainted with – foods like flour, coffee, sugar and others. On account of this, the *Diné* really suffered hardships. Then some man, like Manuelito, became real unsatisfied with the existing situation; and other *Diné* helped to make plans. These men begged the government, "Please permit us to go back. We want to go back to our country. If we are to continue to be like this, it seems that something will annihilate us."

The *Diné* begged the government in this manner; consequently, an agreement was made. The government asked the *Diné*, "Will you be this way: Be obedient, when you leave here and when you get back to your country? Will you make it a point to send your children to school in the future? Will these things be carried out?" Again the

Smoke signals were the only means for fast communication over long distances.

government questioned them, and the *Diné* agreed to what was said, "Yes, forever we will obey one another, in the future we are not going to do this again. We are not going to think of each other in the old way again. You, our government, what you command us to do, we will obey it."

That was what the *Diné* had to say. Consequently, their begging was acknowledged after a few more questions by the government, "Do you mean it?" "Yes, we mean it," responded the Navajos. "We are not going to do it again; we will live according to your commands, and you will be our guidance." When the *Diné* made these statements or declarations, they were quickly released from Fort Sumner and removed to Fort Defiance, Arizona. There, some of them stayed for a while, and others left soon for their old homes. All continued to be cared for by the U.S. government. It was said that sheep were given out – probably two sheep to each family. The *Diné* were told, "If you take care of them, they will grow" (referring to the sheep). Tools were given out also, mainly farm tools, and the Navajos were told, "You will now go back to the places you like, you will move back where you think you will find your subsistence, so you can once again support yourselves."

So, finally, the *Diné* were let free to go back to various parts of the Navajo Reservation, where they planted corn, melons, etc. for food. Another point that I forgot: At the beginning of the enemy attacks before Fort Sumner, the *Diné* always had guards. Smoke was the only signal. *Diné* who lived on the tops of the mountains were in rugged areas. But, even though the places were rugged, the *Diné* planted corn, which they would store in a pit and take out during the winter time.

Howard Gorman, Sr.

A medicine man at Nazlini, Ariz., Howard Gorman, Sr., describes his "Long Walk Period" narrative as having come down to him through his menfolk forebears. He is 92 years old and a member of the *Kinyąą'áanii* (Towering House People) clan.

I WANT TO TELL YOU A STORY pertaining to some of the things that happened in the past. I would guess it has been more than 200 years since the *Diné* lived without any enemies.

They lived in a good way upon their lands. They herded sheep. There were always sheep then, as well as horses. And they planted their corn patches. All of a sudden the enemies came, and the Navajos' sheep were taken away – every one that the enemies could lay their hands on. Some sheep were hidden over the hills.

We didn't have rifles, just bows and arrows, used mostly just to hunt with, such as to kill rabbits and other animals that are eaten. The arrow was the only weapon we had, and not all of the Navajos had arrows, just those that hunted.

I'm from a place called *Nazlini*, in Navajo they call me *Bicheiini' Biye'* (Grandfather's Son). That is who I am. Ever since I was very young quite a few menfolks told me stories. They used to say that the *Nóóda'í* (Utes) were our first enemies when we lived at the *Dibé Nitsaa* (La Plata Mountains) and at the *Dził Ashdlá'ii* (La Sal Mountains). Even though it was a good place to live, because of the Utes the Navajos fled, mostly to the west, from the La Plata Mountains and the La Sal Mountains. After the sheep were taken away from the Navajos, enemies mistreated our people. Some of those who escaped the mistreatment came here to *Nazlini*. *Lók'aahnteel* (Ganado), *Dził Łijiin* (Black Mountain) and *Tsélání* (Salina) were some places where the Navajos lived a good life before they were mistreated by the *Nóóda'í* (Utes). There had been no enemies. Our forefathers just used to hunt, and at times, they went to where the enemies drove their horses; so they started raiding back and forth, not every day, just very seldom. They didn't do much in what they were trying to accomplish because there weren't any rifles. Even though the enemies were like the Navajos in many ways, they were larger people, according to our late forefathers. After several years more enemies began to journey into our land — from the country of the *Naakaii* (Mexicans) (they were the ones who attacked right after the Utes), as well as the *Dziłghą'í* (Apaches — the general name given to White Mountain and San Carlos Apaches), also a tribe called *Góóhniinii* (Hualpai-Havasupai) that lived on the Grand Canyon floor. All of these became our enemies, and life was an extreme hardship almost every night and day for many years. After that time there were not many Navajos left. They had few clothes, such as shoes, pants and shirts; and there was very little food. They were pitiful. The Navajos ate anything that they could find to eat. And, of course, the women suffered as much as the men. Their only source of clothing material was cedar bark that was softened by hand. Enemies were against them from all directions, and they were using rifles. Somewhere up around Salt Lake there was a leader just like the President of the United States in *Wááshindoon* (Washington).

Most Navajos had only bows and arrows for weapons, used mostly to hunt animals such as rabbits.

From Salt Lake the Utes were saying, "All of these people called the *Naabeehó* (Navajos) shall be killed, as the agreement was made and approved. They shall all be killed because they steal too much." The Utes were given guns from Salt Lake.

One of the places the Mexicans journeyed to was *Tséyi'* (Canyon de Chelly), where the Navajos were sitting in *Adahódooníłí* (a cave which is known today as Massacre Cave). They were not angry. There was snow on the ground, and they were attacked suddenly. The Mexicans blocked their path down the cliff. It was a great distance down, and it was very, very hard to reach the foot of the cliff. If you were standing at the edge of the cliff, looking down, and if someone was walking down there he would be very small; and if a horse was there it also would be very small. Because it had snowed, the Navajos had not come down the cliff. They had spent the night in the cave.

There they were attacked; and it is called Massacre Cave because all the Navajos were killed except two. They both pleaded for their lives. One of them had been wounded by the side of the ear, and, though the blood was flowing from his ear, he pleaded. He was a member of the *Tsénííjíkiní* (House Beneath Cliff People) clan. The other man was small, and he was a member of the *Mą'ii' Deeshgiizhnii* (Coyote Pass) clan, and they were related to each other. At Massacre Cave the two pleaded for mercy, saying, "What are you going to do with us? In some way help us." The one who got the wound by the ear was a boy. He died about 70 years ago. According to the story, one of the Mexicans understood Navajo. He

The *Diné*, trying to hide in what is known today as Massacre Cave, were attacked from above and from below.

was to become known as *Naakaii Tsiisch'iłí* (Curly Mexican) because he had curly hair.

The Mexican who was their leader asked, "What is he saying over there?" Curly Mexican answered, "He says you will not kill us." Then the Mexican who gave all the orders when to kill, where to kill and what not to kill, said, "Okay, come up here." The two Navajos went from under the cliff, and they said again, "You've killed us all; as you see, there is blood everywhere. Some of the Navajos have rolled down the cliff into a canyon. Why did you do this to us? What are you going to do with us?" The Mexican leader told them that they could live since they pleaded for mercy, but he wanted to know whether there were more Navajos in the cave of another cliff. And the two Navajos told him it was not known because, as it had snowed the night before last night, probably they were snowed over somewhere.

The two Navajos then were told, "We now are making a settlement at *Ch'ínílí* (Chinle), and, if you still want peace, tell the others who presumably are around, and quite a number of you come out to Chinle. There we will talk to each other, and we will plan the right, friendly, peaceful way." That was the way it was planned, and "peace" was made between the Mexicans and the Navajos.

The Mexicans made camp for their settlement at *Tsébina'azalí* (Things Flow Around the Stone), near the mouth of Canyon de Chelly north of what is now the Canyon de Chelly National Monument Headquarters, where there was a good place to corral the horses. Back in the canyon, some of the Navajos talked about being at the Mexican camp the next day. Some were afraid to go out to Chinle. They said, "He's just going to kill us, for no reason is he saying." Even though some told each other of what was being said, 13 of the Navajos went out to where the Mexican leader had told them to be at noon. As they came out they told the leader, "The ones of us who have survived are here, please don't hurt us any more than you have to." They were told again that there would be no more enemies. They were to tell each other, and they were to meet at a place called *Tséhootsooí*, where there would be a tent, and a bugle would make a sound that there would be no enemies. They also were told not to be scared of the garrison camp and to be there in about four months, or less. He was referring to *Tséhootsooí* (Fort Defiance – Meadows Between the Rocks).

After four days at Fort Defiance where the Navajos were housed in tents, again a bugle made a sound and they said to each other, "They've told us that now is the time to meet with us," and the Navajos were gathered together. At a place called *Tó Dithił*

(Whiskey Creek), also at *T'iis Naasbas* (Round Grove), they were told that they would be moved to *Hwééldi* (Fort Sumner). That was what the Mexican leader known as *Naakaii Tsiisch'iłí* (Curly Mexican) told the Navajos; and he explained what it was like at that place. Under his supervision, the Navajos were moved to Fort Sumner. The number of Navajos who were gathered at Fort Defiance is unknown. They were given rations. Because some Navajos had been dying of hunger, they had gone to Fort Defiance; and some of them had died on the way. Others died of the extreme cold.

Four times as many Navajos were driven to Fort Sumner the next summer. There they were taught everything, and they again were given rations. With some Navajos their crotches were barely hidden, and they were ashamed. Torn cloth was given them to wrap around their waists. There already were Navajo leaders at the confinement camp. They were taught everything, as they are teaching us today, but everything wasn't fully approved for them.

After several years at Fort Sumner, life became very hard for the Navajos. There was no wood for fires; there weren't enough seeds to grow their crops, which hardly could grow in the poor ground, anyway; and insects ate what did come up. The White Man used to kill cattle for them, but there was not enough meat to go around, just a small piece for each person. In this way, some cow meat, as well as some from pigs, kept the people from starvation. After another year at Fort Sumner, things became even worse. As they had done before, the Navajos pleaded, "Release us back to our lands, back to our patches that we used to eat upon. There must be still some of our native foods that were left, such as sumac berries, prickly cactus fruits, and yucca from which we made yucca fruit cake, as well as wild potatoes that used to grow along the *Dził Łijiin* (Black Mountain). Such plants used to be our food; let us return there."

Again they were told, "We will not let you return there; instead we will let you go to *Halgai Hatéél* (Oklahoma – Wide Plains); that is the way we will let you go."

Some Navajos were wondering which way *Halgai Hatéél* was.

But our forefathers kept on trying their best to convince the leaders at Fort Sumner, as they had been pleading for four years. But they always were told that they were to be let free to go to Oklahoma. After four terrible years at Fort Sumner they all said, "We've tried hard, but we must meet again just one more time"; and a date was set for another talk. One of the Navajos got angry and said, "Why not cut my throat now, since I am just nothing." Then he sharpened his knife, and he told the white leaders, "Here, use this to

Massacre Cave from floor of Canyon del Muerto, looking approximately north. Soldiers shot into cave from top of cliff at extreme left. Extent of cave is indicated by arrows.

Part of Massacre Cave as seen from cliffs where soldiers were stationed to shoot down into it. Cave, shown by arrows, extends to left of photo. Photographer was facing almost due east, with portion of Lukachukai Mountains in upper right background.

Cleft in rocks high on cliffs from which soldiers shot Navajo women and children in Massacre Cave below. Teddy Draper, Sr., Navajo translating consultant and one of book's storytellers, stands in opening.

Looking eastward and down into portion of upper reaches of Canyon del Muerto, showing eastern end of Massacre Cave at left. An idea of height of cave and cliffs is derived from fact that cottonwood trees on floor of canyon (lower right) are 80 to 90 feet high.

cut my throat. I've asked you to release us; still you will not do it. I've tried hard to plead for my people, but still you say 'No'; here, use this on my throat now if I fail again in pleading with you. This is the way it will be; if not, let me have your permission to leave. If I don't have your permission, I will not have another day to live." The man, called *Yichi'dahyiłwóh* (Barboncito) as he had two names, once again spoke to the White Man, a general, "Please, my grandfather, don't tell me to wait. We will send word back to *Tsii'báligaii* (Grayhair), our leader (as we were told once) who lives beyond Salt Lake." The Mexican who spoke to them in Navajo in Canyon del Muerto's Massacre Cave was still their interpreter, as it happened.

A reply to the message was returned. It stated, "The people who are called Navajos are under your jurisdiction as of this date, they are no longer under our control." That was the way it happened, and from then on we went under the control of the U.S. government.

Finally, an agreement was made at Fort Sumner, and it included putting their small children in school, the first school to be at Fort Defiance. Later they were to be established in all agencies, such as Keams Canyon and Shiprock, as well as at Fort Wingate. After the agreement was approved and made legal, the Navajos started back to their beloved land. They went first to Fort Wingate, where they were given rations, as well as clothes.

Before they were let free to return to their land, the Reservation line was drawn up for them from *Tsoodził* (Mount Taylor) onward to *Dibé Nitsaa* (La Plata Mountains), to the west at *Dook'o'oosłííd* (San Francisco Peak) and back east to *Sisnaajíní* (Blanca Peak).

Scott Preston

Mr. Preston, a well-known medicine man and a former Vice Chairman of the Navajo Tribal Council (1955-1963), lives at Klagetoh, Ariz. He is 78 years old. He was born into the *Tódich'íinii* (Bitter Water) clan.

I WAS A MEMBER of the Navajo Tribal Council for many years. Before I became a member of the Council, I used to hear some of our forefathers telling stories. My late father didn't go to *Hwéeldi* (Fort Sumner). My fathers' father was called *Dahjoléeh* (Rope Him).

Four relatives of my father who were with the thousands who walked the Long Walk to Fort Sumner were called *Hastiin Yáásání* (Mr. Old Throat), *Hastiin Bigishii* (Mr. Cane), *Dahjoléeh* (Rope Him) and *Béésh Łigai Yits'idii* (Mr. Silversmith), and they didn't even know that their sister also made the walk, along with other Navajos known as *Hastiin Tł'ízí Sizíní* (Mr. Standing Goat) and *Asdzą́ą́ Tł'ízí Sizíní* (Woman Standing Goat) who used to live at *Lók'a'deesh'jin* (Keams Canyon) and near *Tódínéeshzhee'* (Kayenta, Arizona).

As the story really starts, the first enemies who came around and started raiding the Navajos and their sheep were the *Nóóda'í* (Utes). Some say that the *Naakaii* (Mexicans) used to steal their sheep, but none was known to have done this to them in the beginning. The Navajos used to live, without suspecting any enemies, in such places as *Tsé'azhoosyaachii* (Red Sliding Rock – near Piñon, Arizona), *Béak'idbaa' Ahoodzáná* (Piñon, Arizona), as well as with the *Kiis'áanii* (Hopis). Then, all of a sudden, the Navajos started raiding the *Bilagáana* (White Men) who had sheep, even though they were told not to steal. They also used to kill Mexicans who herded sheep for the White Men, and stole their flocks. Also, at that time, gold had been discovered in *Hoozdo Hahoozó' Hazą́ą́jí* (California – Area Where It Is Hot), and the Navajos even killed White Men who were journeying to California by wagon train.

A Navajo leader who was raiding with his men and stealing from the White Men was known as *Hastiin Yidéez* (Mr. Burned of Skin), a member of the *Tótsohnii* (Big Water People) clan. They used to kill White Men and Indian enemies as far as Salt Lake and Kanab in Utah.

The Navajos even used to kill each other, even though they were told over and over not to do it. Every horse and sheep they killed would be eaten because at that time hunger was in the midst of the Navajos. At the same time the Mexicans, under the orders of the United States government, were journeying into Arizona from New Mexico to attack the Navajos and to take them as prisoners and slaves.

At Navajo Springs near Marble Canyon, Arizona, where some Navajos, along with some Hopis, used to herd horses, a number of Navajos were killed by the Mexicans. Some of the Navajos fled to *Tsé'łizhiniiha'í* (Black Knob – west of Tuba City, Arizona). Those on horseback fled farther, to *Dziłdiłhiłii* (Shadow Mountain).

After the Navajos were attacked, some of them fled down to the floor of the *Bidááhá'ázt'į'* (Grand Canyon) to be hidden from the attack of any enemies. Others continued to journey in different directions. Some went to Canyon Diablo, Arizona, and eastward to *Kin Łigaaí* (Baca, New Mexico), and on to *Hwééldi* (Fort Sumner).

At Fort Sumner they were driven by force into adobe buildings where they were accounted for. Some of the Navajos did not arrive until two years later. The number of Navajos who were driven to Fort Sumner is unknown. Still, the enemies used to come around and attack them. In return they used to kill the enemies when they could. They were issued rations such as flour, coffee, sugar and beans.

The number of years the Navajos spent being rounded up and at Fort Sumner was really five. Some of them didn't like it at Fort Sumner; so they ran away. A good number of Navajos had remained behind in the steep arroyo areas near *Ts'ah Biikin* (Inscription House) near *Naatsis'aan* (Navajo Mountain).

According to the stories told about Fort Sumner, some Navajos spent one year, some two years, some three years and some four years there; and the number of years that some spent was five. Some Navajos were enemies of their own people, and they used to scout around with the White Men to capture Navajos – men, women and children.

At Fort Sumner the Navajos were driven by force into adobe buildings where they were checked in and counted.

Eli Gorman

A medicine man and a member of the Nazlini School Board, where he lives, Eli Gorman, 72, says that his lengthy account of the events of the Long Walk period came from his father and other menfolk. His main clan is *Kinyą́ą́'áanii* (Towering House People).

I'LL TELL YOU ONLY WHAT I KNOW. I don't know much about history. We don't really know how people lived in the past. We began, not long ago, to realize what is going on. It was not until after the *Diné* came back from Fort Sumner that we began to understand things. We know only what we have heard. There used to live men and women who told stories about the Navajos and their past. Now they are gone (dead). They told me stories; so all I know of past history is what I heard from those deceased people.

There used to be people of many races. We lived among them, and lots of events took place. The tribes were: *Nasht'ézhí* (Zuni), *Kiis'áanii* (Hopi), *Chíshí* (Chiricahua), *Naałání* (Comanche) and *Nóóda'í* (Ute). We lived among these other Indian tribes — tribes of the same general race — that's what I was told. Also, before us were the *Anaasází* (Ancient People). They lived approximately 1,500 years ago, pretty close to 2,000 years ago. In *Tséyi'* (Canyon de Chelly) there is a place called *Kinnii'na'ígai* (White House Ruin) that is said to be one of their living places. Farther up that canyon, there used to be a lot of houses built by the *Anaasází*. Throughout each and every canyon there were more houses, lived in by the same people. They also lived in the *Tooh* (San Juan River) area, as well as around and under *Dibé Nitsaa* (La Plata Mountains) according to our forefathers.

Even though we have been living among many other Indian tribes, we always have kept our own culture. It is said that there was a time when we got over-populated. That was pretty close to 2,000 years ago. Anyhow, tornadoes, flood, hunger and many kinds of sickness almost annihilated man completely. All of this came about as a result of people's misconduct. At least, that is the way our stories go. When a few people survived from each tribe, they

Navajos, in spite of troubles and much moving around, kept their own culture and ways of life.

separated and started living their various ways as groups. Each group of people was very few in numbers.

Navajos, during this period, were living around *Dziłna'oodiłii* (Huerfano Mountain) in New Mexico. When we were living at *Dziłna'oodiłii*, we started moving around, but we never got too far away from the region. We just kept on living and moving right around *Dziłna'oodiłii*. While the *Diné* were living there, the population started to increase and a lot of events took place. There are many stories about this place, and the stories go from there on over to *Dook'o'oosłííd* (San Francisco Peak). While the *Diné* were living at *Dook'o'oosłííd* the population continued to increase tremendously; and it was around *Dook'o'oosłííd* that the *Diné* first developed four different clan systems. The *Diné* were re-created there. Then division began to take place, and soon there was a clan increase, such as: *Tsinsikaadii Tódich'íínii* (Spreaded Tree Bitterwater), *Bįįhbitoónii Tódich'íínii* (Deer Spring Bitterwater), *Tsébek'e'eschįįn Tódich'íínii* (Marked Rock Bitterwater), *Tł'ogí Tódich'íínii* (Fuzzyhair Bitterwater), *Yo'oh Tódich'íínii* (Beads Bitterwater), *Tódík'oshí Tódich'íínii* (Sour Water Bitterwater) and *Tsinsikaadii* (Spreaded Tree).

Re-created *Diné* from *Dook'o'oosłííd* is what we are today. From that place the *Diné* moved back to *Sisnaajíní* (Blanca Peak). From *Sisnaajíní*, we spread in every direction, and our population kept on increasing. Most *Diné* next moved to Canyon de Chelly and to areas around Canyon de Chelly, *Dził Łijiin* (Black Mountain) and other mountains in the Black Mountain area. At the time, the main sources of food of the *Diné* were deer and mountain sheep.

During that period there were no white men, not even one was seen around. After discovering us, they started living among us all over the country. *Diné* were living in Canyon de Chelly, as well as around Canyon de Chelly, Ganado, Steamboat, Tuba City, Lukachukai, Shiprock, and areas close to Albuquerque when the White Men made a settlement at New York. Other Indian tribes also were living among us. We would visit them regularly.

Tools were lacking. There were no iron hoes or axes. Bows and arrows were our only weapons. With them, the *Diné* would kill deer, mountain sheep, rabbits, prairie dogs, rats, porcupines, badgers, bobcats, etc. These animals made up much of our forefathers' food. Also eaten were small and big grass seeds, wild spinach, wild bananas and small wild potatoes. Those potatoes were common in prairie areas in those old days. Wild berries were used for food, too; and corn was planted in small fields or patches. It was impossible to raise more than enough. Because of lack of modern tools and farm equipment, the *Diné* raised just enough food to survive.

White Men were living far from us at a place called Santa Fe. After making a settlement at New York, some of them had moved over to Santa Fe. Because the *Diné* were far away from the White Men, their tools were the planting stick (*gish* – hand-made) and the hoe (hand-made). Hoes often were made of wood. Sometimes goat, sheep or horse shoulder blades were used as hoes. So there were small corn patches on which the *Diné* depended. This is the way the stories go. So these were our foods. We survived through all the hardships and gradually moved ahead.

Navajos, at the time I am telling about, were born to lives of hardship – not into the world of prosperity. Our people had been living in poverty. They visited other Indian tribes such as the Hopi, Zuni and Mescalero. Soon they started raiding cattle and sheep from other tribes living around *Tsoodził* (Mount Taylor); and the Navajos, in turn, were raided, and they lost many of their women and children who were captured by the other tribes and by the White Men and Mexicans. Some *Diné* would take off at night, saying, "We are going on the warpath."

One time an Indian agent from Santa Fe (a Mexican) came up with a plan that the Navajo people should be issued food and clothing. One day several wagons full of those things were pulled into Fort Defiance. From there the supplies were taken on to *Tódildon*

(Bubble Spring), a little way south of Fort Defiance. The *Diné* were told to meet there so they could be issued food and clothing. Unfortunately, the *Diné* just rushed it. They were asked to wait for the things to be distributed systematically, but the Navajos rushed in and took over all the supplies. The men that had brought in the things just moved off a little way and watched the Navajos in action. Soon nothing was left. The supply runners just went back to Santa Fe and reported what had happened.

As time went on the *Diné* continued to raid, and the U.S. government was getting tired of the situation and looked at the Navajos as real potential trouble-makers. A white leader probably said, "There is nothing but trouble ahead for them. We will have to round them up because, as time goes on, they will decrease in number. Many of them will be killed, especially the belligerent ones. If we round them up peaceful ones will not be killed; children will not be killed; only the warlike *Diné*." The message probably was sent to *Wááshindoon* (Washington, D.C.) At least, that is what the old people used to tell me. I wonder if other people tell the story like this, but I doubt it. Telling the true story like this is worth it. It is what I had been told in the past.

As time went on, the plan was kept in mind: "Navajos will have to be rounded up." Other Indian tribes were informed of the plan – Comanches, Apaches, Zunis and Hopis, as well as the *Naakaii* (Mexicans). Then the other tribes and the Mexicans declared war on us, raided us and sent us running all over the place, especially to the mountains. There was no safe place. Soon there were dust clouds in places like Steamboat, the whole Black Mountain region and the Lukachukai Mountains. The Gray Mountain area was not so bad, and some *Diné* there never went to *Hwééldi* (Fort Sumner). They were at their homes all the time when others were at and returning from Fort Sumner.

As the raiding went on, many Navajos were killed. All we had for weapons were bows and arrows, which were almost useless because our enemies had guns. They had guns called *bii'ná'jíhí* (old-fashioned rifles). To load the rifle, powder would be dumped into the barrel. Other rifles also were used. They had copper bullets, round like small balls. All that was needed was to drop a bullet into the barrel and push it down with a special rod made for loading. The rods always were kept handy. There are still some of these in Ganado at the house of *Hastiin Jéékałí* (the late Mr. Deaf). Anyway, the enemies killed a large number of *Diné*. Besides their rifles, the Utes used bows and arrows, as did the Comanches. With those weapons, the enemies really made the Navajos suffer. A large number were killed. I don't know how many.

The war went on for many years. All that time the Navajos were running all over. Some starved to death. There still are bones at *Deeslį́* (Water Starts to the Nazlini Wash), around the Nazlini area. Human skulls can be seen underneath the rocks, sticking out, some crushed to pieces. Peaceful *Diné* were picked up peacefully, but many women were killed. Men were slaughtered. Children usually were not killed. They were taken as captives and often sold as slaves. My late father told me, "Finally, when the snow got to be knee high at Canyon de Chelly the enemies moved in." He said that he was living at a place called *Tsédeeshzhaí* (Rocky Cliffs), a little way south of Chinle, when he heard that the enemies were coming down hard on them, and there was no safe place to be. Someone in the family suggested, "Let's go over to *Tsébo'osni'í* (Rock Struck by a Lightning) and to a cave full of bushes which is there. It is a hard place to get around to and pretty hard to get into."

So the people moved into the cave, and then it started snowing again. As the blizzard got bad, the *Diné* gave up their sheep at a place called *Tónáhakáádí* (Waterfalls).

Before letting the sheep go loose on the open range, only two were butchered for meat. Besides the meat, the people had few food supplies. One day, the people heard a gunshot down in *Tsébo'osni'í* just before noon. Then another shot was heard, and another and another. The firing gradually picked up, and soon it sounded like frying, with bullets hitting all over the cave. This went on nearly all afternoon. Then the firing ceased, but, by that time, nearly all of the Navajos were killed. Men, women, children, young men and girls were all killed on the cliffs. Some just slid off the cliffs down into *Tsébo'osni'í*. At the bottom were piles of dead *Diné*; only a few survived. Blood could be seen from the top of the cliffs all the way down to the bottom. This was about 108 years ago. Our people never had a chance to kill any of their enemies, even though they had bows and arrows. However, one man was sitting by a rock near the cliff bottom when he saw a portion of an enemy's leg; so he shot an arrow at it, but all he did was wound the heel of an enemy's foot. With the few who were living when the enemies' firing ceased, my grandfather, grandmother and my father waited and listened. While my grandfather, grandmother and my father were in the cave, waiting and listening, they could hear people talking. The waiting went on through the night, with the survivors staying in the cave.

At dawn the next morning, a man was heard yelling from the edge of Canyon de Chelly, from a place called *Aláhdeesáh* (Last

Point). The man said, "Nearly all of us are killed, my fellow men. Is anybody still alive? Our men disappeared just before noon yesterday. They were all killed, and that was the last of us *Diné*. There are piles of dead at the bottom of the canyon. What shall we do? Our men are all gone. They are all killed. We must figure out a way to contact our enemies. They have moved out to *Ch'ínílí* (Chinle)." [They had moved to where the present Catholic Church stands, and the soldiers had camped where the Navajo Police Station is now.] There were a lot of soldiers and horses on the hillside. Wagons were not used – only horses.

Among the survivors there was a man named *Hastiin Biighaanii* (Mr. Backbone), a woman and another man. These three left the cave and walked through the Canyon de Chelly wash. They had decided to give themselves up, no matter what happened. They thought it would be all right if they were killed.

When the three got to Chinle they saw a multitude of soldiers and many Enemy Navajos* – *Diné* who had joined the soldiers some years back. The Enemy Navajos understood English, and they later interpreted for the *Diné*. As the three approached the camp, the soldiers just stood and stared. As the *Diné* got closer, they spread out. One soldier gave the *Diné* a hand signal to go right into a tent; so they went in. When they got to the center the three sat down. Surrounding them was a crowd of soldiers, staring at them. Then one of the *Diné* spoke to the commander and his officers. When the Navajo spoke, one of the officers asked, "What?" Then the Enemy Navajos began to interpret. *Hastiin Biighaanii* said, "You have killed most of us. There are no more *Diné* now. They are gone. Maybe a few are alive in other areas. You have killed us, and there is nobody left for you to kill. Besides, we have nothing; we are suffering very much from hardship. We want to stop here; we want peace."

The officer replied, "There will be peace. Some other *Diné* probably survived. Bring all of them out here so that they can be together. We do not know about those who will refuse to come out, but we really want you to be saved. We will have food and everything for you people here."

The Navajo spokesman said that would be all right, and the three were given food. They never had seen coffee, sugar, flour, baking powder, salt and other ingredients. They did not know how to fix those things; so the *Diné* were shown how to use and eat them before taking them back. Then the three Navajos went back to Canyon de Chelly where the message was passed on to the few

*Navajos who generally lived east of Mt. Taylor.

survivors who could be found. Some of them went to where the soldiers were camped, but not many. After several days of waiting for others to come in (only a few arrived, one by one), they were moved on. Big mules and horses were driven ahead in the deep snow on a trip to Fort Defiance.

It took a number of days to get there. The *Diné* who already were there were told, "Those of you who were here before and are here now, tell the newcomers to join us."

Then the trip to Fort Sumner began. My ancestors said that a lot of *Diné* already had been taken there. Food supplies were brought in from Santa Fe. As they started on the trip most of them walked. They had no shoes other than moccasins. For clothes the *Diné* wore deer hide and *biił* (woven wool dress). The *biił* resembled an overcoat. It was pretty warm. *Yistł'é dootł'ish* (blue legging) and *yistł'é yiilchíí* (red legging) hides were wrapped around men's and women's legs. They still are used in some areas today.

The trip went on for many days and nights, and there were many *Diné*. As the people were traveling near *Tsoodził* (Mt. Taylor) they came to a bridge. It is a little way beyond Mt. Taylor. I believe the place is called *Háák'os* (Curve Neck). Anyway, there was a wash with a bridge. The road was blocked by two White Men with red complexions. They ran a big chain across the bridge and started scolding: "What's the use of taking the worthless Navajos on the trip with you? Just kill them! Horse thieves! Foxes! Crows!"

They named all the thieves there are and said, "That's what the *Diné* are. They killed our sisters, mothers, brothers and many relatives. They drove off our sheep, cattle and horses. They have been stealing from us for a long time. For heaven's sake, kill them all."

The road was blocked by two white men who put a chain across the bridge.

That is what the two White Men said to the commanding officer. But he replied, "Calm down; we have peace. What you say probably happened. It has been going on in the past, but from here on, it will not happen again. The *Diné* will kill no more White Men. They have been raiding back and forth with other Indian tribes. Now there is peace among them. The *Diné* will kill no more Indians of other tribes, nor will other Indian tribes kill any more *Diné*. That is the rule now. What's left of them, let them live in the days to come; let them increase in number. It is not right for any Indian tribe to disappear."

That is what the commanding officer told the two White Men, who then became calm. The officer went on to say, "If any person speaks like that in the time of peace, it will cost him a jail sentence. That is the rule."

The White Men dropped the chain and let the people through. The trip continued for many days and nights, for how many I don't know. White people never said how many days it took to get to Fort Sumner. All they said was, "We went there." When the *Diné* got to that place they saw that there were lots of soldiers and officers. They were issued food, cattle were taken from them and slaughtered. They were talked to. Some Navajo chiefs were *Hastiin Dahgaa'í* or *Yichi'dahyiłwóh* (Mr. Mustache – Barboncito), *Ats'ą́ą́ Béstł'oni* [English not known], *Hastiin Ch'il Haajiní* (Mr. Man of the Black Plants Place), *Hastiin Bigod Diiłídí* (Mr. Burned Knee) and *Askii Bilį́į́'láni* (Many House Boy). I have forgotten the rest of them. There were more, of course. They were the people who talked with military officers while the *Diné* were at Fort Sumner.

At the beginning of the third year (and even earlier), the Navajos started asking humbly to be sent back to their own country. They had brought the matter up tentatively in the second year. During the third year women, young men and girls cried, and the men said, "We miss our country; give our country back to us." They said this to the leader from Santa Fe. He was one of the officers who visited Fort Sumner often. Another man who visited was a Ute Chief. Once he shouted, "Navajos shall all be killed; not even one of them shall live, each and every one of them shall die."

He was told to quit saying that by the leader, who defended the Navajos. "For what reason," he asked, "shall the *Diné* be killed? We will kill no more *Diné*." He added, "No, they will not be killed. It is peace time now; you are thinking about the past which is all forgotten or dismissed." Then the *Diné* were told, "We will discuss your request and let the people in Washington, D.C., know about it."

All this time the *Diné* were crying, "*Tséyi'* (Canyon de Chelly)! Send us back to Canyon de Chelly. We did not want to leave it, and we miss it very much."

The *Diné* did a little raiding while at Fort Sumner. They would go over to *Naałání* (Comanche) territory and the Comanches also would raid the *Diné*. The Navajos even stole from each other at Fort Sumner. There also was a group of *Diné* called *Tsédeé'aał* (Chewing Stones). They killed four White Men, but the incident was dismissed. The last time those White Men were seen they were heading up a hill toward the south. A moment later the four horses returned with four dead men on their backs. The men had been shot in the back with bows and arrows by the *Tsédeé'aał*. *Tsínaajinii Hádiłch'ahłí* (Dark Tree Extended Talker) told me this story. He had been at Fort Sumner, and he knew the facts. It affects me as though I had been to Fort Sumner myself. I was told the following story, too: *Hastiin Hádiłch'ahłí* said, "While I was at Fort Sumner I was guilty, too. There was a time we herded cattle for a Mexican man at a place called *Walla* (Wallace). We were very hungry, and our children had little to eat. One day, while herding, I injured a cow and then killed it. We ate some meat and took the rest back to Fort Sumner and distributed it among our relatives."

Hastiin Hádiłch'ahłí said he was young – about fourteen years of age – at the time he went on the Long Walk. This is the way his story goes: "It was said a peace treaty had been made. The *Diné* were told 'You people will start back to your country within the next ten days.' The Navajos were very happy on the ninth day – the day before they were let free. They were wild, jumping around and saying, 'We are going back tomorrow.' "

When the day came, wagons were filled with children. One of the men's wife gave birth to a child. Some women were taken in the wagons, pulled by mules and horses. Some *Diné* rode horses. Others walked the whole way back. It took many days and nights to reach *Tséhootsooí* (Fort Defiance). When the *Diné* got to Fort Defiance they were counted. Other *Diné* were there. The chiefs and sub-chiefs gave speeches, among them *Hastiin Ch'il Haajiní* (Manuelito). There is a statue of him in Gallup, New Mexico. The Navajos were told by their leaders, "We have peace now. We have been to Fort Sumner, and you people were talked to. You understand what we have done in the past. Some men, women and children died of famine, and some of them were killed because of our own faults or mistakes. We were punished for our own misconduct. From here on, none of you will do it again. Young men and young women shall multiply. From now on you will live better lives. Sheep will come back. Your livelihood will come back. Wagons will be given to you. Horses will be given to you. Sheep will be given to you; and plows, hoes and axes will be given to you. This was what you were told and it was agreed on."

All of these promises were carried out. Some wagons were given to the Navajos. White sheep were given, ranging in number from two to four, depending upon the size of families. The people took these sheep back to their places on various parts of the land which the government had set aside as a Navajo Reservation. The *Diné* were told, "If you think and plan ahead for your sheep and take good care of them they will increase. They will be your main source of livelihood. You and your children will live off them."

This proved to be true. After the people came back from Fort Sumner they had a new interest in life, and they split into groups and headed for various parts of the Reservation. Some moved back to Canyon de Chelly.

Two Navajo men were told by the government to mark boundary lines for the Reservation.

I don't know how large a territory our people are living in today. When the *Diné* came back from Fort Sumner, some white leaders told our people to mark off land that would be theirs for many years to come. Our people were told, "There will be a good piece of land for you people to live on." It probably was the people from *Wááshindoon* (Washington, D.C.), who said, "Mark off the land, live on it, it will be your land. Where you want to put your boundary line is all up to you. Mark off a large area; your population is not going to stay the same."

When the *Diné* who were present at a meeting when a survey was made were counted they numbered 1,500. The people were told, "It is because of these reasons that you will have to mark off a good piece of land. After you mark it off and get to be overpopulated, then it will be all right for you to overflow your boundary line."

The *Diné* said that was all right. One man who helped lay out the boundary line was named *Damóós* [Name of Mexican origin]. He and another man were told to do it. (I forget the other's name. I have heard it mentioned. If it were written down on a piece of paper, it would be easier to remember. When someone tells you a story orally, you forget it. That's the way I am now. I am forgetting some of the old stories.) Anyhow, the two men were told, "Fix yourselves some food. Pack food for your horses, too. Leave here, and, when you get to Mount Taylor, split up." *Damóós* was told, "You go to *Ashįįhí* (Salt Lake, N.M.), then over to a place called *Jadíbihiikááh* (north of St. Johns, Arizona). It is toward *T'iisyaakin* (Holbrook). Put a boundary line through those areas. Then extend it to *Dook'o'oosłííd* (San Francisco Peak). Make sure the peak is the center. From there continue to *Tónaneesdizí* (Tuba City) and beyond; then extend the line into the Colorado River."

The other man was told, "As you leave Mount Taylor, make a line through *Ya'níílzhiin* (Torreon, N.M.) to *Tóhajiileeh* (Cañoncito). Bypass *Beehaí* (Jicarilla) territory; then go over to a place called *Dibé Nitááłí*, near La Plata Mountain. From La Plata Mountain, extend the line into the Colorado River and make the river a part of the boundary line."

This was what the men were told, and they agreed to do it. They led their mules off, with packs of food attached to the animals. As they were approaching Window Rock, Arizona, they hardly had started on the journey. They were walking at the present Window Rock housing area when one of the men said to the other, "Brother, look here! This seems to be an unnecessary mission. It's not going to be our country. It will be somebody else's in the future. We are about to die of old age already. Or, maybe we will not die of old age.

You never can tell in this uncertain world. In any case, we will labor for nothing. It will be an unimportant mission; so we will split here."

At Window Rock junction (a little way from the present stores), one of the men said, "My brother, you lead your mules into that *nastł'ah* (beginning of canyon), then down to *Ba'hastł'ah* (south of Tohatchi, N.M.), then back down to *Tsétáák'aan* (Hogback). Myself, I will go through *Lók'aahnteel* (Ganado) and *Na'áshǫ'ìí Tó'ó* (Burnsides) and then to the top of the ridge and along the ridge back down through *Tsindahsikáád* (Spreaded Tree Area) and over to *Be'ek'idhatsoh* (Big Lake) and *Tódinihí* (Moanwater). Then I will go down to another place called *Tsindahsikáád* (Spreaded or Standing Tree Area), *Dibé Bichąąnbii'tó* (Sheep Waste Spring) and, finally, to *Shash jáá'* (Monticello, Utah). That is as far as I will put up a boundary line. So all we are going to include is the Lukachukai area. There are only two of us."

Each said, "All right, my brother"; and they split from there. Today, a government fence runs along the old boundary line from Window Rock all the way up to *Tsétáák'aan* (Hogback). The *Diné* were told to put up a line covering a large area, but, unfortunately, they didn't do it. As time went on the *Diné* started complaining, and Navajo leaders took up the problem. *Hastiin Adiits'a'ii* (Henry Chee Dodge, a man from Crystal, New Mexico) was one of them. Then there were *'Éé'naashoodi Bitsii Yischilíyę́ę* (Curly Hair Missionary), from Saint Michaels, Arizona. He also was known as *Bi'éé Naashoodi Tsoh* (Big Missionary) or *Naat'áani Nééz* (Tall Leader) from Fort Defiance. He had been in Fort Defiance since the *Diné* had moved back from Fort Sumner. These people made trips to Washington, D.C., also *Askiistł'iniiyę́ę* (Spotted Boy). Fortunately, our boundary line was extended to San Francisco Peak in that direction. With a few more extensions the line got to *Tsizizizii* (Leupp, Arizona), and to *Ahideelk'íd* (Top of the World, N.M.) and that is how it is today. The old boundary line contained only a small portion of our present-day Reservation.

This is the way the old men told me the story. This is what they used to say.

About the Treaty (of 1868), the story said:

From this day on you *Diné* will kill no more White Men; likewise, White Men will kill no more *Diné*. That is the way it is going to be from now on. We want to be real friends; we want to be one people; we want to have one language; we want to have one government so that we all can live better lives."

When the government said this, the *Diné* said, "All right. This time give our country back. We will go back to it."

It had been said that the Navajos were going to be sent to an area somewhere near Phoenix, Arizona, but our forefathers said, "No, we want Canyon de Chelly."

As they were pleading strongly for Canyon de Chelly, they were told, "You lost the land; you were conquered. The land that you lost now belongs to the U.S. government. Therefore, the land will be leased back to you for your use temporarily."

So it was said that we went back to our land temporarily. This is how it is stated on a paper of old regulations or the Treaty of 1868. The *Diné* also were told, "Your children will be educated. You will send them to school so that they can learn the White Man's language. That is the way it is going to be now. This will continue forever in the future, even beyond one hundred years."

The *Diné* said, "It shall be done," and the agreement of 1868 was adopted.

I am now a member of a school board. This is the way it has been every now and then. I have been presented with a piece of paper, and I have been told that the writing on it says it is one of the agreements that has been made at Washington, D.C. One hangs on the wall in my house now. They say the various agreements were made and not subject to change.

As a result of the Treaty of 1868 peace and beauty came back to being. Then things gradually changed to be as they are today. Back in those days there were no roads. When I was old enough to know what was going on, there were some roads but no automobiles. I am 72 years old (1972). There was a road leading from *Be'ek'idhatsoh* (Big Lake) to *Ch'ínílí* (Chinle), and there were other dirt roads going in various directions, but few vehicles used them. Horses were everywhere; cattle were everywhere. There were many sheep. At the time I began to know what was going on, I noticed that the *Diné* were enjoying the privilege of raising all the livestock they wanted. At my house, there was this man named *Hastiin Háahastááłí* (Mr. Flat Area). He was my father. He raised a lot of cattle and sheep at *Háahastááłí*. His sheep numbered over a thousand. Herding sheep was my work as a youth. My brother, sisters and I have been herding sheep through all the years.

Fred Descheene

Fred *Deeschíínii*

A retired range rider who now lives in Wheatfields, Ariz., Fred *Deeschíínii*, in his middle sixties, says that his historical accounts came from his grandfather, *Adiits'a'ii Sání* (Old Interpreter). He was born into the *Táchii'nii* (Red Streak Extending Into the Water) clan.

THE STORY THAT I WILL TELL will be about my late grandfather, named *Adiits'a'ii Sání*, whose real name was *Naakaii Adiits'a'ii* (Mexican Interpreter). He told it this way:

It was when they were small – *Diné Nééz* (Tall Navajo – his brother), one of their sisters, and the boy who became my grandfather. They went with their mother from a place called *Tsénideelzháh* (near Chilchinbito) and on to *Tsélání* (Salina). The Mexicans were scouting for them, and the best place to hide was *Tsélání*, atop some steep rocks. However, some Navajos were captured around there, and so their mother started with them for another place. They went down near *Tséhilį́* (Tsaile) to a place called *Ye'ii'bidooghą́ą́n* (Killed Gods), herding a few sheep, with seven other *Diné*. They herded to *Séí Heets'o'sí* (Wheatfields Butte) and on to *Ye'ii'bidooghą́ą́n*.

The story is told of a Ute leader, known as *Tsii'bálígaii* (Grayhair). He was scouting for the Navajos; and he took the heart out of a baby and put it in a crow's heart, and he shot it up a canyon cliff. After that, the Navajos were no longer strong. Sometimes we hear that the Navajos were strong, but, in a way, the Utes were the strongest of all.

The man named *Tsii'bálígaii* hunted (scouted around to find the Navajos). He was a friend of the Utes and Mexicans. From *Tséyi'* (Canyon de Chelly) all the Navajos were driven to *Hwééldi* (Fort Sumner). Only a few survived, and they said, "We will go to Chinle to surrender. A few *Diné* still are wandering around there."

At a place called *Mą'ii' Chąąłání* (Plenty Coyote's Waste – about 15 miles southeast of Fort Defiance), as the Navajos were camped, the enemies attacked them, and all of their sheep and the people were killed except for two. One of them was my late grandfather. From *Mą'ii' Chąąłání* they continued with a few other Navajos who had survived (including my grandfather's sister, as well as *Diné Nééz*) to *Tséghádinik'ąí* (Burned-Through Rock). But they didn't go to *Tséhootsooi* (Fort Defiance). They went to *Shash Bitoo'* (Fort Wingate), where they surrendered. At Fort Wingate my grandfather was sold to the *Naakaii* (Mexicans), also *Diné Nééz*. They were taken to the *Tooh* (Rio Grande River), where my grandfather herded sheep for the Mexicans. *Diné Nééz* herded sheep at another place.

They spent a year at the Rio Grande River herding sheep for the Mexicans, while the other Navajos were driven to Fort Sumner for confinement there.

After a year the brothers said, "Let's run away." They had been saving some meat jerkies, but they didn't go just then because the Mexicans were really watching them. My grandfather stole a gun from the Mexicans and saved all the gunpowder that he could. They didn't run away because the men whom they were herding sheep for might kill them. During that time the sister got wed to a Mexican.

After more years at the Rio Grande herding sheep they made another plan to run away. My grandfather was ready again. *Diné Nééz* went to see him one evening, and they planned with their sister, saying, "We will make the sound of an owl across the river from under a rock. There is where you will meet us."

They made the sound of an owl all night, but she did not come; so they spent another day there, and still she did not come. Then, when darkness appeared, they went out to the river across from where there were some horses tied up at a village. My grandfather said to *Diné Nééz*, "Don't hesitate to jump on one of those horses that are tied. Just cut the rope and jump on."

So they crossed the river to where the horses were, cut the ropes, jumped on and started back across the Rio Grande. They went away from the river, riding all night toward Fort Sumner. The one my grandfather was riding had a crack in his hoof; the other horse was all right. My grandfather was carrying his gun; also lots of food. They had forgotten about their sister. Close to Fort Sumner they left the horse that had the cracked hoof, and both boys rode one horse. When they arrived near Fort Sumner, some of their relatives recognized them and said, "Stay out there; stay out there."

They stopped, and both of them undressed and went in naked to the confinement area. Their uncle took and hid the gun; so for no reason had they carried it a long way. Inside Fort Sumner the people washed the boys and told them that if, when Navajos went to the land of the enemies they returned to a house dressed, they undressed outside. Even though there were a lot of Navajos at the fort, still the enemies used to attack them.

At Fort Sumner my grandfather learned how to speak Mexican, and he used to interpret in Mexican. His name, *Naakaii Adiits'a'ii* (Mexican Interpreter), was given to him, and his name was given to his grandchild.

As the years went by at Fort Sumner it was said by a few Navajo leaders by the names of *Ch'il Haajiní* (Manuelito), *Tsóiini'* (Big Man), *Dahghaa'í* (Barboncito), and *Milyaanani'* (Mariano) to the white officers, "We are lonesome for our land; how can we return to it?" All the Navajos were suffering a great need; and it was said among them, "We will perform the *Mą'ii' Bizéé'nast'ą́* (Put Bead in Coyote's Mouth) ceremony." So they went out to look for a coyote, and, within a short time, one was brought back, and then the *Mą'ii' Bizéé'nast'ą́* ceremony was performed. The little coyote sat like a dog on the deerskin, and in that way spoke to the leader.

Soon after that, agreements were made with the White Men, and the Navajos started back to their beloved homeland. Most *Diné* traveled by foot; some who had traveled by horse from Fort Defiance traveled back by horse again. Some Navajos decided to remain at places along the way. They are called *Tsédee'aałhi* (Chewing Stones) today. Some are called *Chísí* (Mescalero Apaches) and *Dziłghą'í* (Apaches). My late grandfather said that he came back to the homeland along with most of the others.

When the two boys, riding on one horse, came to Fort Sumner relatives recognized them, ran out and cried, "Stay out there."

Dugal Tsosie Begay

Dahghaa'í Ts'ósí Biye'

Dahghaa'í Ts'ósí Biye' is an 85-year-old sheepherder near Valley Store, Ariz. The following narrative came from a grandfather and other ancestors. He was born into the *Ashįįhí* (Salt) clan.

I AM GOING TO TELL YOU my grandfather's and great ancestors' story. They said it was our own fault that we were rounded up and taken to Fort Sumner. They said we used to kill Ute Indians, Pueblo Indians and Mexicans and bring their sheep back, and that those actions caused the wars between us, the Army and other Indian tribes. As the wars went on between us and the others, the number of our people decreased and the government noticed it. They talked about us and they said, "What if all Navajos starve to death, or what if they all are wiped out by other Indian tribes and the Mexicans? What's next?"

As the talk went on, it was decided from Fort Sumner that we be rounded up and taken to that place for security. So, a trip was made by soldiers from Fort Sumner to *Chásk'éhatsoh* (Nazlini Wash) near Canyon de Chelly. The camp area, by the people from Fort Sumner, was at upper Canyon de Chelly. They came there so that the Navajo people could be moved to Fort Sumner. A number of big wagons were pulled in by steers. In the wagons were supplies of all kinds of food. The reason these people came over from New Mexico land was the fact that we were starving and being raided by other Indian tribes. Because they were very hungry, some of our people started moving into the camp area of the people from Fort Sumner. A man named *Hastiin Káák'ehé* (Mr. Wounded Arrow) came in, too. This man was sent out around the whole region to tell the Navajos that the people coming in were harmless and that they were there to provide our people with food and security. So he went around and told the people that there was plenty of food for them at the *Tséyi'* (Canyon de Chelly) Army camp.

When most of the people had come into the area, and when it was said that there were no more people out in the field, the trip to Fort Sumner began. Food was taken in the wagons, and some children and older people also were taken by wagon, but most Navajos walked all of the way to *Hwééldi* (Fort Sumner). Eight steers were used to pull each wagon. A long piece of wood was attached to the front center of the wagon, and across this one long piece of wood were four more shorter pieces fastened with straps. On one side of this long piece of wood were four steers, and the same number were on the other side. Because there was no way to control the steers that were pulling the big wagons, people walked on each side with whips to control them.

From *Ch'ínílí* (Chinle), the Long Walk went through *Tséhootsooí* (Fort Defiance), *Na'ní'zhoozhí* (Gallup), *Shash Bitoó* (Fort Wingate) and then on to *Hwééldi* (Fort Sumner). There was no attack by other Indian tribes during this long trip, but sometimes our children and women disappeared. Every so often a rest stop would be made so that people could rest or fix their meals. Many of these stops were made between Fort Wingate and Fort Sumner. At one particular rest stop, people left several things, according to some people. The rocks that were used to make bread on still are standing or sitting there. Also left were stones used to grind corn. Because of the slow trip, overnight camps were short distances apart.

When people got to Fort Sumner they noticed that there was a big river nearby. Along the river banks were many trees. Our people did not know that they were going to stay there for the next four hard years. It had taken them approximately sixteen days to travel from Fort Defiance to Fort Sumner.

When the Navajos got to the fort they started making shelters. They used tree branches to make their homes, just as they still sometimes do today. Women did not know how to use the White Man's flour and coffee; so they mixed flour and *tó* (water) and ate it uncooked. They did the same with *gohwééh* (coffee) – just mixed it with water and drank it without boiling. It is even said that some people thought that the White Mans' flour was used the same way as Indian corn meal; so a number of other things were added as ingredients in making bread. As a result, terrible stomach aches were common, from which a lot of people died. A few people were made chiefs and sub-chiefs at Fort Sumner. One of them was *'Kinyinaagał* (Walking around the House – another name for Manuelito), whose statue is in Gallup.

Seed corn also was issued at Fort Sumner, and soon people started farming. They did not use plows to loosen the soil; they used sticks for planting the corn. They say that, back in the old days before Fort Sumner, farms were very productive because of using planting sticks. However, at Fort Sumner we had very poor crops. Everybody was hungry. In slaughtering cattle large holes would be dug; wood or branches would be laid across the holes, probably to keep the meat from touching the dirt or sand. The cowhides would be dried, and then used as doors to the small shelters.

Most homes at Fort Sumner, however, were made by digging holes in the ground. Laid across the holes were logs and branches. On top of the logs and branches were piles of dirt.

Squaw Dances were held. At one place would be the first night of the Squaw Dance ceremony, while the very same night would be the second night at another place. The only difference between a *Ndáá'* (Squaw Dance) at Fort Sumner and back here was that rattle carrying was for a very short distance there. A big problem was the lack of horses; so people used sticks as their horses. While people were going on a rattle-carrying ceremony they would ask the *Diyin Dine'é* (Holy People) for the bringing back of horses. Other ceremonies like the *Ye'ii' Bicheii* (Yei-be-chai Dance) and the *Azniidáá'* (Fire Dance) were carried on at Fort Sumner.

Because hunting was permitted at Fort Sumner, buckskins were common. Women's clothing and footwear were made of buckskins. Men's clothing was made of white flour sacks. Living conditions were bad. Beef was distributed every so often. There were very few sheep, goats and horses.

(This is my grandfather's story. He used to exchange stories with other old men all night long. I would listen with much interest and keep the fire going to keep them warm.)

As time went on at Fort Sumner, some people started saying, "I want to go back to my country. I miss my country and I feel very homesick."

Pretty soon some people ran away. The only thing other people noticed was that they were missing, and it was assumed they had run away. Some well-known chiefs and sub-chiefs, were *Hastiin Adiits'a'ii* (Mr. Interpreter, or hearing or understanding Person – Henry Chee Dodge), a man named *Askiitł'inii* (Freckle Boy – Charley Walker) and Manuelito. Manuelito was the chief. People kept on crying and saying that they wanted to go back to their country.

Firewood was hard to find. Only one kind of wood was used, called *nááztání* (mesquite). It was found a long way from Fort Sumner. It was the root part that was used for firewood. In other words, people had to dig out their firewood. The nearest places where wood could be found were about three to four miles distant.

(Some accounts say that the Navajos had to walk as far as 25 miles away to find firewood after the nearer supplies had been used. – Ed.)

Because there were no horses or anything to haul the wood, two men would leave early in the morning to bring in some of it. Braided yucca was used to haul it. There also was real danger in bringing wood alone because wolves were around. Probably not too much wood was required because of the small size of the fireplaces.

As I said earlier, a big river was nearby. From this river ditches were made so that some people could do farming. Cantaloupe, watermelon and corn were raised. Seeds were given out by the white people, and it was said that cantaloupe, watermelon and corn were the main food sources. Because some corn was raised, the *Kinaalda'* (Puberty Ceremony) was conducted for young ladies.

Regarding the population situation, the place was not too crowded. The Army did not guard the Navajos much. Our people lived there as they did back here. They were looked over just to make sure they did not run away. There were some guards walking around.

Our people did the very same thing at Fort Sumner which they did back here in that they started going off and stealing livestock from the *Naałání* (Comanche) and other Indian tribes. Soon those Indian tribes started raiding our people. They would recover or take back some of the livestock that was brought in by our people. It was said that the Navajos would be attacked early in the morning. A big round stone wall was built up for protection against the enemies. The Navajos were attacked twice. As most of our people got inside the big stone wall during enemy attacks, it got real crowded. A few of our men probably hid out in the cornfields, for a number of our enemies were killed. It was found that when a warrior of the *Naałání* tribe was killed, they never left the body there. They recovered the body and took it back with them. During the attacks two women at the back of the enemy battle line blew whistles, and then the enemies would attack our people heavily. The enemies' horses were highly decorated; so were the enemies themselves. They dressed in hides. Their shields were made of cowhide, which was hard and as slippery as ice. When the Navajos shot at them, the bullets would not go through, and arrows also would just fall back. As I said before, the Indians who attacked our people were highly decorated – with feathers and bells. The feathers and bells scared our people. Some almost fainted.

Among the captives' other troubles there were lice at Fort Sumner. They mostly were found in rocky areas, living in small holes

Some captives got away by quietly crossing the river at night and escaping toward the west.

in the rocks. A lot of people got lice at Fort Sumner, especially in their hair. The men's hair, like the women's, was pretty long in those days.

As time went on, our people continued to beg that they be sent back to their own land. Many of them were very homesick. Finally, an agreement was made between our chiefs and sub-chiefs and the United States government, represented by white officials. The agreement was that Navajo parents would send their children to the White Man's schools to be educated in the White Man's way of life. Navajo parents were warned not to interfere with the Whites educating their children. Our people also were told that they were not really free. They were under the United States government. After the agreement was made, our people were freed from Fort Sumner. When they left they were informed as to what was expected of them when they returned to their own country.

Back at *Tséhootsooí* (Fort Defiance), white sheep were given out, as were some horses. Some people took good care of their sheep and soon had good sized flocks. It has been said that our great grandparents bought more sheep from Morman country. Two men would take a rope to bring back ewes. Woven rugs were exchanged for the sheep. The Navajos bought cattle from the Spaniards.

Living conditions improved with the coming of more goats, sheep, horses and cattle. To ride the horses men made male and female saddles. Stirrups were made from pieces of wood; so were the whole saddles, with cowhides covering them. Also, goatskin was braided to be used as reins. Goatskins and cowhides also were braided into ropes, as were horse tails. It was said that horsetail ropes were the strongest of all.

Hosteen Tsosie Begay

Hastiin [Hastįį́] Ts'ósí Biye'

At 80 years of age this gentleman describes himself as a self-employed sheepherder. He lives near Kayenta, Ariz.

SOME NAVAJOS LEFT for this area from *Tséyi'* (Canyon de Chelly), somewhere around Chinle, Arizona. They made one overnight camp at that rocky point which is visible near Dennehotso, Arizona. My late grandfather on my father's side said, "When people started on the journey I was left at home to care for the hogan. Then I thought to myself, 'Why should I stay home? No way!' "

So he roped his fastest horse, rode off after the group and caught up with them early the next morning where the people had camped for the night.

The purpose of the trip was to annihilate the *Nóóda'í* (Ute Indian) tribe. Earlier, an enemy *Naakaii* (Mexican) boy had been killed, and, because of that, a great number of Navajos were killed. What was left of the Navajo people got real angry, but, unfortunately, only eight Navajos survived. The other Navajos on this second journey got annihilated. Most of them probably were from the *Dził Łijiin* (Black Mountain) region, and 40 were killed by the Utes. The other Navajos – eight men – were not killed. They all survived and got back safely. These were from Canyon de Chelly. After that, the Navajos were rounded up and driven to Fort Sumner. Among them was my grandfather. He told me that some Navajos were put on necessary details like butchering cows, cutting up the meat, issuing rations to the people, and mixing mud for adobe houses. He and other Navajos said they spent four winters and four summers at Fort Sumner.

There was one *Diné* who understood the Mexican language. And there was a Mexican who understood the English language. Thus two interpreters were used in carrying out the begging conversations between the Navajo people and the White Men. First, the *Diné* begged the Mexican, the Mexican then told the White Men what the Navajos were begging for, which was to go home. Then they reversed the talk. Four Navajo leaders begged that their people should be moved back. They explained that, if their staying there continued, a lot of unusual things would happen to them. They would not survive. Finally a peace was made.

My grandfather said he saw and heard this happen. He made the journey back with his wife and son. That was the only family he had then. He got more children after coming back from Fort Sumner. They all passed away as menfolks.

To go back to the beginning of the trouble, at a place called *Mą'ii'deeshgiish* (Coyote Plain) a Mexican leader would have meetings, like nowadays chapter meetings, where Navajos were issued *na'ajaah* (rations). But a stupid fellow did what he did. He was a boy by the name of *Askiiłizhin* (Black Boy). I was told he was a young man. It was he who killed the son of the Mexican leader who was in charge of the Navajo people. Consequently, a war broke out. It was said that the Mexicans gave guns to the Ute Indians. Who knows? Nobody saw it happen. It's my grandfather's story. He told me it was said that Utes were provided with guns to fight the Navajos. The Utes defeated the Navajos by using guns. Then we were rounded up and driven to *Hwééldi* (Fort Sumner) where we suffered very much and barely survived.

It's not true that the Navajos were punished because they had stolen livestock from other tribes. It's just a made-up story. After the Navajos were allowed to go back to *Tséhootsooí* (Fort Defiance) they were given sheep. Later, they were accused of having stolen sheep, but the truth is that the Navajos acquired sheep in the first place with much effort and hardship. They took good care of them, and they became a main livestock. So did horses. I have heard that horses were bought, not stolen. They were bought in *Gáamalii* (Mormon) territories. Mares and stallions were bought, and the mares had offspring, just as ewes do, every year. And the number of horses increased rapidly.

This concludes the story that I will tell.

At Fort Sumner some Navajos were put on tasks such as butchering cattle, cutting up the meat and issuing rations to the people.

The Mexicans provided guns to the Ute Indians to help fight the Navajos. [The White Men, especially the military, also did it.]

The storyteller's grandfather told him that when people started on the journey to the north he was left behind to take care of the home.

Hoske Yeba Doyah

Hoské Yibádooyah

Hoské Yibádooyah, about 70 years old, still herds sheep in the Ganado, Ariz., area. He refers to his account as a "menfolk story." He is of the _Tsénahabiłnii_ (Sleep Rock People) clan.

I AM FROM GANADO – *Hoské Yibádooyah* (Killed All Angry Chief). I have a wife and children – *ashiike ashdla'* (five boys) and *at'ééd t'ááłá'í* (one girl). I also have lots of grandchildren by my father's side.

It is true that I came to the world when there were still some older Navajos from whom I used to hear stories about hard times they had had.

The story begins when the Navajos were unsatisfied with their lives, and our menfolks used to go to the lands of the *Naakaii* (Mexicans) and raid them, steal from them, and drive *dibé* (sheep) and *łį́į́'* (horses) from their territories; and, because of our stealing, we were driven to *Hwééldi* (Fort Sumner). Not all of us were put there; some stayed behind in the *Wedahgo Kéyáh* (highlands) areas of *DziłŁigaii* (White Mountain).

After four years at Fort Sumner, they were lonely for their own land, especially for the region around Chinle where many of them were from.

At Fort Sumner the menfolks pleaded for the Navajos to be returned to their country. One of the Navajo leaders was called *Hastįį́ Dahghaa'í* (Barboncito) and was also called *Yichi'dahyiłwóh* (Barboncito). So they pleaded, and they promised not to steal again. After they were granted freedom, they traveled by wagon back to what had been made a reservation, in the days of the ox wagon, all the way from Fort Sumner to *Tsétah* (Tse Bonito), a place near *Tséghánoodzání* (Window Rock). And, while they were being hauled back by wagon, they heard of a meeting to be held within four days at *Tséhootsooí* (Fort Defiance). Everyone said, "We want to attend that meeting, stop here"; and they were just dumped there at Tse Bonito, and the ox wagons went back to *Hwééldi* (Bosque Redondo – Fort Sumner).

After the wagons departed, they stayed at Tse Bonito along with the children (close to fifty of them), and the children were crying with thirst, and there was no place to get water.

While the children were crying, a *Ye'ii'* (Holy Person, or a God) said, "*Wó Hó Hóówóóó', Wó Hó Hóówóóó',*" and everyone said, "For no reason, or cause, did the *Ye'ii'* speak"; and, within a few more minutes, he again said, "*Wó Hó Hóówóóó', Wó Hó Hóówóóó'.*"

The thirsty Navajos were led by the *Ye'ii'* (Holy Person) to a hollow in the rock that was filled with water.

After the *Ye'ii'* spoke a second time, everyone started on down below from the hill that they were sitting on (near Tse Bonito) and on around the rock where there now is a *naalyéhébá hooghan* (trading post). Something was going on, and it was dark. Because of the darkness, everything was uncertain; and, as they were listening, the *Ye'ii'* again spoke in the same way, and everyone said it sounded over where the rock was. They scattered, and, as they were looking around, they saw a hole in the rock filled with water. The women got their dippers, and fed all of the children water; so they all survived the thirst.

Finally, on the fourth day, they all journeyed to Fort Defiance for the distribution of rations.

The *Ye'ii', Haasch'ehewaan* (Second Talking God), and the *Ye'ii', Haasch'eełti'í* (Talking God), said, "For the future of life, for our beliefs, for our progress, may you be our sacred ceremonial rituals." For this purpose did the *Ye'ii'* make the sound. Before then no *Ye'ii' Bicheii* (*Yei-be-chai* Dance), chants or rituals were heard anywhere.

At Fort Defiance they were given ground flour and the side slab of a pig; and they saw things called potatoes. Some who didn't know the use of flour ate it in a mush-like form, and a few later were killed by the flour. Some others prepared it well enough to eat. Coffee beans (unground) were distributed also. Some Navajos boiled the beans unground; others ground the coffee beans and boiled them. That is when the use of these foods was learned. Before that time, we didn't know their use or how to eat them. Today we eat just like the White Man does.

Dibé T'ááłá'í (one sheep) was issued to some Navajos, along with the food. Some Navajos decided to spend the night there; others, loaded with food, left for *Ch'ínílí* (Chinle) the same day, and from there on they were free.

The Navajos were told not to do any more stealing, to go back to their land, and think of work and the use of their land; and they were taught how to raise sheep which were given to each member of a family.

At Bosque Redondo they had promised to have their children put in the *'ólta'* (school) so that they could be educated, and that was one reason why the Navajos were released.

Fort Defiance was the place where many plans were developed for us after we returned back from Bosque Redondo.

Notah Draper

Naat'a Draper

His father told the following story to *Naat'a* Draper, a 70-year-old sheepherder of Valley Store, Ariz. He was born into the *Táchii'nii* (Red Streak Running Into the Water) clan.

WHEN THE NAVAJOS (*DINÉ*) were raiding tribes, or *'ana'í* (enemies), in other parts of this territory they would take the livestock and drive it back here. At the scene they would kill the sheepherder or the stock owner. Many of our people asked, "What is going to come of it?" So, the *Nóóda'í* (Utes), *Naakaii* (Mexicans) and White Men started looking for the Navajos and were on the kill or warpath.

Some of the *Diné* fled to *Tséyi'* (Canyon de Chelly) to escape from the enemies. The Navajos didn't have food at that time like we have now. They always were seeking something to eat like grass seeds, yucca fruit and piñon nuts. That was before Fort Sumner, and there were not very many *Diné* at the time – not like today when we are growing and increasing fast and there are homes all over the Reservation. Not a house could be seen. The people would build something like huts out of rock high up in the cliffs in the sunshine area, and from there they went out to hunt food. They also went out to steal from *'ana'í* (enemy tribes). That's what my deceased father used to say. That is the reason why the *Diné* were being attacked by enemies and why there were only a few Navajos left. Then it was decided not to kill or invade the Navajos any more. The White Men gave an order, and it was said that the *Diné* were to be driven to *Hwéeldi* or Fort Sumner, and they were taken first to *Tséhootsooí* or Fort Defiance. During their stay at that place they were issued rations like flour, baking powder, etc. The *Diné* didn't know what the food was or how to go about using it. They mixed all of the

Many Navajos built huts of rocks high up on the cliffs in the sunshine area.

baking powder with some flour and put it in hot ashes to cook. It gave them diarrhea and stomach trouble, and some died of it.

After a while, the *Diné* were taken to *Hwéeldi* (Fort Sumner). They didn't travel on horses that they had. All but some little children and old people had to walk. My deceased father went on the Long Walk. He was in his young boyhood at the time. He said some of the first action took place in the Chinle area, where many Navajos were killed or taken captive. Those that refused to turn themselves in died of starvation there.

Four years were spent at *Hwéeldi* and, during most of that time, the Navajos pleaded to return to their homelands.

My deceased grandmother did not journey to Fort Sumner. She was taken captive by the *Nóóda'í* (Utes) here in the Chinle area during her adolescent years, and she was taken to the Ute territory. I don't know how far and where that was. She spent ten years among the *Nóóda'í*.

At about the same time there was a young Navajo who also was taken captive by the Utes. Afterward, the girl who became my grandmother met the young *Diné* and, years later, she gave birth to a baby to that Navajo. In time, she brought the baby back with her, and it was to be my mother. When my grandmother was taken as a captive to the *Nóóda'í* territory she was sold to the *Naakaii*

(Mexicans), and she spent ten years among them. After she came back the people called her *Naakaii Asdzaan* (Mexican Woman), and she lived here among our own people.

After the Fort Sumner *Diné* had returned, the people started recovering from the terrible hardships that they had endured – somewhat like a tree blooms after a hard winter. The *Diné* were in bad condition at first; so they were given sheep, some to each family; and that was how the Navajos began to raise and increase their new flocks.

My deceased father told me about happenings that took place at Fort Sumner, like the Comanches invading the Navajo confinement area, and how some of the *Diné* hunted game in the mountains as they had done back in their homeland. Also, some chants or ceremonies were performed, like the *Ndáá'* (Squaw Dance) and *Na'akai* (Nine Nights Night Chant).

Getting firewood was the worst problem because there was hardly any wood of any kind, and it was very hard to get. There was some sort of brush called *nááztání* (Mesquite). Its roots were dug out and brought home – sometimes for many miles.

During their stay at *Hwééldi* the *Diné* pleaded to return to their homelands. So, after an agreement was made, the Navajos were told to put their children in school to be educated throughout future generations. This agreement was made between the *Diné* and the peace commissioner. I don't know when schools got started after our ancestors returned from Fort Sumner, but I remember when I was in my teens that some parents enrolled their children, and our parents used to hide us. The reason was they didn't want us to attend school.

That's how it was. The *Diné* had got some stock from the Ute territory, and they began to increase their livestock like we Navajos are increasing today. At that time sacred ceremonies were being held, and they were done right. Now our people aren't performing some ceremonies the correct way because they get hold of the bottle and drink too much wine. That's the trouble with us Navajos. A long time ago, when our ancestors performed a ceremony, it was holy for them and no alcoholic beverages were used.

However, the *Diné* are living better lives now and have almost everything they need. Back in the old days large numbers of our people died of starvation. My deceased father told me these stories. I asked my brother about my age not long ago, and he told me that I am about eighty-six years old. I am blind now and can't see any more. My wife passed away three years ago.

The Comanches attacked the *Diné* at Fort Sumner several times.

The Navajos had to walk many miles from camp to dig mesquite roots for firewood.

Hascon Benally

Hasgaan Bináli

This Crownpoint, N.M., medicine man is approximately 90 years of age. His Long Walk narrative came to him from *Asdzą́ą́ Łibaii* (Gray Woman), his late mother. He is a member of the *Hashtł'ishnii* (Mud People) clan.

OUR LATE FOREFATHERS, those that were wise, begged their fellow *Diné* to stop going around stealing horses, sheep and cattle from the Mexicans; but the stealing went on. One of the men who was begging the *Diné* to quit stealing said, "Don't be sorry when we get enemies like a road covered with ice – starvation, poverty and cold. You will suffer; then you will understand."

Later, the prediction came true. Lots of people starved, and others froze to death. Finally, the U.S. government was informed of the situation, and it probably said, "What if the *Diné* vanish? It would be bad; so there must continue to be some *Diné*."

Then the government probably set out to make a temporary settlement. That was done a little way beyond *Naatoohsik'ai'í* (Grants, New Mexico) at a place called *Tósido* (Hot Springs – on the Acoma Reservation in New Mexico). The government, thinking of assisting the Navajo people, said, "Some *Diné* probably are still alive; so scout them out and bring them in." Right away, the *Diné* started scouting for other *Diné* that were thought to be still in the land.

Some *Diné*, by that time, were said to be helpless due to not eating or hardly eating anything. At *Tósido* plenty of food was provided for the incoming Navajos – food such as bacon, coffee, sugar and flour. As the *Diné* were not acquainted with these foods, lots of them died after eating it. That is the way my late mother used to tell the story.

Scouting and bringing in of *Diné* to *Tósido* went on for some time. There was one man that I used to know. He had one eye.

Anyway, he and some other men were the leaders at the time. He was the person who suggested the place called Fort Sumner for the *Diné*. He said, "No farther than Fort Sumner." And it was agreed that the *Diné* would be moved to that place. The move went on for some time. My ancestors said that the journey went through Albuquerque. My late mother said that the Navajos spent a few years at Fort Sumner.

At first, there was some firewood like *nááztání* (mesquite root). As time went on, it all disappeared. *Ta'neets'éhii* (cockleburs) then were used. My late mother said that she brought bunches of them in an old sheepskin. She used to say, "Cockleburs were our firewood."

As time went on, the *Diné* started begging to return to their land. *Hastiin Ch'il Haajiní* (Manuelito) was one of the leaders who begged. Finally, their pleading was acknowledged, and the *Diné* were told, "Now you will go back to your land." One man, a member of the *Tł'izíłaní* (Many Goats) clan, said that at the meeting school supplies and clothing were put on display – pencils, paper, old shoes and old pants. One man was giving a speech. When he got stuck, he asked for help and said, "Where are you, *Naabaah Tsíłkéé* (Manuelito's name then – meaning Youth Warrior)? I am stuck in giving a speech." Manuelito came by, picked up a pencil and some paper and said, "This is what I want. I'll put these shoes and the whole outfit on."

So the agreement was made. The pencil, paper, shoes and clothing seemed to symbolize education and living in their own country. Thus, the *Diné* were authorized to go back to their country.

While our people were at Fort Sumner the Comanches attacked them. The *Diné* were issued rations. Cattle were butchered for them, with a small piece of meat for each person. Coffee and flour were also issued, and the *Diné* lived on those things. Finally, they started back, with their belongings hauled in wagons pulled by oxen and mules. Many *Diné* walked to *Tséhootsooí* (Fort Defiance), carrying their belongings on their backs.

That was the way my late mother and her husband told their story. My mother's name was *Asdzą́ą́ Łibaii* (Gray Woman). The man she started going with after returning from Fort Sumner was *Tł'izíłaní* (Many Goats). The *Diné* continued to be cared for after being moved to Fort Defiance. Rations were distributed to them, and cattle were butchered for them. How long this went on, I don't know. Later, some leaders asked, "How long will this go on, the distribution of rations?" The distribution then ceased. It has been said that two sheep were issued to each Navajo family. The number of sheep increased rapidly, especially when one family went to live with another. *Hastiin Tł'izíłaní* (Many Goats) also said, "We were told to pick out good pieces of land on which we could raise corn, vegetables, fruits, etc., so we could have food for ourselves."

The Navajos raided and stole horses from Mexicans in New Mexico.

Herbert Zahne

Herbert Zahne herds sheep to some extent in the Coal Mine, Ariz., area. He is 65 years old. The original narrator of his story was a grandmother – *Asdzą́ą́ Ałt'isí* (Little Woman). On his mother's side his clan is *Bįįhbitoónii* (Deer Spring People); on his father's, *Táneeszáhnii* (Tangle) clan.

I AM FROM *TSÉ'KǪ* (COALMINE). My clan is *Bįįhbitoónii Táneeszáhnii* (Deer Tangle).

I am asked to tell a story concerning my ancestors. This is the story that my grandmother told me. I remember only a small portion of it. Her name was *Asdzą́ą́ Ałt'isí* (Little Woman). Her husband was named *Hastiin Néézí* (Tall Man), clan *Tł'izíłaní* (Many Goats). They lived around this area over a hundred years ago – areas where there are mountain regions like *Naatsis'aan* (Navajo Mountain) and in the deep canyon of *Bidááhá'ázt'į́'* (Grand Canyon).

It came as a surprise to the many people living around here that the Navajos were stealing from other tribes, causing fights with *Naakaii* (Mexicans), *Nóóda'í* (Utes), *Naałání* (Comanches) and *Bilagáana* (White Men). My grandparents told me that the Navajos were so accused, and they placed the blame on the people for stealing from other tribes. It is not true that all of our people were a bunch of thieves. This was just an excuse, perhaps for other reasons beyond our knowledge at the time. Of course, there were bands of Navajos who took to raiding, and the whole tribe was blamed for their actions.

That false blame placed on the people brought the white soldiers upon them, scouting around, gathering the Navajos in bunches and herding them to *Tséhootsooí* (Fort Defiance). Later, they were marched to *Hwééldi* (Fort Sumner). The people were in the poorest condition, at the point of destitution. *Hastiin Néézí* used to describe how they went to *Hwééldi.* There was much suffering, and many died – a lot of them from starvation. His brother, named *Atsídízhííhí* (Tree Bark Silversmith), was a little boy, not old enough to travel on foot; so he carried the boy on his back the whole way.

He said it seemed like years before they arrived at the place, and then they found it in the worst condition, with nothing there. Everything was bare, and, worst of all, there was little food. What food was issued to them was unfamiliar to their diet, and it caused a lot of deaths among the people. While traveling to *Hwééldi*, people went through all kinds of suffering, death resulted to masses and masses of people, a lot of them from starvation.

While at *Hwééldi*, the guards, some looking like men from other tribes, mixed with White Men, would give orders, herd the people around to make them work. At the same time, they would separate husbands and wives, and they would herd the womenfolks away and rape them, taking them by force. You hear about government laws now which are against that kind of action and which protect people, and we wonder where those laws were then. Did anything like that exist? Or was it just another way of punishing the Navajos?

My grandparents were very young and not worried at the time, even though living was terrible and there was a lot of suffering. But most of the people somehow managed to endure life there. After four years, there, somehow or some way, they were told that they could go back to their own homeland. The unfamiliarity with White Men's food still had been causing a lot of deaths, especially the powdered white flour which we eat a lot today. People would try to cook or fix it different ways, but it caused dysentery and resulted in deaths.

Some men were considered to be the leaders among the Navajos, and they were the spokesmen for the rest of the people. They would meet with the white leaders to discuss problems, and somehow they came to a decision that the people should be released.

All of a sudden, after four years, word came that the people could start moving homeward. *Łį́į́'* (horses) were very scarce; so the only means of transportation was on foot. Once in a while a Navajo man or woman would be seen riding a horse, bareback, of course. Also, once in a while, used red clothing was issued, but, still a lot of people went naked except for a *Tłeeschoozh* (breechcloth) or whatever could be found to wear on the front part of the body — and barefooted. Sometimes, somehow, some way, some people would manage to collect yucca leaves and braid them to wear on their feet.

The journey back was not much different from the one that had been made in the opposite direction four years before. A lot of people couldn't make it all the way back to *Tséhootsooí* (Fort Defiance) because of various reasons. Some people were traveling with small children; others were sick, and some old people couldn't walk any farther; so with these various problems involved, they stayed behind and began living there outside the Reservation

Many Navajos escaped the Long Walk by living in deep canyons such as the Grand Canyon.

boundary line. There was no line then, of course; or, if there was a line, the people were not aware of it. Some still reside there now.

This is the way my grandparents told about the tragic events that they went through. It has been about 47 years since I last heard the story because they both passed on soon after telling it to me.

Also, my late father used to tell me of these events as he had heard of them through his grandparents. His stories pertaining to *Hwééldi* were similar to those I had heard. He explained that while the people were confined at *Hwééldi* they held their sacred ceremonials and their prayers, asking the *Diyin Dine'é* (Holy People) to take them back to their homeland.

Going back to before the Long Walk, a lot of our people had been captured by other tribes and enemies, and they became slaves. Some of them were recovered, but many just vanished and were never found. Then, during the walk to *Hwééldi*, a lot of people were left behind, dying; and many were killed by the soldiers when they became sick, starved or helpless and couldn't make the full journey.

Some Navajos never went to Fort Sumner. A lot of them hid in deep canyons or on the mountains, such as at Navajo Mountain and other rugged areas where they couldn't be found. They managed to avoid the enemies and survive. This all happened over a hundred years ago.

Later, the *Kiis'áanii* (Hopis) became our worst enemies. And what they are saying today is this: "We never made the journey to

Hwééldi. For that reason, the land is ours." But that is not true. The land rightfully belongs to the Navajos because our ancestors suffered and died for it. That is the way the Navajos feel.

Our ancestors told us that they didn't have any weapons before the Long Walk, other than bows and arrows and long spears. Navajo men were very expert in handling those spears. Today, we would never match them. And, in running, they could go as fast as a car and get to destinations in no time, especially when looking for enemies.

Right after the return from Fort Sumner, school was initiated for Navajo children, according to our ancestors. One wonders, if schools were started then, how come, after over a hundred years, there are very few Navajo people who are considered to be highly educated. I imagine this is the fault of the government.

After schools were opened on our land, bad incidents occurred here and there. Some parents didn't want to place their children in school, and government men or policemen were sent out to find them and force them into school. This caused resentment and trouble between the Navajos and the government people. A lot of us never went to school because our parents kept us home to take care of the sheep, bring water and wood and do endless chores that needed to be done at home.

I am now 65 years old; so I was born about *dzidiin* (forty) years after the journey back from *Hwééldi*.

On the homeward journey some Navajos braided yucca leaves and made "shoes."

Fort Garland in Colorado as it looks now, situated about 30 miles east of Alamosa in the extreme south-central part of the state. Established to protect settlers from Indians in that area, Kit Carson was its commanding officer from August, 1866, through 1867, after many of the Navajos had been rounded up and herded to Fort Sumner. General William Tecumseh Sherman was hosted at Fort Garland by Carson in the fall of 1866.

Friday Kinlicheenee

Friday *Kinłichíi'nii*

A farmer and stockman of Ganado, Ariz., Friday *Kinłichíi'nii* is active at the age of 75. The following story came to him from his father, *Kinłichíi'nii Néez* (Tall) and a grandfather, *Hastiin Bi Łį́į' Łáni* (Mr. His Many Horses). His main clan is *Tsénahabiłnii* (Sleep Rock People).

THOSE WHO JOURNEYED to *Hwéeldi* (Fort Sumner) were our ancestors, our deceased grandfathers and all. They had been scouting, stealing and packing their horses to Salt Lake and far away from *Shash Jáá'* (Monticello, Utah). They went in groups – maybe two of them, three or even four; and that was the way they were doing it back then. They even used to steal from the White Men whose horses were in corrals. They would come at dusk and steal during the night. They used to bring back the horses from the White Men's territories; and, because of this, they raised a conflict.

The White Men used to come and look for the Navajos. They would spend a night, and sometimes they failed to find the Navajos who had stolen their horses. At that time hunger was among the Navajos. They were without shoes, and they had few clothes. My father, whose name is *Kinłichíi'nii Néez* (Tall Redhouse), told the story of Fort Sumner; and, also, my deceased grandfather, *Hastiin Bilį́į'łání* (Mr. Many Horses), when he used to visit us at *Kinteel* (Wide Ruins) would say, "And that was the way it was back then. It was hard, and we came down through hardship."

After the conflict with other tribes and the White Man, something was planned against the Navajos. They were captured and taken to *Tséhootsooí* (Fort Defiance), and from there to Fort Sumner. I do not know the number of days they traveled, but it was by ox wagon, which was the only way to travel.

It was originally from *Lók'aahnteel* (Ganado) that some started for Fort Defiance and on to Fort Sumner. Others came from *Ch'ínílí*

(Chinle). The Navajos were just captured and rounded up. After four years everyone started saying, "We are lonesome for our land. How can we return to Chinle?"

Meanwhile, some Navajos who had been living at *Dził Łibaii* (Gray Mountain) stayed behind there and hunted for small animals like rodents, chipmunks and squirrels. That was the way they ate for four years, and they survived.

As I said before, the Navajos brought on a conflict against themselves. It wasn't just a one-time case of stealing. They used to raid homes everywhere they went, not only here but everywhere, even at Salt Lake and in the lands of the Apaches. They killed each other, and the Apaches as well. They took their horses and sheep. At least, that was the way my deceased father used to tell me the story.

At Fort Sumner there was a leader called *Binii'teeshchii'* (Ash Face) and another one called *Ch'il Haajiní* (Manuelito), and there is a statue standing with a striped blanket atop the Zuni theater in *Na'ní'zhoozhí* (Gallup, N.M.), and he is called *Ch'il Haajiní.* He was the in-law of the man called *Lahona Baadaaní* (Lahona-in-Law).

Ch'il Haajiní was the man who discussed with the White Men how the Navajos could return to their land. It was said, "Perhaps two of you will go back and check the land"; and two men went to Chinle where they found that some peach trees still lived in the old orchards, with rodents, chipmunks and squirrels the only ones eating the peaches. Then the men returned to Fort Sumner from Chinle, *Hááhastéél* (west of Cottonwood) and *Lók'aahnteel* (Ganado); and they said, "The land still is all right, untouched since we left four years ago. No one is around."

After the two men returned, the men hunted for a coyote. They found one, circled it and it was caught, and the Coyote ceremonial was performed. After that, the Navajos' talks convinced the White Men to let them be free from Fort Sumner.

The men who used the Coyote ceremonial rituals were the only ones who had straight stories about Fort Sumner, and it is very hard to find anyone who knows how to perform Coyote ceremonies. Back then they performed it somehow, but no one knows how. Anyway, the Navajos were brought back to Fort Defiance, and the number of days they traveled from Fort Sumner to Fort Defiance is unknown. (I think it was quite a while.)

At Fort Defiance rations were distributed, such as side slabs of pigs. Just a little while back I first saw sliced bacon. Now, today, they're just taking our money for those little pieces of bacon, but back then sides of pigs were given free, and that was what they called "distributing food (rations)." Corn and beans also were given, and wagons, axes, harnesses and sheep. I guess two sheep were given to each member of a family. After the rations and things were distributed, the Navajos scattered for their homelands.

Back at Fort Sumner our ancestors had given up our children by agreeing that they be sent to school. On account of that we were allowed to leave that place and return to our beloved lands.

Our weapons were taken away from us, and they told us that, forever, we would not lay our hands on any more weapons; and then the White Men lied and gave back our weapons. For no reason our children (boys) went to war, suffering without any sleep just because of us. And here we just sleep. That was where they made a lie.

After the agreement was approved at Fort Sumner, now, after our children reach the age of schooling, they are put in school, girls and all; and that is the way it is today. I used to sit by my father all night just to hear his stories.

After the Navajos took the sheep that were given to them back to their lands, they produced a lot of sheep. They were told that forever they would depend on sheep, that they should not hate them, but raise them. That is why the sheep were given into our hands.

Later, I saw the sheep when they were overstocked. I am approaching my 75th year of life as I am telling my story. So you see, the Navajos have produced a lot. They were told at Fort Sumner that there again would be more boys and men, girls and women; and that was the way it was discussed according to the Coyote ceremonial. Likewise, there again would be sheep, and the Navajo people again would spread out.

Two head of sheep were given at Fort Defiance to each family that returned from Fort Sumner.

After the Treaty of 1868 children, both boys and girls, were put in school.

Corn, side slabs of pig and other rations were given out at Fort Defiance.

Mose Denejolie

Mose Dijóólii

A rancher who lives near Piñon, Ariz., *Mose Dijóólii*, who is in his seventies, says that he learned from his grandparents about Navajo life on their own land and the sufferings of Fort Sumner. His clan is *Tł'izíłaní* (Many Goats People).

I LIVE THREE MILES SOUTH of Piñon Trading Post, and I haven't been too far away from it. A long time ago I worked at the trading post. I resigned when I had earned my retirement benefit. My late great-grandmother and great-grandfather told me, "We did not make the trip to Fort Sumner. We fled up to the top of Gray Mountain."

I had a grandfather known as *Hastiin Jáád Chǫx'í* (Mr. Bad or No-Good Leg). That is, he got that name later in his life because he had a leg out of which came pus. As a youth, he learned how to use bow and arrows effectively, and he spent most of his boyhood with his father. So, during the roundup of Navajos for Fort Sumner, as the enemies were approaching, *Hastiin Jáád Chǫx'í* would move slowly along with a walking cane. He kept his son a little way behind him, while women would be walking in front, carrying children on their backs. *Hastiin Jáád Chǫx'í* probably knew certain ceremonial rituals because the enemies never caught up with him. Fortunately, but with great difficulty, his people finally made their way to the top of the Gray Mountain. Navajos who continued to live in this area were said to have been wiped out or captured.

In those days, messages were passed on by word of mouth – which still is true and common now. People would tell one another this and that. That is how it was known that a number of people made their way to the top of Gray Mountain. As far as I know, no enemy ever got to the top of that mountain. I have heard that all of the people who stayed in this area (around Piñon) were rounded up and driven to Fort Sumner. That's what the people who made the

Long Walk said. They also told us that they helplessly walked the whole way to Fort Sumner. Between here and Fort Sumner some *Diné* were killed along the way. It has been said that some of them were killed at a place called *Bisdootł'izh Nideeshgiz* (Blue Gap), only a few miles east of the Piñon Trading Post. At *Bigiizh* (the Gap) one lady left her baby and ran up the hill toward another place called *Dóó Yaánastł'ah* (Box Canyon). When she came back the baby was still there, but she found a dead man (an enemy) nearby. Then there were a man and a deaf lady who were captured and taken as *yisnaah* (slaves). The rest of the people were all driven to Fort Sumner. The U.S. Army surrounded them all the way. It was said that some Navajos starved to death during the long, tiresome journey. At the time of the Navajo roundup, some *Diné* got pretty weak, especially while on the Long Walk. When they chased a rabbit into its hole they would start digging after it. When a Navajo got hold of a rabbit's hind leg, the rabbit would just run off his hands; or, when a rabbit ran out of a hole and bumped into a man, the man would fall down, and the rabbit would run over him. The U.S. Army fed corn to its horses. Then, when the horses discharged undigested corn in their manure, the *Diné* would dig and poke in the manure to pick out the corn that had come back out. They could be seen poking around in every corral. They made the undigested corn into meal. Plenty of hot water was used with a very small amount of corn; and it was said that hot water was the strongest of all foods. The *Diné* spent four years at Fort Sumner living in a most miserable way.

Back here, the *Diné* hid in rugged areas. The enemies had to hunt for them, or, rather, had to track them down like lost horses before they could be taken along with other captives. It was said that the *Diné* living in this region had Hopis, Apaches and Comanches as their *'ańá'í* (enemies). They had to flee around from these enemies. In those days when the *Diné* heard a real owl hoot at night, they believed the direction from which the owl was hooting was the safe direction to take. Often, an unusual hooting of an owl could be heard. If the *Diné* suspected the hooting to be done by an enemy they would flee away from the sound. When the *naak'idoolwoshii* (bird who whistles) made its noise – "ahoo, ahoo, ahoo" – the *Diné* would say the enemies must be approaching, and they would flee in the direction the *naak'idoolwoshii* was flying.

Another direction indicator was the *mą'ii'* (coyote). The direction from which a coyote howled was another safe direction to flee. The enemies would imitate the howl of a coyote, but the *Diné* easily could tell whether the howling was by a real coyote or by an enemy. If the howling was thought to be by an enemy, the *Diné* would flee away from the direction. An owl was a safe path indicator when it hooted at night. The *dzidiłdǫǫlhíí* (hawk), when it made its sound, was a bad, or dangerous, path indicator. So, when the *Diné* heard the noise of a *dzidiłdǫǫlhíí*, they would flee away from it. Also the crow. When it called "*gáa, gáa, gáa*" ("caw, caw, caw"), that was another sign of danger, and the *Diné* would remain calm and not move around. Another kind of crow, called *gáagiinilchiní* (a smaller type of crow), that crowed with a high pitched voice, was another indicator. At least, that is the way I was told the story. About Fort Sumner, those who came back said, "We spent four years at Fort Sumner being issued flour, etc. – just enough to survive on."

There was this thing called *nááztání* (mesquite root) which people used as firewood. They were watched over, and they were forbidden to burn mesquite; so the *Diné*, in groups of three or four, would slip out to dig mesquite roots. While one man did the digging the other two or three would stand by as guards. Another thing, if one person went out to dig mesquite root, he easily could be killed by a wolf. In such a way the *Diné* spent four helpless years at Fort Sumner.

Another thing, at ration times each *Diné* would be given one slice of bread. At times, they would kill a rabbit or a rat. If a rat was killed, the meat, with the bones and intestines, would be chopped into pieces, and twelve persons would share the meat, bones and intestines of one rat. (People probably were given a small piece of rat meat each.) Back here was all right as far as food supplies were concerned. People who fled up Gray Mountain depended on yucca, a large pinnacle of white blossoms that was cooked (boiled) and eaten. *Tsintaht'ah* [part of tree bark between the outside bark and the wood] was eaten, too. *Łe'éze'* (a kind of weed) was dug out and eaten. Wild carrots, which grew year 'round, also were food. The people must have had a hard time living, but most of them survived. Near starvation was the real cause of weakness, especially in the knee joints. At times, a Navajo would find a horse, or, if he saw another person riding a horse, he would shoot the horse. When the owner of the horse demanded payment for his injured or dead horse, all he was entitled to get was two arrows (handed to him). Or, if the owner of the horse demanded that he get a share of the horsemeat, he was entitled to get nothing else if he accepted a share of the meat.

Back at Gray Mountain, the *Diné* who survived told one another what was happening to those who were driven to Fort Sumner. They learned this from the few who escaped and returned to their homeland. Toward the end of four years at Fort Sumner, some Navajos were saying, "We were a lot better off when we were in our own country." So there was this man named *Yichi'dahyiłwóh* (Barboncito), also called *Dahghaa'í* (*Mą'ii' Deeshgiizhnii* – Coyote Pass Clan). He and his people (the *Diné*) discussed the possibility of being let out from Fort Sumner. After discussing the questions, "How and in what way, or what can we do, to be released?" *Yichi'dahyiłwóh* said, "Tomorrow, we'll go hunting in a fence-like movement." So, early the next morning, all *Diné* ran off in every direction. Some went this way, others went that way. They formed a big circle and started closing in. When they had closed in to about the size of a sheep pen, they had a coyote within the circle. *Yichi'dahyiłwóh* or *Dahghaa'í* (Barboncito) told the *Diné* to stay calm, and he approached the coyote. When he walked up to it he made, or did, what is called *Mą'ii'Bizéé'nast'ą́* (Put Bead in Coyote's Mouth) ceremony. The coyote, a female, was facing east. Barboncito caught the animal and put a piece of white shell, tapered at both ends, with a hole in the center, into its mouth. As he let the coyote go free, she turned clockwise and walked off timidly, with her tail between her legs – toward the west. Barboncito commanded the *Diné* to make way for the coyote, and they did. Once she had gone through the circle, the coyote started running westward, and Barboncito remarked, "There it is, we'll be set free."

Four days later the commanding officer asked the *Diné* if they really missed their country. The *Diné* responded noisily, "YES, we miss our country very much and would like to go back." Soon after that, they were set free and walked back to Fort Defiance, Arizona. There they were issued some sheep. Some *Diné* then moved back to Canyon de Chelly, while others departed for their former homes in various parts of what was then their Reservation. When the *Diné* who had hid at Gray Mountain heard of the distribution of rations and sheep at Fort Defiance some of them went there.

After the *Diné* returned from Fort Sumner they started thinking about living better lives.

After the ceremony (Put Bead Into Coyote's Mouth) the female coyote walked away timidly – toward the west and Navajoland.

Tezbah Mitchell

Round Rock, Ariz., is the home of 70-year-old *Tezbah* Mitchell. Her story came down from various forebears. She is of the *Táchii'nii* (Red Streak Running Into the Water) clan.

NÓÓDA'Í (UTES) WERE TALKING with harsh words against the Navajo people, and at *Tsétáák'aan* (Hogback – east of Shiprock, N.M.) there were many Navajos who had moved there from here. The bad words continued, and, for that reason, the Navajos fled. As they moved along the river, beyond *Tsébít'í* (Shiprock, the pinnacle) they crossed the river where there is now a bridge.

The large group of Navajos moved slowly westward, through *Dziłdiił* (near *T'iis Názhas* – Teec Nos Pos, Ariz.) and across the valley through *Tsé Awé'é* (Baby Rocks) and over the north end of *Dził Łijiin* (Black Mountain) toward *Tééhnidééh* (Long House Valley). The journey continued through *Ahidiilk'id* (the Shonto region) and straight westward. I've forgotten the names of the places that the journey covered from there. I do not know how many people made the journey, but some of my own ancestors were included. There was a large number of people and livestock (sheep, goats and horses).

Somewhere, south of *Nato'hdził* (Jacob Lake Mountains) the people crossed a canyon, after which it was decided that they would spend several days in the area. So the people prepared to settle down, unpacking horses, etc.

My own great-grandfather was known to be a bad raider, and he was the leader of a large band of Navajo men and women. He went raiding for his band, and it was in this canyon that his nephew killed him.

My great-grandfather's nephew's wife and his children had been left on foot, and they were trying to cross the canyon, walking up a steep hill. The children were tired and crying. His nephew and another man were walking some miles behind when he got the message that his uncle had forced his wife and children off the horse and left them on foot and killed the horse. My great grandfather's name was *'Ahidigishii* (Finger, or Hand, Signal). His nephew was told, "The band butchered the horse and took the meat behind the bend over yonder. Your wife and children are left on foot, walking up the steep hill, crying."

Many Navajos fled from the Utes, crossing the San Juan River where a bridge now stands.

The wife and two children struggled up a steep hill after some Navajo raiders had killed their horse.

The two men took off right away toward the area where the incident had taken place. My great-grandfather was sitting there sharpening his arrows, with a gun beside him, when his nephew walked right up to him. The nephew grabbed the gun, poked him hard on the forehead with the stock, pushed him to the ground and shot him to death. The men then took the weapon and left the body and headed for the steep hill across the canyon.

My great-grandfather's friends (members of his band) came back to where his body was; some were crying, grieving over the death of their leader. This is how our great-grandfather died. Some people were standing at the edge of the canyon, watching. They said, "He deserved what was coming to him; it is his own fault."

That is what my grandfather used to tell me.

After what happened there, the people started their journey back toward the east. While there, they did not encounter any enemies, but the news got around that a lot of enemies were raiding the people in that eastern region.

Upon their arrival at *Hahaz'teel* (Top of Cottonwood) they met some enemies who raided them of their livestock. It was said that a large crowd of enemies camped by *Tséhilį́* (Tsaile) lake one night, and a large number of captive Navajo men, women and children were held. The enemies had with them some babies in cradle boards. Probably their mothers had been killed. The enemies also had obtained a large number of sheep and horses which they were driving with them.

My ancestors survived on top of *Báálok'aa'í* (a mesa south of Black Mountain) to which they had fled at night after they encountered the enemies at *Hahaz'teel.* The news then got around that the enemies were gone; so they moved immediately toward their old homestead, which was *Bisdootł'izh Deez'áhí* (Round Rock). Finally, they arrived home where there were hogans and a sheep corral.

The rest of the family, including my old great-grandmother, were left behind at the place where they had lived previously.

During the troubled time of over a hundred years ago, word got around that the White Men wanted all the Navajo people to go to *Tséhootsooí* (Fort Defiance) as soon as possible. A number of Navajo men were sent out on horseback to tell the people to report, and word came to us that a lot of Navajos had arrived there already, including some of our relatives. It was said that, if and when all the people reported to *Tséhootsooí*, the enemies, including the White Men, would not bother us any more, that we would be left alone to live peacefully.

Word got back to my great-grandmother that the family of a close relative had arrived at Fort Defiance and that the family was living there. It was assumed that everything was well and that no danger was involved; so plans were made to move to Fort Defiance.

It had snowed about a foot when the family started toward the new living place. There were three people on foot, carrying little packs on their backs and driving a small herd of sheep. The journey took several days, and, on the way, it snowed again. By the time the group reached what is now *Ni'íijiihásání* (Old Sawmill) some relatives came out from Fort Defiance looking for them, and they met at a small mountain in that region.

Upon their approaching Fort Defiance, they came up over a ridge from where could be seen a lot of smoke rising from many camps against the slope of a mountain. My great-grandmother was told that this was the place where individuals were to report, and she also learned that some people had moved on to Fort Sumner on the far side of New Mexico.

Soon that long journey began for my ancestors. A wagon was provided to haul some of our personal belongings, including dry

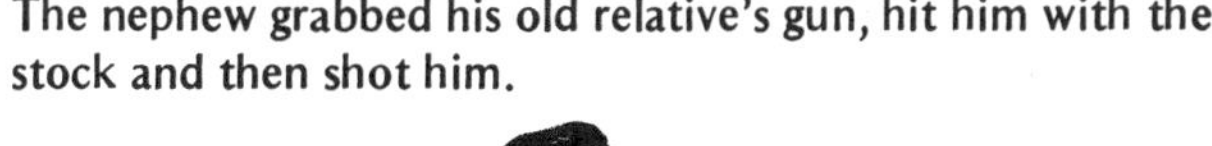

The nephew grabbed his old relative's gun, hit him with the stock and then shot him.

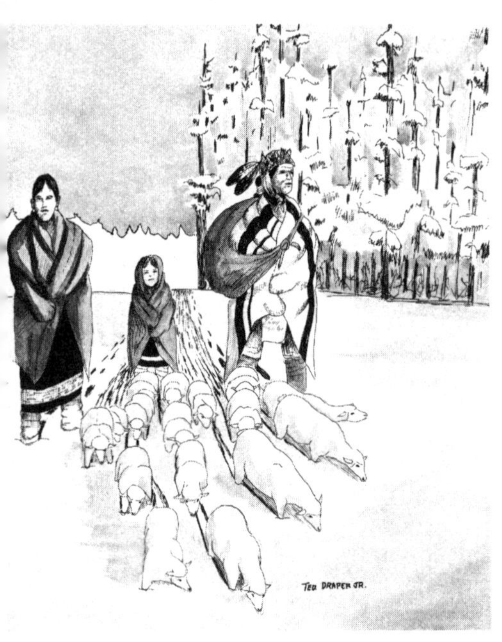

The family of three started for Fort Defiance in about a foot of snow.

corn, beans and some oak grain (acorns) which was something like horse feed.

Included in the large group were a lot of children, young and old men and women. The journey continued straight east. My grandfather said there were many groups of Navajos who went to Fort Sumner and that the people spent from two to four years there before those who survived were allowed to return to their own land. I have been told that, while there, each person received daily a small amount of food, like a cupful of corn — just enough for one meal. And they worked like slaves. Some Navajos would hoe and pick weeds in the gardens and fields for white people who lived there.

I have forgotten most of the incidents that happened there. It has been a long time since I heard the stories. I do remember hearing it said that several raids by other Indians on the Navajos occurred. The raiders probably were from Oklahoma or out that way. The soldiers tried to protect the Navajos, but death and wounding resulted from the fights. Once an attack took place at early dawn. The soldiers shot back, however, and a lot of enemies died. The rest fled.

My grandfather (my mother's father) herded horses near the huge camp. The animals belonged to a number of people. One time, when he and two other men were herding, they became involved in a card game, and the enemies came. My grandfather got to the horses in time to round up a few. The enemies took the rest, including a beautiful stallion which was used to keep the herd together. "After the enemies took off with the horses, I heard the stallion whinny from a far distance and that was the last I heard of him," my grandfather used to say. While our men were trying to take the horses away from the enemies, the latter got hold of one of the Navajo men while they were aiming to get his horse. He was yelling for help; so my grandfather went back to try to rescue him. He caught him just as the enemies threw him off the horse. Some horses were recovered after the fight, but most of them were gone – also some Navajos who had been captured. It is not known how many people were captured at that time, or at other times, or how many were killed or wounded. Once, two Navajo men were walking at early dawn when they were ambushed and killed. The enemies scalped one of the men who had hair which went clear down to his ankles. They took his scalp, along with his long hair, and left his bare skull.

After four years a treaty allowed the Navajos to make the journey back. Everything was in very poor condition, including the people. Some old men and women – helpless ones – were permitted to ride in wagons, but a lot of them had frozen to death or had died of *dichin* (starvation or sickness). It must have been around midsummer when the people arrived in their land because the sunflowers were in full bloom.

My great-grandmother was one of the few survivors among my ancestors who made that journey both ways to and from *Hwééldi* (Fort Sumner). My grandmother and three of her brothers also survived those terrible years. My mother was born at Fort Sumner; she was a year old when they returned.

I cannot remember much that was told to me about things that were said before the *'aha'deetą́* (treaty – of 1868) was signed, but I knew that for years talks constantly were going on, like they do at Chapter Houses today. Every morning at dawn people would gather to listen to speeches and instructions made by white leaders and by some Navajo men.

Upon the return, the people gathered at Fort Defiance where one sheep was issued to each family. In some cases it was discovered

A large number of captives were held by the enemies at Tsaile.

that one member of the family would be an only survivor. In cases like that some of them gave their one sheep to another family. The people were told not to butcher these sheep to eat, but, rather, to breed them and raise more sheep. My great-grandmother was a great weaver. She wove belts, saddle blankets, etc. and she exchanged these products for sheep. Before long, she owned quite a number of sheep, and, of course, they quickly grew into a large herd.

During the Fort Sumner years a lot of Navajos escaped. They were both men and women. They escaped on foot and walked the long journey home; and I've heard a lot of their stories when they were still alive as to how they got away and managed to survive. Two of them were my grandmothers by clan.

One of my grandmothers told me how she made her escape, and her story was like this: After running away from Fort Sumner she reached some big mountains where she saw a red (brown) bear. It appeared friendly. They stood looking at each other for a while. Then, because the bear acted like he was motioning to her to follow him, she did so. This big animal was her guide and protector for three days and nights as they traveled together, he always some distance ahead of her. Sometimes the bear would stop, climb a tree and eat something. It seemed to be a sign to her; so she would sit down and eat a bit of food that she had brought or gathered.

One time, while resting and eating, a big black bear appeared and came toward her, advancing slowly, showing his long white teeth. In an instant, the brown bear attacked and killed the black bear by chewing its throat.

The following day, about noon, the bear stopped under a tree and ate berries from the bushes. After a while he walked away a short distance, turned and looked at my grandmother. He stood there making motions with his head as if to say he was leaving, which he did. My grandmother told me that she used to talk to the bear during their journey together and that it seemed to understand what she was saying.

She continued the journey alone, crossed the *Tooh* (San Juan River) and, finally, after many days and nights, she arrived in *Tséyi'* (Canyon de Chelly) where some of her relatives still were living. They decided that a night sing should be performed over her before she continued her journey homeward.

Many persons who escaped had exciting stories to tell about their long and dangerous trips home.

When my grandmother got away most of the Navajos still were at Fort Sumner.

Chahadineli Benally

Ch'ahádiniini' Binálí

[See sketch at beginning of third story, page 57.]

FOUR NAVAJO "RAIDERS" ran around loose, mostly in *Tséyi'* (Canyon de Chelly), and the man named *Dibéyázhí Bich'áhí* (Lamb Cap) was head of these four men. They would raid the rest of the Navajos at night; and, during the day, they would hide or split from one another and do their raiding separately. They were feared greatly by the people who lived down in and above *Tséyi'*. These men would raid a camp and take the best horses from its herd, and then they would kill the rest of the horses for food. Sometimes they would go up to the top of the canyon and raid the people who lived close to the edge, taking their sheep.

These same men eventually left the canyon and went down into the territory of New Mexico, where they met up with some Mexicans. They told the Mexicans about life in the land of the Navajos; so three Mexican men got interested and followed the Navajos back to *Tséyi'*.

Soon after, one of the Mexicans brought up the fact that some of the people in his country owned lots of sheep; so plans were made to return to New Mexico to kill the owners and take their sheep. This began the warfare between the Navajos and the Mexicans. The seven men headed back to New Mexico to carry out their plans. They dressed one of the Mexican men in a Navajo costume to resemble a Navajo, and they sent him on a mission to kill a certain Mexican man who owned many sheep. He killed the owner of the sheep and the two sheepherders who were tending the animals at the time, and he took some rifles and ammunition. When the men got back together, they started to drive the flock of sheep northward. Somewhere along the way they broke up the herd and brought the smaller flocks to *Tséyi'*.

After the sheep were brought, a lot of trading went on between the men who brought them and the *Tséyi'* people.

Navajo raiders attacked Mexicans in New Mexico to steal sheep and horses.

At about that time the Navajos had learned the skill of silversmithing from the Mexicans; so, after the flocks of sheep were brought to the canyon, hand-made jewelry was exchanged in some cases for sheep. In the meantime, people began to wonder and ask where the Navajo outlaws had got the sheep, and word got around fast about where the animals had come from.

Plans were made among the Navajo outlaws and the Mexican men to go back to New Mexico, and some old army rifles with long sword edges were obtained. Two separate groups of men started out on the journey. As they were approaching New Mexico, they met another group of men heading in the same direction. Upon reaching the border of New Mexico, they were attacked by a group of Mexicans who were out looking for them, expecting them to return after discovering what they had done.

During the surprise attack, the Mexican man who killed the sheepherders got shot. The fighting continued until sundown, with rifles and bows and arrows. After most of the Mexicans were killed, the Navajos managed to obtain a large flock of sheep, and they were herded back to their land in groups.

These journeys had been made on foot, and several trips were made afterward by other Navajos. One trip was planned and made by a large band of Navajos, the idea being to get hold of as many sheep as possible.

Once more, the Navajos and the Mexicans got in a fight. The two remaining Mexicans who had joined the Navajo outlaws suddenly changed their minds about being part of the Navajo raiders, and they left to join their own group, the Mexicans.

During the attack a lot of Mexicans were killed and it was discovered that the two who had helped the Navajos with raiding had been killed. It got to the point where Navajo bands were attacking the Mexicans farther into New Mexico, most of the attacks occurring during the night when everyone was asleep.

Raiders surprised a group of Navajos eating fresh corn near Chinle.

(Replying to a query as to whether the Navajos had sheep before the raids described in this story, *Hastiin Ch'ahádiniini' Binálí* said "yes" – and continued his account.)

Each family had a few, something like 10 to 20 head of sheep.

These raids continued until the Mexicans asked for help from tribes, like the *Nóóda'í* (Utes), who joined them to attack the Navajos. Two traitor Navajos joined the *Nóóda'í* to guide them to the land of the Navajos to search out the hiding places of members of their own tribe to kill them off. The two Navajo men who joined the *Nóóda'í* were named *Tsii'bálígaii* (Grayhair) and *Binii'teeshchii'* (Ash Face). With the help of these two men, a lot of massacres took place at different places; and, at this same time, many *Diné* were captured and taken away as slaves. Then more tribes moved in to kill off Navajos, to take their livestock for their own and to capture women and children for slaves.

After a time, though, the Navajos were winning the battle against the other tribes, but more tribes were coming in from different directions.

For example, one time two main raiding parties were moving up the left side of the Chinle Wash toward the south. (This incident happened in the Chinle Valley). Farther up the valley (referring to the vicinity of Chinle) there was a small corn patch where a group of Navajos were relaxing and eating freshly grown corn, when all of a sudden a group of raiders came upon them. The Navajos were surprised and fled in different directions, but generally in the direction of two hills called *Tséshi Jááh* (Piles of Rocks), not far from the corn patch. The people ran toward *Tséshi Jááh* for protection. While being chased by the enemies, a group of Navajos ran back and forth between the two rocky hills, and a lot of people were slaughtered. The rest fled for shelter toward a small canyon near *Tsénáádoo Tsós* (Hissing Rock).

While this attack on the group of Navajos was going on, another raiding party of enemies was heading south near the *Tsénáádoo Tsós* canyon, probably having come down from *Dził Łijiin* (Black Mountain), where they had attacked various camps and had taken all the livestock they could get.

Another incident that occurred during this same period was the shooting down of a woman near or right above *Tsélání* (Many Fortress Rocks – Salina). She had left her home on top of *Dził Łijiin* (Black Mountain) early one day, just when the morning star was rising, for the nearest water hole. The woman's name was *Abé Tsoh* (Big Breast). She was one of the few women who knew and practiced sorcery, like in the "Enemy Way" ceremony and the *Tsosts'id Ha'oodzii* (Seven Words Will Kill a Human Being, or an Enemy), and she could use *anitįį'* (poison pollen). Water was scarce in the region of her place; so the nearest waterhole was at *Be'ek'idhatsoh* (Big Lake, or Cottonwood Wash). Hastily, she filled her jug with water and started back up through *Tsébeenii'dzíní* (Rock Standing Against the Cliff).

Just as she was approaching a cedar-covered area, four enemy riders advanced from behind her. They had found her tracks by accident and followed her.

From another direction, almost the opposite, a small band of Navajos was moving, when they happened to see a woman walking in the distance carrying something on her back. It was decided that someone should find out where this woman was going and where she was coming from. So one man took off to see. Just as he was approaching the woman he saw some riders going toward her; so he quickly vanished in some tall grass and hid among big rocks. From this point he watched what happened to the woman. According to his report, this was the way they treated her before they shot her to death:

The riders were approaching the woman rapidly and found her where she stood among some tall grass. They rode up close and started circling around her on horseback, and they grabbed at her clothes and soon ripped all the clothes off and left her completely nude except for the water jug which still hung from her neck. When they ripped off the waist band they saw something tied to her waist with a strip of deer hide – two small bags. She started singing one of her witchcraft songs, and the enemies understood then that she was a witch and that she had her poison pollen in the two small bags. When her song ended, she told them they all would vanish at exactly noon. Then she was shot in the head, slowly fell to the ground and died. One of the raiders went to her and cut the two small bags away from her waist, taking care not to touch them, and pushed them into a fire, which was built for that purpose, and burned her poison pollen. They took her water jug and rode away.

In the meantime, one raiding party that was out to kill Navajos was moving slowly toward the place called *Chooyéégííghaní* (Hunchbacks murdered), while the other party took its route toward Chinle. The plan must have been for the parties to meet at *Chooyéégííghaní*.

One party of Mexicans, Apaches and White Men had set up camp for a feast over near *Tsélání* (Many Fortress Rocks). They had a small band of Navajo captives with them. It was planned that the raiding parties would join up later.

The other raiding party (Mexicans, Utes and White Men) had settled at *Chooyéégííghaní*, where smoke was rising from several fires that were built to cook for a feast. Several sheep were slaughtered, and the intestines were thrown away while the meat parts were roasting over open fires. Some enemies were taking naps after the horses had been unsaddled and put out to graze, including the ones that had been taken from the *Diné*. All the gear – saddles, bridles, blankets and guns – was carelessly scattered all over. Captives were being watched and guarded closely, however.

A small group of Mexican raiders was moving slowly up the Chinle Valley toward where the old dam used to be. They were to join the others who already had established camp. Several Navajo women captives were riding behind the main party with small jugs of water tied to their saddles.

All of a sudden, as the Mexican raiders joined the larger group, right over a small hill near the camp came a lot of Navajo riders who rushed into the midst of the enemies. Surprisingly, it was a large group of Navajos, and a terrible battle followed among Mexicans, Utes and Whites on one side and Navajos on the other.

Some were fighting on foot and some on horseback, shooting with bows and arrows and guns and using swords. The Navajo captives got loose, grabbed enemy guns and swords and started fighting. Two enemies took off on horseback, followed by two Navajo men – *Biighaaníbiye'* (Backbone's Son) and one of his friends. The enemies headed for a mesa some miles away. The four were chasing and shooting at one another until they came to a small canyon where one of the Mexicans went over the cliff on horseback. However, he managed to survive and escaped. The other Mexican was shot in the eye and died instantly.

The Navajos had been aware of the enemy search parties long before, and they planned to follow and kill the invaders. The Navajos watched them from the high mountains as they moved up the Chinle Valley where the parties separated. Plans were made to attack both enemy parties at the same time; so, while one party was being attacked, another attack was starting down the valley. The Navajos hid in a long, deep ditch, some on foot and some on horseback. They were ready and waiting when an enemy caravan came over the hill, and they opened fire. Some enemies tried to escape and headed for the mountain toward *Dziłghaahaskai'í* (Utes' Trail on Top of Hill). Three of the enemies (of the four who had killed the woman sorcerer) had reached *Dziłghaahaskai'í* and were ready to go over it when they all were killed. Some *Diné* say that the three enemies escaped, but, according to my great-grandfather, all three were killed by some Navajos who were hiding up there at *Dziłghaahaskai'í*.

So you see, *Abé Tsoh's* evil power had worked after all because all of the enemies vanished as she said they would, except for the one who escaped.

Enemy bodies were scattered in a large area, along with their dead horses, after the fighting. The Navajo survivors gathered, collected all the livestock, guns and saddles and divided these among themselves. Some claimed their own stock and went on their way toward the mountains.

The Mexican who escaped reported to his leaders, telling about the massacre that had taken place and how he escaped. The leaders decided that there would be no more raiding by the Mexicans against the Navajos. Instead, a different approach would be used. The plan would be to use the Army and round up the Navajos and take them to *Hwééldi* (Fort Sumner, or Bosque Redondo) in what is now New Mexico.

A large party of Navajos rushed into the midst of the enemies (Mexicans, Utes and White Men) who were camped, winning the hard battle that followed.

Eventually, a camp was set up near Chinle over toward Canyon de Chelly where the Navajos were to meet of their own free will. Gradually, as word got around, the Navajos did come out of their hiding places and started gathering. This was like a trap because free food was announced and given out like it was nothing. It really was a trap because the Navajos had no knowledge of the White Men's plans to take them to Fort Defiance. From surrounding areas they came, a few at a time, some from *Dził Łijiin* (Black Mountain), but mostly from *Tséyi'* (Canyon de Chelly).

Finally, a day came when it was decided that it was time to move the Navajos from Fort Defiance to Fort Sumner. Some large wagons arrived, with ox teams pulling them. Some Navajos rode in the wagons, but most walked, with the enemies escorting them. It was several weeks before the arrival at Fort Sumner, and the Navajos found a lot of other members of the Tribe already living there.

Food was distributed among the people, and more food was promised if they would cooperate. Because the Navajo did not know how to fix the strange foods in the proper ways, and perhaps because of the change in diet and climate, many deaths occurred. There were medicine men, but they did not have herbs to cure the nutrition sickness. Different types of diseases also caused a lot of deaths. There was much suffering among the people.

During these years some men would slip out during the night and go into Apache territory to visit. It was from the Apaches that they learned and adapted one of their sacred ceremonials which is still used today. The sacred ceremonial is called *Chíshíjí* (Apache Wind Chant), named after one of the Apache Tribes.

It has been said that a Navajo man called *Ch'il Haajiní* (Manuelito) who, for a while in his younger days had been with an Apache Tribe, became a leader of his own people, and, partly through his friendship and leadership, the Navajos got their land back in Chinle. After he became a leader in *Hwééldi* the Navajos were released from Fort Sumner. A statue was made of him, and it was placed in Gallup.

My own great-grandmother told me that she never went to Fort Sumner. During that terrible period she spent four years on top of *Tséhilį́* (Tsaile) mountain along with my other grandparents. They survived mostly on goat and horse milk, also on some wild animals that could be found nearby. Both of my grandfathers were *naalchí'í* (spies or watchers), and they would go out daily to look for enemies. They had lookout points from various places on the ridges.

Three years after the Navajos were herded to Fort Sumner both of my grandfathers decided to go there. They left one morning, taking some food that my grandmother had prepared for them. Upon their return after many days they said that the people would be released the following year, either in the spring or fall.

Life went on as usual after my grandfathers returned to the mountains, and they continued their hunting daily. Hunting was more favorable, animals were more plentiful than today, and they went out without much fear of the enemy.

The following year all of the Navajos who had survived returned from Fort Sumner to Fort Defiance where several sacred ceremonies and prayers were performed asking the *Diyin Dine'é* (Holy People) for guidance as the *Diné* went back to their land.

These prayers were answered as the situation today proves because the Navajos are by far the largest tribe in the United States and Canada, and they gained abundantly after Fort Sumner until the time of the Stock Reduction about 35 to 40 years ago. And today there are many changes for the better.

Upon the return of the People from Fort Sumner to Fort Defiance, some farm tools were issued to them by the government, and each family received two head of sheep. Agreements were signed. One was that the Navajos would send their children to the White Men's school to get educated; but there was no agreement as to abuse of the Navajos' livestock.

As it happened some forty years ago, thousands and thousands of the Navajos' animals were taken away by force, and they got nothing in return. First, it was the reduction of horses that took place, and most of the people never knew whose idea it was. There was mass slaughter of horses; some were shot down because they had bad blood, as the Navajos were told. Then the same thing happened to the sheep. Some were burned alive, great numbers at a time. It was a tragic time that never will be forgotten – when the livestock went to waste, which was the only means of survival and which still is treasured. The Navajos were robbed and deprived of much of their livestock, and, since then, they have not been able to raise livestock as they did before; also, it seems like the rains from the heavens will cease.

So now the Navajo wonders what will come next! What will the White Man want? Perhaps our Reservation land!

Hosteen Tso Begay

Hastiin [Hastįį] Tsoh Biye'

Seventy-seven-year-old *Hastiin Tsoh Biye'*, a medicine man in the Many Farms, Ariz., area, heard the following historical events from a grandmother. He was born into the *Tł'ááshchí'í* (Red Bottom People) clan.

AS FOR ME, I HAVE NOT BEEN AROUND too long yet. I am 76 or 77 years old. In trying to think back about 72 years, I feel as though I am dreaming. I think that I remember things around home when I was about four years old, like herding sheep, but not too clearly. I barely remember people carrying me on their backs when they herded the *dibé* (sheep). Soon, however, I realized that I had a mother, a grandmother and a father.

As I was growing up, my grandmother and I used to move a lot with our sheep. During the winter nights my grandmother would tell us stories about events that took place prior to the Navajo roundup for *Hwééldi* (Fort Sumner). At first we did not understand the stories, but, later, we did understand. She said that people once lived here and there and did a lot of farming. Just to mention two places – *Ch'ínílí* (Chinle) and *Tséyi'* (Canyon de Chelly). She would tell us about where other Indians lived and how our people would steal sheep, goats and horses. According to her story, Navajos in groups of 10 or more would say, "We are going to steal more sheep," and they would take off. When they encountered Mexicans with flocks of sheep or goats, they would kill the sheepherders and bring back all their sheep and goats. This went on for some time.

Then one day, at *Tsoodził* (Mt. Taylor), a *Naakaii* (Mexican) named *Chąątééłí* (Wide Belly) found his two husky sons killed, and the war between the Mexicans and the Navajos really began. As for weapons, the Navajos used bows and arrows, which were not very effective because of their short range. The Mexicans used guns –

probably rifles and pistols. As the war went on, many of our people were killed, and the Mexicans got back some of their sheep, goats and horses. In addition, the Mexicans captured many of our women and children. They were used as slaves.

One time a *Ndáá'* (Squaw Dance) was held at Chinle, and an important man gave his people a talk concerning stealing stock and going on the warpath against Mexicans and Indian tribes. This man kindly asked the people to stop going on the warpath because he wanted everyone to live in peace and to feel secure at all times, rather than having to be on the alert every night and day. He also told the people he had heard that, if the Navajos did not stop stealing and raiding, all other Indian tribes would be allowed to raid the Navajo people. He added that a number of reports about the Navajos'

Navajos killed the two sons of Wide Belly, a Mexican.

bad conduct were on the way to Washington, and he asked those present to please behave themselves. However, while he was talking, a number of Navajos said, "We are going on the warpath on such and such a date." They were just like drunken people. The important man said, "Pretty soon not very many of us will be left. Our enemies will attack us early in the morning while it is still dark. Some of our people have had their hearts taken out while still alive."

Later it was said that a report went to Washington, probably by the Mexicans, saying that there were only a few Navajos left. The government, or the people in *Wááshindoon* (Washington), decided not to have us wiped out completely. Instead, they decided to have us rounded up and taken to Fort Sumner. Military personnel moved in with big wagons which were pulled by eight steers per wagon and were used as transportation to Fort Sumner. Many of our people walked because there were only a few wagons. The shipping point

During a Yei-be-chai Dance the *Ye'ii's* were killed by raiders from another Indian tribe.

was at Fort Defiance. From Fort Defiance groups of soldiers were sent out to various parts of the Navajo country to round up the Navajos for Fort Sumner. A lot of the people were afraid of the Army, but not much trouble developed. Some people say we did fight with the Army. Anyway, the long journey to Fort Sumner began from *Tséhootsooí* (Fort Defiance), then on to *Tségháhoodzání* (Window Rock), *Na'ní'zhoozhí* (Gallup), *Be'eldííldasínil* (Albuquerque) and finally to the place called *Hwééldi* (Fort Sumner). At the end of two years some people still were coming in.

Even at Fort Sumner, though, we were attacked by other Indian tribes.

As for religion and ceremonies, our people practiced them as usual, except that they were considered especially sacred and were respected very much. Squaw Dances, Fire Dances, *Ye'ii' Bicheii* (Yei-be-chai) Dances and others were held. Back here on what is now the Reservation, before the trip to Fort Sumner, one time, a *Ye'ii' Bicheii* Dance was held at the top of a mountain, and, toward morning, the *Ye'ii' Bicheii* were killed by the raiders (the place now is called *Ye'ii'bidoogání* (Yei-be-chai Massacre).

Somewhere toward the end of two years and the beginning of the third year at Fort Sumner, lots of people became homesick, and they wanted to go back to their land and homes. They started asking the officers in charge at Fort Sumner to let them go back because they missed their country very much, but there were no results until toward the end of the fourth year of captivity – in the spring. Some medicine men conducted a ceremony in connection with the request to be sent back to their homes. After the ceremony was over some men went again to see the officers in charge. This time the request was considered, and, a few days later, the treaty between the Navajos and the United States was signed. *'Aha'deetą́* (the treaty), as we know today, is called the "Treaty of 1868." It provided that the Navajos be freed from Fort Sumner, from where they were taken or escorted back to *Shash Bitǫo'* (Fort Wingate). From there the people spread out to go to their homes in various parts of the Navajo country. Some made their permanent homes around Fort Wingate. That is why we see some Navajos living in that area today.

We should remember that not all Navajos went to Fort Sumner during the Long Walk period. Some hid in the canyons and mountains. We should remember that, before Fort Sumner, the Navajos not only stole other Indians' livestock and killed the Indians but that they also stole from their own Navajo neighbors. And, finally, we should remember that other Indians and the Mexicans stole Navajo women and children to be used as slaves.

Earlier, I talked a little about a Squaw Dance that was held in the Chinle area before the Long Walk. As I said, a man gave a talk about not stealing, raiding, etc. As he talked to the crowd, some people kept saying, "We are going on the warpath on such and such a day." Finally, the man got pretty upset, and he said, "Okay, go ahead. Go on the warpath, but just remember, when you do, everything will turn against us. Every living plant, animal and person will be our enemies."

This turned out to be just about true.

Some foods during the Fort Sumner period were wild potatoes, yucca fruit, wild onions and grass seeds. People probably did some hunting, too, but it was never brought out. Also, when the Navajos got back to Fort Defiance from Fort Sumner two to four sheep were given to each family. People who took their herds to Fort Sumner also brought some of the animals back. After they had settled down and started to make their permanent homes, more sheep, goats and horses were given out. Medicine men conducted ceremonies asking for blessing of the sheep, goats, horses, water, land, etc. They did this because they wanted to increase their livestock, to have more water, as well as more useful and productive grazing lands and farmlands. The humble wishes, wills, hopes and prayers of our great-great-grandfathers and grandmothers have been fulfilled. Those ancestors also said, "One of these days the same thing is going to happen again." I assume they meant another hardship like the Fort Sumner period.

To go back – during the wars among different Indian tribes, the Navajo people felt very insecure. Two men always would be on guard, while others were working or sleeping at night. When the guards got tired and sleepy, they were relieved by two others. It also has been said that four years before the main wars broke out among the Navajos on one side and the Army and other Indian tribes on the other, a small mountain slide took place high on the slope of *Dził Łijiin* (Black Mountain), nearly above the present *Tséch'ízhí* (Rough Rock Demonstration School). This was a sign indicating something bad was going to happen. It also has been said that there was hardly any sickness before Fort Sumner. It is true that some colds and sickness came upon the people, but they came only once a year. Suddenly, after Fort Sumner, all kinds of sickness came, but our medicine men conducted their ceremonies.

Many years ago, at a ceremony, three or more old men with gray and white hair would sit around and discuss stories of the past. They also would talk about present conditions and the future. Back then, there was no vehicle of any kind other than a few wagons. They were issued at the same time that the sheep, goats and horses were given out. The treaty of 1868 also stated that there would be no interfering with educating Navajo children. Parents were to send their children to school so they could learn to read, write and speak the *Bilagáana bizaad* (English language). The treaty also stated that Navajos would not make any more war on anybody from that day on. It was said that old Navajos had predicted a lot of things that are taking place today. Long before the Navajos saw a *chidí* (automobile), a man once said, "Sometime in the future there is going to be something running on the road and it will run by itself, and there is going to be a new system of communication something like the *Diyin Dine'é* (Holy People) once used. A wire will be used for communication. That is the telephone today. Also, people will start traveling in the air. Then there will be councils to counteract these wild actions, but they will not work. People will keep going forward. They will not turn back. When the clan system is forgotten, this will be the end – just like walking off a cliff."

Who or what told these men what it was going to be like in the future, no one knows.

Curly Mustache

Curly Mustache of Wheatfields, Ariz., heard this story of a tragic period in Navajo history from a grandmother and a grandfather. He is a medicine man and livestock owner and is about 85 years old. His clan in *Mą'ii' Deeshgiizhnii* (Coyote Pass – Jemez – People.

PRIOR TO THE LONG WALK to Fort Sumner, some people seemed to be thinking of trouble to come. As you know, hunger can make a person think of anything; and there was this man named *T'ááłá'í* (Number One) who was almost starving. For that reason he started going around picking out men like himself – those that were suffering from poverty. After he was joined by some men, they started taking livestock from their neighbors. *T'ááłá'í* and his men, using bows and arrows, also shot and killed a number of horses while other Navajos were riding them. By doing these things, the group made enemies of their own people. In the same way, they made enemies of the *Kiis'áanii* (Hopis), *Nóóda'í* (Utes), *Naasht'ézhí* (Zunis) and *Báyóódzin* (Paiutes).

As a result, the U.S. government sent its army to fight the Navajo people. At the same time, the government gave rifles to the Utes, probably with the idea that the Navajos were courageous, hard to conquer and should be rounded up. The Utes probably were told something like: "This land, from this day on, shall not be taken away from you. It will be yours forever. All the government asks in return is for you to help us conquer the Navajo people."

Right away the *Nóóda'í* started to raid the Navajos. While the fighting was going on between the Utes and the Navajos, the Army made a settlement at *Tséhootsooí* (Fort Defiance) from which to issue or provide food for Navajo people who came there and were peaceable. The government probably did this with the idea: "If we provide food for the hungry Navajos they will come to Fort Defiance on their own without being looked for or rounded up." Lots of Navajos came to Fort Defiance to be issued food and clothing, but as soon as they received those things they would sneak away at night.

To stop this habit the Navajos were moved to a place on the far side of New Mexico Territory called Fort Sumner.

Some of our people spent four years at Fort Sumner. Some spent less time. They were issued food and clothing. The government probably put the Navajos in this camp to tame them, but our people kept on doing what they had done back here. They took sheep from the *Naałání* (Comanches) who already had stolen them from the Navajos. The Comanches, in revenge, raided the Navajos, using their rifles. As to whether the Army helped the Navajos when they were being attacked by the Comanches, the Army probably was afraid to help because the stories to not tell that when the Navajos were raided the Army came to their assistance. The U.S. Army probably was pretty weak then. For example, one time the Navajos attacked a part of the Army. The soldiers were riding horses and shooting guns, while only a few Navajos had rifles, probably acquired from dead soldiers. When the soldiers retreated a large number of them were killed. As they rode wildly back to their camp the survivors just put rifles over their shoulders and took wild shots at the Indians.

My grandmother and grandfather told me this story, which happened before they both went to Fort Sumner. Shortly before the roundup for Fort Sumner, some Navajos went to live with the white people and the Mexicans. They were called *Diné 'Ana'í* (Enemy Navajos). It was these members of the Tribe who told the Whites and *Naakaii* (Mexicans) that other Navajos were their *'ana'í* (enemies). Soon afterward, these Enemy Navajos started to bring in raiding parties of their own people. They probably were being paid for acting as guides for soldiers throughout the Navajo country. They helped to round up Navajos for Fort Defiance, although most Navajos were not rounded up. They went to Fort Defiance of their own free will. It is said that, even before the coming of the *Bilagáana* (American white people) some Navajos had sheep and horses. When Stock Reduction was going on in the 1930s, it was said that the government claimed sheep were under its control because the government had given a few sheep to the Navajos after their return from Fort Sumner. In my opinion the people in *Wááshindoon* (Washington) were wrong.

Before Fort Sumner, some people had sheep and horses, and they warned others to stop stealing the sheep and horses from *Bitsí Yishtłish Dine'é* (other Indian Tribes). They probably said this for their own protection because they were thrifty with their livestock, and that is why they told their starving neighbors to quit stealing. But the reply was, "It is a real suffering to die looking out through the smoke hole; so I am going on the warpath on such and such a day." Then a group of men (usually young ones) would take off. A few days later they would bring back a flock of sheep that they had taken away from the Mexicans or the Hopis, or they would have cattle from the White Men. Some of our great grandfathers did those things, and it was because of this that they were taken away.

At last they were released reluctantly. *Ch'il Haajiní* (Manuelito) was an outstanding Navajo head man. He humbly asked that his people be sent back to their country. *Dahghaa'í* (Barboncito) also was a chief. In fact, there was no single main chief. It was more than one person. There were these men: *Ch'il Haajiní* (Manuelito), *Dahgaa'í* (Barboncito), *Bitsii'naneesk'éé'* [English not known] and *Hastįį́ Łtsoí Ts'ósí* (Slim Yellowman). The other men's names I have forgotten. Anyway, there were four important Navajo leaders. One time a man named *Hastįį́ Naat'áani* (Mr. Narbona) was killed at a place called *Bisdahłtsóí* (Yellow Hill, near Newcombe Trading Post, N.M.) on the eastern side of the Lukachukai Mountains. *Hastįį́ Naat'áani* was one of the four important Navajo leaders, but the U.S. Army killed him under a flag of truce. When the white commanding officer asked the Navajo people who their leader was, with all this stealing going on, Narbona was sitting on a horse; and there was a Pueblo man nearby. Anyway, this Pueblo man said that the horse which Narbona was riding was his horse. A Mexican, who probably understood Navajo and Pueblo, told Narbona that the Pueblo man said, "The horse you are sitting on is mine; so give it back to me now." Twice the Mexican interpreted and told Narbona to give the Pueblo his horse, but both times he refused to do so. The second time, he said, "No, I will not give up the horse. It is my horse!" By that time the commanding officer was pretty upset. He ordered his men to shoot *Hast'įį́ Naat'áani*.

When *Hast'įį́ Naat'áani* was killed, by the order of the commanding officer, the rest of the Navajos rode off. Only Narbona was killed. After the incident, the Navajos started moving to Fort Defiance. From there our people were walked to Fort Sumner. Most of them spent four years there; some say they spent five years. Those who spent five years at Fort Sumner were the ones who sneaked out to join the Mexicans. Those that spent four years were those who moved to Fort Defiance. After spending four years, the people were finally released. *Dahghaa'í* was the chief who was most important in signing the treaty with the commanding officer of the soldiers. After the treaty (of 1868) was arranged, the commanding officer told *Dahghaa'í* (Barboncito or Mustache Man), "From here on you will carry no more guns; guns you will give up. If guns are still in your hands, the days ahead are going to be the same. Things that came up in the past will continue to come up in the future."

Dahghaa'í replied, "No, we must have our guns. Guns are not used only against Mexicans or other enemies. In the first place, Navajos do not make guns. You are the people that make guns. Why don't you give up guns, too, and quit making them?"

When I see a picture of *Yichi'dahyiłwóh* (another name for Barboncito) he is sitting without his shirt, and on his upper chest there is a scar. It looks like an arrow scar to me. He has long straight hair coming down to his shoulders. A rifle is in his hand. At the treaty-making he told the *siláo binaníta'í* (commanding officer), "We are going to continue to have guns, and I am not going to give up my rifle. Guns are used to hunt deer, elk, etc. *Bee'eldǫǫh* (guns) are not used only against Mexicans and other enemies; so I am not going to give up mine."

As the years went by, the people kept asking that they be sent back to their own country, but the result was always the same — unsuccessful! Finally, it looked as though there was no more hope, but there was a man named *Dibéyázhí Bich'áhí* (Lamb Cap). He told the people to rope a *mą'ii'* (coyote); so a number of men saddled their horses, and a few minutes later they had found one of the animals. They chased it a little way, roped it and brought it back. When the coyote was on hand a *Mą'ii' Bizéé'nast'ą́* (Put Bead in Coyote's Mouth) ceremony was held. During the ceremony our main leader was blessed with coyote power. Then the leader again talked to the commanding officer about being let free from Fort Sumner, and this time the officer approved the request and the people were released. An old book or old paper was made for us. It contained an agreement between and by the Navajo people and the U.S. government. One provision of the agreement concerned education, saying that the Navajo children would go to school and that the government would provide teachers. The officer said, "Your children must learn to speak the English language. When you get back to your country you must put your children in schools." *Dahghaa'í* (Barboncito) said it would be carried out, and the agreement was made.

A few years after our people returned from Fort Sumner the agreement concerning education went into effect. Some people thought it was fine; so they put their children in schools. At the time there was no school at Fort Defiance, and pupils went to *Yoo'tó* (Santa Fe) and Albuquerque to be educated. Some students were older. Others were quite young, between the ages of six and ten years. However, as the schools got under way, some people started opposing them. They said, "No, my children will not go to school. We do not want them to be away from us. Besides, we need them to work around the hogans and to herd the sheep."

One case where the school officers tried to take children to school by force involved a man named *Biłį́į́łizhinii* (Black Horse) from around *Bisdootł'izh Deez'áhí* (Round Rock, Arizona). His clan on his mother's side was either *Ashįįhí* (Salt) clan or *Dibéłizhiní* (Black Sheep) clan. Anyway, Black Horse was one of the men who refused to send his children to school. He was joined by other Navajo parents. They said, "No, we will not send our children to school."

Other people living around *Bisdootł'izh Deez'áhí* (Round Rock) had started to send their boys and girls to school; others already were there. The trouble started over attempts to take more children away. They studied first at Fort Defiance; then they were taken to Santa Fe or Albuquerque. Black Horse did not like the idea of sending children to the last two places. He really got angry.

What happened – back at about the turn of the century – was that some people living on the other side of the Lukachukai mountains came over to this side to join Black Horse. A white school official and *Hastiin Adiits'a'ii* (Henry Chee Dodge) came to Round Rock from Fort Defiance. Mr. Dodge was an interpreter for the official, and I believe *Chaalátsoh* (Big Charley) was the other interpreter. Anyway, when the interpreter told the people that the official wanted parents to send their children to school Black Horse said, "No!" Then he and his men grabbed the official and nearly threw him into a deep wash. Black Horse and his men might have killed the school man, but some Navajos protected him and helped him escape. Then men from the other side of the mountains kept riding around on their horses, and soon there were a lot of people at the Round Rock incident. Part of the crowd sided with the school man; the others were for Black Horse and his followers. Plans to take more Navajo boys and girls to school from that area were not carried out for some time. Later, *Diné siláo* (Navajo policemen) were used. School officials and these policemen went around to peoples' homes and asked them to send their children to school. This approach was very successful. The first approach had been cruel.

There was a time when the *Chísí* (Mescalero Apaches) and the U.S. Army were at war. The Mescaleros were living on the top of a mesa. There was only one trail or passage up the mesa. The U.S. Army rode up through that trail one day, and the Mescaleros blocked it off by stacking stones across the trail. They then sent one of their men to the bottom of the mesa and a little way out on the prairie. When the soldiers saw the man, they started chasing him. As he was being chased, the Mescalero ran back up the mesa through a narrow trench. At the same time a bunch of Mescaleros were waiting around the blocked-off trail to ambush the soldiers. The Mescaleros used guns they had acquired from dead soldiers, and when the soldiers were riding up the blocked-off trail, they were killed by the Mescaleros.

As the soldiers were having an unsuccessful war against the Mescaleros, the U.S. Army decided to make soldiers out of the Navajo people so they could get some help from us. The headquarters for recruiting Navajos was established at *Ałnaashiihááłidę́ę́* (Spring on Both Sides – east of Gallup, N.M.). The Army probably thought we could defeat the Mescaleros because the Navajos were real strong and tough, even though they didn't have guns. They would hide behind objects and kill enemies. In other words, the Army used the Navajos so they could round up the Mescaleros. The dream of the soldiers was fulfilled one night when the soldiers and the Navajos went to the top of the mesa while the Mescaleros were asleep.

It was after our people had come back from Fort Sumner that they helped the U.S. Army in rounding up the Mescaleros. It really was the Navajos from *Ałnaashiihááłidę́ę́* who defeated the Mescalero Apaches. Later, Navajo police came into being with the establishment of the Navajo Police Headquarters at *Ałnaashiihááłidę́ę́*.

That was the way life was in those days. There was great hardship, but, as time went on, things took shape and gradually got better. As of now, people probably are leading a better life in the Navajo way along with the White Man's culture. I think we are living much better, and I imagine it will be even better in the future with the advancement of education. These days, I hear that many of our students graduate from high school. I often wonder how many of them will continue their education beyond high school. In some places things are taught in the English way and in the *Diné* way. It is best when our children learn both.